Best Hikes
with
CHILDREN™

NEW
JERSEY

SECOND EDITION

NEW JERSEY

SECOND EDITION

ARLINE ZATZ

THE MOUNTAINEERS BOOKS

THE MOUNTAINEERS BOOKS
is the nonprofit publishing arm of The Mountaineers Club,
an organization founded in 1906 and dedicated to the exploration,
preservation, and enjoyment of outdoor and wilderness areas.

1001 SW Klickitat Way, Suite 201, Seattle, WA 98134

First printing 1992, second printing 1994, third printing 1995, fourth printing 1996, fifth printing 1998, sixth printing 1999, seventh printing 2001, eighth printing 2002. Second edition 2005.

Published simultaneously in Great Britain by Cordee, 3a DeMontfort Street, Leicester, England, LE1 7HD

Manufactured in the United States of America

Project Editor: Margaret Sullivan
Copyeditor: Joeth Zucco
Cartographer: David A. Zatz
Cover and book design: The Mountaineers Books
Layout Artist: Ani Rucki

Unless otherwise noted, all photographs are by Joel Zatz.

Cover photograph: *Young boys on hike* © Getty Images/Photodisc
Frontispiece: *Cartographer David Zatz began hiking at an early age and enjoys it now with his children.*

Library of Congress Cataloging in Publication Data
Zatz, Arline.
  Best hikes with children in New Jersey / by Arline Zatz.— 2nd ed.
      p.   cm.
  Includes index.
  ISBN 0-89886-820-3
  1. Hiking—New Jersey—Guidebooks. 2. Outdoor recreation for children— New Jersey—Guidebooks. 3. New Jersey—Guidebooks.
  I. Title.
  GV199.42.N5Z38 2004
  917.4904'4—dc22
                                          2004024625

A journey of one thousand miles begins with one step.

—Confucius

To my granddaughter, Zoe Zatz—

For the joy you've given me on all the walks we've taken together,

and all those yet to come;

and for sharing my love of hiking and writing books.

I hope, while on your trail through life,

you'll remember holding my hand,

the fun we always have, and our great walks and talks.

CONTENTS

LEGEND

TRAILS

··········· Featured trail   ·········· Other trail

ROADS

——— Main road

——— Secondary road

(195) Interstate

(9) US Highway

(94) State Highway

[529] County road

SYMBOLS

Ⓣ	Trailhead	♦♦♦	Restrooms
Ⓟ	Parking	▪	Building
➚	Direction of hike	•	Point of interest
➶	Reference off map	⚤	Playground
⚑	Campground	⚲	Tennis courts
禾	Picnic site	⚘	Soccer field
⊷	Gate	Ⓐ	Aqua blaze
⊨	Footbridge	Ⓑ	Blue blaze
▬	Dam	Ⓖ	Green blaze
⌒	River or stream	Ⓚ	Black blaze
▬	Body of water	Ⓝ	Brown blaze
⩊	Marsh or grasses	◎	Orange blaze
📷	Scenic outlook	◎	Pink blaze
┼┼┼┼	Railroad	Ⓡ	Red blaze
·········	Power line	Ⓢ	Silver blaze
—·—·—	Boundary line	⊗	Teal blaze
— — —	Pipeline	Ⓦ	White blaze
– – – –	Fence	Ⓨ	Yellow blaze

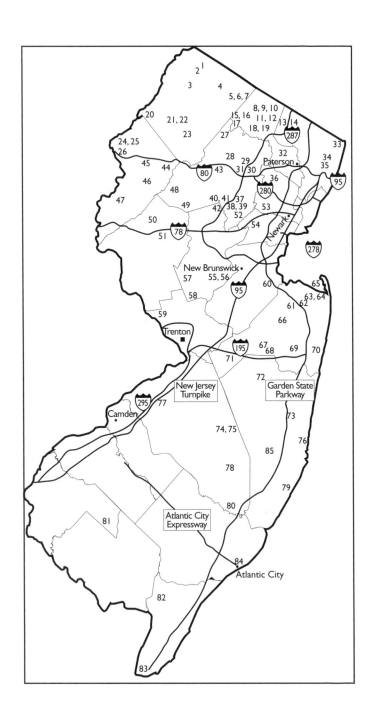

ACKNOWLEDGMENTS

Heartfelt thanks, big hugs, and lots of love to my husband, Dr. Joel L. Zatz, for his valuable contributions to this book, including providing directions to each trailhead so no one would get lost; his super photographic skills; for helping me with computer problems; and most of all, for his enthusiasm, love, and the pleasure of his company on each of these hikes.

Tremendous thanks, too, to my son, Dr. David A. Zatz, both for his expertise in designing the excellent trail maps as well as his helpful suggestions. And to my daughter-in-law, Dr. Kate Zatz, for her great ideas, sense of humor, and support and encouragement.

I am very grateful to the organizations and individuals who helped me gather valuable information both for the original edition and in this revised edition, including the Appalachian Mountain Club; New York–New Jersey Trail Conference; Rails to Trails; and Karl Anderson, naturalist, Rancocas Nature Center; Mike Anderson, Scherman-Hoffman Sanctuaries; Pete Bacinski, director, Sandy Hook Bird Observatory; Steve Barnes, director, Poricy Park; Patty Bertach, director, Watchung Reservation; Christian Bethmann, superintendent, Brendon T. Byrne State Forest; Frank Bopp, ranger, Bass River State Forest; Melissa Brown, chief ranger, Ringwood State Park; Jane Bullis, naturalist, Merrill Creek Reservoir; Tom Card, chief ranger, Ringwood State Park; Dianne Bennett-Chase, Island Beach State Park; George Chase, historian, Island Beach State Park; Chris Chidichimo, ranger, Clayton Park; Rab Cika, supervisory park ranger, Kittatinny Point Visitor Center; Chris Claus, naturalist, Cattus Island; Cynthia L. Coritz, superintendent, Bass River State Forest; Madeline Dennis, Flat Rock Brook Nature Center; Dave Donnelly, Batsto Village; Mimi Dunne, naturalist, Pequest Natural Resource Education Center; James Faczak, naturalist, Cheesequake State Park; Elizabeth Faircloth, Forest Resource Education Center; Thomas E. Fobes Sr., parks manager, Manasquan Reservoir; William Foley, superintendent, Wawayanda State Park; Don Freiday, naturalist, Scherman-Hoffman Sanctuaries; Brian Hardiman, ranger/naturalist, Delaware Water Gap Visitor Center; John Keator, superintendent, High Point State Park; Lynn Groves, naturalist, Kittatinny Valley State Park; Jim Hall, superintendent, Palisades Interstate Park; David Hauenstein, public information assistant, Monmouth County Park System; Wayne Henderek, interpretive specialist, Washington Crossing State Park; Tom Hoffman, historian, Sandy Hook; Bob Jonas, supervisor, New York–New Jersey Trail Conference; Ernie Kabert, superintendent, Worthington State Forest; Tom Keck, superintendent, Belleplain State Forest; Laura Kirkpatrick, public relations director, Monmouth County Parks; Bill Koch, manager, Great Swamp National Wildlife Refuge; Tom Koeppel, chief forester, Pequannock Watershed; Joe Kolucko, naturalist, Wawayanda State Park; Bill Laithner, superintendent, Kittatinny Point Visitor Center; Debbie Long, naturalist, Edwin B. Forsythe National Wildlife Refuge; Joseph Lanzara, archivist, Essex County Department of Parks; Deborah J. Long, deputy project leader, Edwin B. Forsythe National Wildlife Refuge; David M. Lord, chief ranger, Stephens/Allamuchy Mountain State Parks; Scott Mauger, superintendent, Parvin State Park; Lorraine M. McCay, interpretive specialist, Allaire State Park; Janet McMillan, trails coordinator, Morris County Parks; Kathleen Meyer, Belleplain State Forest; Gilbert Mika, naturalist, Wharton State Forest; Maggie Mitchell, secretary, Stokes State Forest; Kate Monahan, naturalist, High Point State Park; Brian Moscatello, naturalist, Tenafly Nature Center; Eric Nelsen, naturalist, Palisades Interstate Park; Rand Otten, office manager, Newark Watershed Conservation Development; Kim Russ, community service specialist, Round Valley Recreation Area; Joseph Schmeltz, naturalist, Mercer County Parks; Catherine Schrein, manager, Lord Stirling Environmental Education Center; Gregory F. Smith, chief ranger, Morristown National Historical Park; Paul Stern, superintendent, Stokes State Forest; Ed Talone, American Hiking Society; Paul Tarlowe, senior biologist/information officer, Pequest Trout Hatchery; Liz Turrin, Colts Neck Trail Riders Club; Douglas Vorolieff, naturalist, Pyramid Mountain Natural Historical Area; Lee Widjeskog, supervisor, Land Management, Division of Fish and Wildlife; Rebecca Williams, supertintendent, Washington Crossing State Park; James Zollitsch, chief ranger, Bass River State Forest.

Thanks, too, to my publisher, The Mountaineers Books, for agreeing to revise *Best Hikes with Children in New Jersey* and to staff members, including Director of Editorial and Production Kathleen Cubley for her infinite patience and understanding in extending deadlines; New Editions Editor, Deb Easter, an extraordinary gal who never failed to cheer me with her constant flow of emails filled with words of wisdom and humor. Special thanks, too, to the countless men and women who blaze the trails and maintain them for all of us to enjoy!

NEW JERSEY FACTS

Date of Statehood ▪ December 18, 1787

State Capital ▪ Trenton

Nickname ▪ Garden State

Land Area ▪ 7504.8 square miles

Total Coastline Area ▪ 127 miles

Highest Point ▪ High Point, 1803 feet

Lowest Point ▪ Atlantic Ocean, sea level

Greatest Length ▪ 166 miles from High Point to Cape May

Narrowest Width ▪ 32 miles from Trenton to Raritan Bay

State Tree ▪ Red oak, adopted 1950

State Bird ▪ Eastern goldfinch, adopted 1935

State Flower ▪ Purple violet, adopted 1913

State Fruit ▪ Blueberry, adopted 2004

State Insect ▪ Honeybee, adopted 1974

State Animal ▪ Horse, adopted 1977

State Dinosaur ▪ Hadrosaurus Foulkii, adopted 1991

State Fish ▪ Brook trout, adopted 1992

State Seashell ▪ Knobbed whelk, adopted 1995

State Dance ▪ Square dance, adopted 1983

PREFACE

Best Hikes with Children in New Jersey has proved to be a favorite among hikers of all ages and is written for individuals, couples, groups of friends, families, and grandparents. As the only New Jersey hiking book with children in mind, it has gone through eight printings.

While hiking these trails over and over again, I realized that nothing, not even trails, stays the same forever—for I found a couple of trails that suddenly infringed on private property; changes to the color of blazes; or park personnel making minor changes or completely rerouting a trail. Due to the popularity of *Best Hikes with Children in New Jersey*, I realized it was time for a revision, and in this new edition, you'll find I have removed five original hikes and have added fifteen brand-new hikes.

In addition to incorporating new websites, where available, and the name of the county where each hike is located, I've added more useful tips on hiking with and without kids that include safety measures, environmental awareness concerns, and up-to-date information on black bears, ticks, and snakes, plus how to avoid them. You'll also find new photographs, information on how to dress for the hike, and a lot more.

The fun, educational, and exciting hikes that have been chosen range from 1 to 8 miles. I will guide you every step of the way, pointing out places to enjoy a gorgeous view, listen to birds chirping, admire a gurgling brook, or find a special boulder that's perfect for taking a break.

From the highlands in the north to the beaches and pine barrens in the south, *Best Hikes with Children in New Jersey* explores the exciting trails of the Garden State. You'll hike the Kittatinny Mountains for unbeatable vistas; scamper over huge boulders while overlooking the Hudson River; discover the best of Mom Nature; spot birds, reptiles, and mammals; look for ersatz diamonds on a Cape May beach; and go out for the day or an overnighter. You'll discover places to camp, fish, or take time out for a paddle before or after the hike as well as many other surprises.

Some trails meander through mature pine-oak forests. On others, hikers can feast upon the sight of mountain laurel and wildflowers; learn how a pond is formed from the upwelling of underground water); and discover why clay mining was an important part of Pineland history on one of the new hikes (Hike 85, Wells Mills) in this edition. Afterward you can enjoy the nature center that's chock full of old farm equipment, a spectacular view of the lake, and the surrounding woodland.

Along Six Mile Run (Hike 55), another new hike in this edition, walk along gently rolling lowland beside the lovely Millstone River where early-eighteenth-century Dutch farmers settled. Eroded shale bedrock has formed impressive ravines along the course of the Six Mile Run creek. In several places you'll pass beside fields where deer can often be spotted, and most days you'll be completely alone.

Let me know how you've enjoyed each hike. Write to me at *azatz@funtravels.com* and watch for the latest information on my website, *www.funtravels.com*.

INTRODUCTION

Webster's Dictionary defines hiking as "a long walk for pleasure in open country." Before I was married, I thought taking a hike meant walking six blocks to the train station! Happily, a few years later when my husband and I realized that weekends and holidays were times to get away from it all, we created our own definition of hiking: enjoying the outdoors on foot, while strengthening the heart, employing all the senses, and communing with Mother Nature. In fact, according to the American Hiking Society, hiking also

- helps burn calories leading to weight loss.
- decreases harmful cholesterol from the artery walls.
- prevents heart disease.
- slows the aging process by helping to maintain the maximal aerobic power.
- helps reverse the negative effects of osteoporosis by increasing bone density and slowing the rate of calcium loss.
- reduces anxiety by helping to release endorphins, which are thought to be natural tranquilizers.
- decreases the pain of arthritis by helping to strengthen muscles.

When I decided to write a book on hiking, friends asked why I included children. The answer was simple: Hiking with our children added a lot to our enjoyment of the outdoors, and in recent years hiking with our grandchildren has added a new perspective. Learning to see nature through their eyes has sharpened our senses, just as teaching them to appreciate and respect the environment has reminded us to set a good example. When our children were younger, they always had a stockpile of questions for us. As a result we were compelled to read more in order to answer typical inquiries, such as "Why is this called a Christmas fern?" or "How did the boulders get here?" And now that I am hiking with our grandchildren, I am constantly learning—not only from the questions they ask, but from my own observations while hiking along fantastic trails. Every adventure is a learning experience for each of us.

Through the years our children—and now our grandchildren—have enjoyed many of the hikes I've chosen for this book. Each hike is perfect for any age, but especially for children—for they can complete the trail with a sense of accomplishment. And if you don't have children, or want to get out to explore alone, these trails are perfect for you too. The hikes were also chosen to appeal to the senses: for the sight of the soothing green of a hemlock grove, the fabulous view into distant valleys, and the sheer variety of shapes found along the trail; for the sound of a churning stream, chirping birds, and the crunch of leaves beneath tiny feet; for the bouquet of fragrant flowers and the pungent aroma of decaying logs; for the feeling of fresh air on a perspiring face and the smoothness of beech bark on the fingertips.

The majority of these hikes can be completed in a few hours, but whenever overnight camping is available, whether you're backpacking, in a trailer, a tent site, lean-to, or nearby campground, I've

Wildflowers light up the forest floor during spring.

mentioned the location. You can find more information on campgrounds in the appendix.

The Garden State offers hikers great diversity—from the flat, sandy trails in the famous Pine Barrens of the south to the mountainous terrain found in the north. I've seen, as you will, New Jersey's hidden gems—the caves, brooks, waterfalls, and dozens of other examples of Mother Nature's finest work. Whether you opt for an easy hike (which all novices should begin with) or head for a rocky uphill scramble, you're guaranteed a rewarding experience.

Taking children hiking brings special rewards. Besides the togetherness, you'll discover all kinds of interesting things. Be prepared, however, to stop often; once a child spots a butterfly, a fallen leaf, or an odd-shaped tree, he or she will be reluctant to move on. Relax, take along a hand lens or binoculars, and enjoy the experience together. I've discovered a way to motivate even the most reluctant child: provide each with a backpack filled with personal belongings; a small notepad and pencil to encourage a diary of the hike; an inexpensive camera for each child to snap photos of things he or she finds interesting; frequent stops, with promises for some goodies if they continue moving along; a friend from time to time, for companionship; and a lot of praise. Be patient with them during those unexpected whiny moments or when they walk at a snail's pace when they get tired.

ABOUT THE HIKES

Each hike begins with a block of information summarizing important details as to the type of hike, difficulty, round-trip distance, elevation gain, and season hikable. Following that are highlights of each hike, directions to the trailhead and how to proceed, and what to look for along the way, as well as addresses, phone numbers, and websites for more information.

Hikes range from just over 1 mile to 8 miles round trip. A pedometer was used for measuring distance. Pedometers aren't exact but serve as an additional aid in case a blaze or cairn is missing or overlooked. I used the mileage readings to highlight interesting places or plants encountered on the trail and places you can turn around if the little ones—or you—get tired. I used an altimeter and topographic maps to estimate the elevation gain—the difference in height between the highest and lowest points. However, altimeters can be fooled by changes in weather. Remember, too, that climbs of successive hills add up, and continuous ups and downs require more energy than the elevation gain suggests.

HIKE RATINGS

The hikes are rated easy, moderate, moderate-challenging, or challenging (from a child's point of view) and are based on steepness, elevation change, and trail condition. For example, an easy hike indicates flat terrain and good footing, while a moderate hike has some climbs, elevation gain, and sometimes rough footing in some places. A challenging rating indicates steep climbs, significant elevation gain, and a rough trail. Don't hesitate to explore sections of hikes rated moderate or challenging; many have easy sections and feature turnarounds—places within reach that lead to a special view or feature so that children will feel rewarded for the distance hiked.

I purposely did not put down the time it takes to complete each hike because what may be easy for one child or grownup may be more difficult for another. Expect to average approximately 2 miles per hour plus half an hour for each 1000 feet of vertical rise. Don't forget to factor in weather, rest stops, lunch breaks, and a child's desire to examine an ant hill or take a dip in a refreshing brook.

TRAIL FOOD AND WATER

Take along adequate food and drink for the entire outing, plus a bit extra in case of an emergency. Make the food simple—the things children are used to and like. During warm weather, peanut butter and jelly sandwiches won't spoil, but if the kids prefer cold cuts, tuna, or cheese, prechill some individual cartons of fruit juice to keep the food cold. Most kids love peanuts,

The author's grandchild, Zoe Zatz, takes a brief rest along one of the trails covered with autumn's leaves.

popcorn, fruit, and raisins; these are all fine snack foods to give them energy boosts. Let them share in the planning and they'll love those snack breaks even more!

Bring plenty of water, which should always be carried in. Due to toxins and chemicals found in even the cleanest areas, children should be cautioned never to drink water from ponds, streams, or rivers. In an emergency, water from these sources should be boiled for at least 20 minutes, treated with iodine tablets, or filtered and purified.

OUTFITTING

Clothing. Children (and adults too) are best dressed in layers so that an outer shirt can be removed if it gets too warm or can be added if it gets chilly. A tee shirt, woolen overshirt, and windbreaker are usually fine for an autumn day, while a down parka or ski jacket would be a good addition for winter. Children love to wear cozy vests under their jackets, too. Remember that fabrics next to the skin have to allow heat to be released and perspiration to be absorbed. Raingear made of new fabrics that repel precipitation but allow perspiration to escape have become popular, although they are much more expensive than more traditional garments. Inexpensive rain ponchos can also be used in case of a sudden downpour and stowed inside the backpack or fanny pack when not needed.

Pants should always fit loosely. Shorts are fine if you apply sunscreen and are walking in open areas or along the beach, but for most hikes they do not provide enough protection against underbrush, sun, and insects.

While gloves are necessary during cool weather, wearing a hat year-round is strongly recommended. Not only will a hat protect young heads (older ones too) from the sun's hot rays, but it will prevent body heat from escaping during cold weather. If you're camping on an extremely cold night, you can even wear a hat to bed. Because a hat is usually one of the first items to disappear on a windy day or when a child bends down to explore a stream, it's a good idea to secure it with a string or use a clip that attaches to the hat and shirt collar.

Bandanas, popular with children, are very useful. Buy a bunch in bright colors and demonstrate how they can be dipped into a stream and used to wash a sweaty face or worn around the neck to cool off. They also can be used as an insect swatter, head covering, pressure bandage, or face mask during a sudden wind, smoke, or hail storm.

Unless otherwise indicated, sneakers will suffice for many of the trips in this book, but when hiking along wet trails, through streams, or in boggy areas, lightweight boots are best. Boots should be comfortable and always broken in before venturing out on the trail. It is best to wear two pairs of socks—a thicker woolen pair over a thin inner pair. Use silicone to keep your boots water resistant. You might also want to consider gaiters—a fabric covering that fits over the top of the boots—to prevent water from getting inside. Gaiters are also good protection against ticks and provide extra warmth.

Walking sticks. Who can resist picking up an odd-shaped branch to carry along a trail? Not only does it feel and look good, but it helps you to keep your balance while crossing streams or walking over a rocky area. Walking sticks also take pressure off your hips and back while you're climbing, and they help to reduce shock on your knees and ankles while going downhill. In fact, many people now carry a stick in each hand! I've found that sticks can also be used to push aside thorny brush or to see if snakes are hiding between rocks or in underbrush. Nowadays you can buy expensive "sticks" constructed of fancy square-sided wood or lightweight aluminum. Some sport a compass attached on the top knob, while others may have a bottom spear for catching fish in an emergency situation, a ruler for measuring the height of trees from afar, and a camera mount built in under the top knob in case you want to use it as a monopod. There are also telescoping paired trekking poles that can be adjusted to your height and, when not needed, stowed in your backpack. Although I own each kind, I still prefer an ordinary but unique branch found in the woods that I can take home, whittle a bit, drill a hole, and attach a leather thong so I can put my wrist through it while hiking or attach it to my backpack!

Ten Essentials. *The Mountaineers has compiled the following list of items to be taken on all hikes.*

1. **Navigation:** Always carry a map of the area that you'll be hiking in. It's also wise to buy a compass for each child. If they learn how to use it at a young age, they'll never get lost.

Benjamin Zatz stirring the water with a walking stick

2. **Sun protection:** Wear sunglasses to prevent ultraviolet rays from damaging your eyes. Remember to bring along a strap to prevent them from falling off when you're bending down or brushing into a branch. Take sunscreen with a minimum SPF of 15.
3. **Insulation:** Extra clothing for changes in weather.
4. **Illumination:** A headlamp or flashlight. To prevent arguments, give one to each child. Use it to signal or find your way if you're out on the trail as the sun goes down.
5. **First-aid supplies:** Your kit should contain adhesive bandages, gauze pads and tape, antiseptic cream, insect repellent, tweezers, and acetaminophen as well as a bee sting kit and any medicines you may be taking. Optional items include duct tape to immobilize fractures, a triangular bandage or bandana, and antibiotic ointment. If you're allergic to insect stings, ask your doctor to prescribe an insect bite kit.
6. **Fire:** Don't forget to bring along matches in a waterproof container or a lighter. A candle or chemical fuel are important for starting a fire if you're stuck overnight, but use *caution* with children around.
7. **Repair kit and tools:** Don't forget a knife—for adults only, unless you're confident younger persons can handle one safely.
8. **Nutrition:** Extra food in case the hike takes longer than planned.
9. **Hydration:** Carry water in a plastic or metal container holding one quart minimum per person and possibly a water purification system if you're camping or backpacking.
10. **Emergency shelter:** A tent or tarp in case of an unexpected overnighter.

Additional items to take on any hike include insect repellent. One containing DEET works best, but it shouldn't be applied directly onto a child's skin, synthetic fabrics, or on your forehead as it might drip into your eyes as you sweat. Instead, spray the brim of your hat. Take whistles, in case a child strays from your group. Give one to each child and advise them to blow it three times in a row in case of trouble—one long blast, one short, and one long. When available, use backcountry toilets. Otherwise bury human waste and waste water at least 200 feet from all water sources.

I highly recommend that you purchase, and carry along on all expeditions, a copy of the *Emergency/Survival Handbook*, by Robert E. Brown. This book not only contains emergency information, but also includes a reflective centerfold that can be used as a signaling device and a cover that can be used as a fire starter! Lightweight binoculars will enhance any hike, and field guides can be educational. Children love taking photographs; you might consider bringing a camera to be shared. Buy each child an album to store memories of their trips and you may end up with another Ansel Adams on your hands!

Sometimes children are reluctant to walk more than a mile or two, so give them a pedometer to keep track of their progress and watch them go! Suggest that they record the miles hiked each trip and add them up at the end of the year. Our sons were so proud of their mileage totals that they bragged about them to all their friends and walked around with ear-to-ear smiles. Remember to reset the pedometer to each child's stride if more than one is using it.

Packs. The variety of packs is endless, from the less costly canvas or nylon rucksack for day hikes to an internal-frame or external-frame pack for overnight trips as well as fanny packs that can hold lunch, water bottles, and personal items. For kids, anything goes. But each child should have his or her own, for it's important to get them interested in doing their share even if they can only tote a couple of items. Over the years they'll be willing to carry more and more. For the tiny tot in your family use a fanny pack for stowing some goodies, an extra sweater, a magnifying glass, or a small canteen, and watch the response!

Overnight stays. Shelter is necessary for overnight trips, and today's hiking family has a wealth of tents to choose from. These range from simple tarps tied onto overhead trees, to lightweight, three-season expedition models for winter trips, to larger, fixed-camp tents. If you're planning on an overnight stay at a lean-to or campground mentioned in this book, there are many how-to-do-it books on the market. You can also check out a variety of items, including packs and tents, in catalogs (such as L.L. Bean) or on the Internet.

ADMISSION FEES

Hiking trails in New Jersey are free, but from Memorial Day to Labor Day, most state parks charge a fee for parking, and national parks charge admission year-round. You can save money if you visit these parks frequently by purchasing a pass.

State Parks

Annual State Park Pass. At the current writing, this pass is available for $50 and provides free entrance for one calendar year to state park, forest, recreation area, and historic site facilities that charge daily walk-in or parking fees. A second family vehicle pass may be purchased for $25 at any time during the calendar year and must be registered under the same address that appears on the initial pass application.

Disability Pass. Available free of charge to New Jersey residents with a disability, it provides free entrance to state park, forest, recreation area, and historic site facilities that charge daily walk-in or parking fees, plus a $2 per night discount on campsite fees (excluding group campsites). This pass is valid for the term of your disability or for a maximum of five years; it can be renewed.

Senior Citizen Pass. For New Jersey residents age sixty-two or older, this pass is available free of charge and provides free entrance to state park, forest, recreation area, and historic site facilities that charge daily walk-in or parking fees, plus a $2 per night discount on campsite fees (excluding group campsites). It is valid for your lifetime.

To apply for any one of these passes, contact the New Jersey Department of Environmental Protection, Parks and Forestry, P.O. Box 404, Trenton, NJ 08625; (800) 843-6420; or fill out an application at any park, forest, or recreation area office. Applications are also available online at *www.njparksandforests. org*, but copies of the required documents must be sent in with the completed application.

Note: Verification of disability, residency, and/or age is required.

National Parks

National Parks Pass. This provides admission to any national park charging an entrance fee. At this writing it costs $50 and is valid for one year from first use. It admits the pass holder and all passengers in a private vehicle, unless a per person entrance fee is charged. It does not cover camping, parking, tours, or concession fees. Purchase it at any national park where entrance fees are charged, at participating park bookstores, by calling 1-888-GO-PARKS; or by sending a check or money order for $50 plus $3.95 shipping and handling to the National Park Foundation, P.O. Box 34108, Washington, D.C. 20043.

Golden Eagle hologram. For an additional $15, your National Parks Pass will also cover entrance fees at sites managed by the U.S. Fish and Wildlife Service, the U.S. Forest Service, and the Bureau of Land Management. Rules are the same as above.

Golden Age Passport. For visitors sixty-two years or older, this is a lifetime entrance pass to national parks, monuments, historic sites, recreation areas, and national wildlife refuges that charge an entrance fee. Rules are as above. Pass holders also receive a 50 percent discount on federal use fees charged for facilities and services, including camping, swimming, parking, boat launching, and tours. Apply in person at a federal area where an entrance fee is charged. There is a one-time fee of $10. Proof of age is required; a state driver's license, birth certificate, or similar document is okay.

Golden Access Passport. For visitors who are blind or permanently disabled, this is a lifetime entrance pass to national parks, monuments, historic sites, recreation areas, and national wildlife refuges that charge an entrance fee. Pass holders receive a 50 percent discount on federal use fees charged for facilities and services as above, but only the pass holder will be given the price reduction.

TRAIL WISE

Stay on the trail. By staying on the trail, you won't crush fragile plants or cause erosion. Please follow these words of advice: "Take only photos; leave only footprints." In this way, others can enjoy the area as much as you did. Should you spot deer or other wildlife, take photographs from a distance. It's important to make everyone understand that flowers, moss or lichen, and other natural features on state park or forest lands are to be looked at, not picked or destroyed. With a camera, these precious gifts can be preserved forever.

Blazes and cairns. Staying on the trail has another benefit—getting lost, even on a short hike, is always a possibility.

A blaze points the way along the trail.

Trails are marked with blazes or cairns. Blazes are usually painted on trees or rocks, with a double blaze indicating a change in direction. Three dots indicate the beginning or end of a trail. Always keep the blaze in view. Should you lose sight of the one in front of you, turn back and find the previous one before continuing. Cairns are piles of stones used to indicate trail direction where there aren't any trees or posts. Again, always keep the cairn in front of you in view. Never try to find the way by straying cross-country.

Staying found. Prepare for the unexpected—getting separated on the trail from your child. Dress your child in bright, easy-to-see clothing, and add a colorful backpack. Pack snacks, a whistle for signaling, and a large trash bag that can be used as a poncho to keep dry and warm. While hiking, point out prominent landmarks and blazes.

Should your child wander too far from you and get lost on the trail, a few simple rules suggested by the Hug a Tree organization (*www.gpsar.org/hugatree.html*) will ensure a safe, quick recovery.

- Instruct kids to hug a tree near the trail and to stay put until found unless they spot a house or people.
- If your child hears an airplane or helicopter, tell them to move into a nearby open area and wave clothing or a backpack.
- If a threatening animal approaches, teach your child to blow their whistle or shout.
- Above all, assure your child that you won't be angry if they get separated

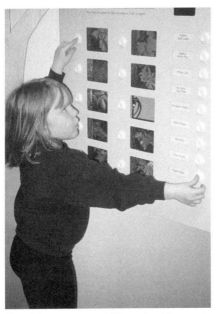

Examining a nature exhibit at the visitor center

from you, so they won't ignore the calls of searchers for fear of being punished.

Maps. Although the maps in this book will normally suffice since the trails are well-marked, it's a good idea to carry a U.S. Geological Survey (USGS) topographic map, which highlights all land features and elevations. For an index of these specialized maps, write to the New Jersey Geological Survey, Map Sales Office, CN 402, Trenton, NJ 08625; or contact USGS at 1-800-HELP-MAP or *www.geography.usgs.gov.* The New York–New Jersey Trail Conference, 156 Ramapo Valley Road, Mahwah, NJ 07430; (201) 512-9348; *www.nynjtc.org,* also sells waterproof, color, topographic maps for a nominal fee.

OUTDOOR MANNERS

Cleaning up. Each time I watched my sons stuffing candy and food wrappers into their pockets or cleaning up after a careless hiker, I felt proud to have succeeded in setting a good example and teaching them to keep the earth beautiful. When you hike New Jersey's great trails, keep the Appalachian Mountain Club's motto in mind: "Carry in, carry out!" In fact, that's the rule in New Jersey's state parks where plastic bags are supplied free of charge so that visitors will take their trash with them. Always bring along your own plastic bag, so if the park hasn't replenished the supply, you can clean up your debris.

Trail courtesy. It's best, even where dogs are permitted, to leave your pet home. Nothing is more annoying or frightening to wildlife or other hikers than a charging, barking dog. If you do bring your dog, please use a leash at all times and check local and state regulations.

Speak softly. Caution your children to speak in a low voice while on the trail, so that everyone can enjoy the sounds as well as sights.

Making fires. Fireplaces are frequently found along the trail; always check to see if fires are permitted in the area at the time of your visit. Never cut down live trees for firewood; instead gather downed wood. Be certain to keep the fire small, and be sure it is completely out before moving on.

WORDS OF CAUTION

Walking alone. The advantages of hiking alone include not having to make conversation and stopping wherever and whenever you please. But walking with your family or a friend is safer. If you sprain an ankle or suffer any mishap, you'll be assured immediate aid. If you don't have anyone to hike with, consider joining one of New Jersey's hiking clubs. Contact the New York–New Jersey Trail Conference at *www.nynjtc.org*.

Your physical condition. When you have small children along or if you're not in top shape, you should plan on hiking no more than a mile and then increasing the length of a chosen trail depending on how well you're feeling. Go farther gradually but don't tax yourself. Remember, hiking is a fun activity, and it doesn't make sense to go home tired with aching muscles.

Leave word. Before starting any hike, whether you're alone or with a friend or family, *always* leave someone with an itinerary detailing how many people are in your group and the approximate time of your return. When you return home, remember to notify that person.

Weather

Before leaving home, listen to the radio or television for the latest weather forecast. Reports are also available via the Internet or newspaper. Since the weather can change at any time, particularly at higher elevations in the northern section of the state, spend some time beforehand learning about the various cloud formations so you can self-predict the likelihood of rain. *Peterson First Guides: Clouds and Weather* (Boston: Houghton Mifflin, 1991) is an excellent guide. Many combination pocket barometer/altimeter instruments are available to help you predict the weather. A reading below 29.92 inches generally means a storm is brewing, while a reading above this is usually an indication of good weather.

Hypothermia and storms. In case you're caught in a sudden storm, be aware that young children are particularly susceptible to hypothermia. Carry extra clothing in case the temperature drops, and watch your children for symptoms. The first signs include crankiness and fatigue, while signs of advanced hypothermia include weakness and shivering. Do not take shelter under the tallest tree during a lightning storm; if you're on a ridge, leave immediately. Also, remove your pack if it has a metal frame. If you're caught in the midst of a lightning storm, the American Hiking Society suggests that you "find a grove of trees, a space between two boulders, or any low spot. Sit or crouch. Do not lie down."

Insects, Snakes, Bears, Rabid Animals

Ticks, mosquitoes, and black flies are pests, and all can cause problems.

Ticks. Ticks carrying Lyme disease can be found in your backyard. Although Lyme disease is as serious a problem in New Jersey as other states, it is more common in the southern part of the state. To safeguard against it, the Lyme Disease Foundation (LDF) recommends wearing light-colored, long-sleeved shirts and long pants when in wooded or grassy areas so you can see the ticks easier. The LDF also recommends tucking your shirt into your pants and tucking the pants legs into socks to prevent a tick from crawling beneath clothing and onto skin. Wearing gaiters can help, too. Stay in the center of paths and use an EPA-approved tick repellent, which should be washed off as soon as you return home. After each hike, help your child check his or her body in case any ticks have hopped aboard, and also examine yourself. The tick responsible for spreading this disease is remarkably tiny, about the size of a poppy seed. If a tick has attached itself to you or your child's skin, use fine-point tweezers to grasp the tick at the place of attachment and as close to the skin as possible. Then gently pull the tick straight out. After removing the tick, wash your hands, disinfect the tweezers and the bite site, and consult with your physician to determine if treatment is warranted.

LDF recommends placing the tick in a small vial (or zipper-locked bag) labeled with the victim's name, address, and date. Have the tick identified and tested by a lab, the local health department, or a veterinarian.

Mosquitoes. This annoying insect is not only responsible for causing itching after it bites, but it can also transmit West Nile Virus, a disease unknown in the United States before 1999. Previously believed to affect horses and birds only, it also infects humans. You can protect yourself when mosquitoes are most active (before sunset) by using proper insect repellants and wearing long-sleeved shirts and pants or a special bug suit.

Snakes. New Jersey is home to many snakes, both poisonous and nonpoisonous, so caution your children to look at them only from a distance and not to stick their hands into any crevices where snakes may be hiding.

Bears. The black bear population has grown tremendously in recent years, and bears are frequently spotted, especially in the northern part of the state. While they are dangerous, they'll usually smell you coming and will probably run for cover before you spot them. If one is close, never coax it toward yourself with food. If a bear approaches you, it's important to keep your cool because a bear can easily outrun you. Make a lot of noise by blowing your whistle or banging stones against a metal canteen. Walk backward while raising your arms so you appear taller and larger than the bear. If you're out in the open, the American Hiking Society suggests playing dead. "Protect your belly, neck, and inside of your arms and legs by clasping your hands tightly behind your neck and lying face down with your legs pressed together." They also warn if the bear rolls you around to "try to stay curled in the fetal position. Don't struggle, cry out, or resist." And if you're tenting overnight, don't leave food or odorous items (such as toothpaste) in the tent; suspend all food and garbage in sealed bags at least 10 feet off the ground and 4 feet from the tree trunk.

Rabid animals. An increasing number of rabid animals, such as raccoons and skunks, have been reported in recent years. It's wise to stay away from even the cutest animal you may meet on the trail, and never pet them no matter how close they may come to you.

Poisonous Plants

Be cautious about coming in contact with plants because certain ones can cause severe skin irritation, blisters, and itching. Learn to recognize poison ivy, poison sumac, and poison oak. *Poison ivy*, which may grow as a plant, bush, or vine on tree trunks, branches, and along riverbanks, has three shiny green leaves, greenish-white flowers, and clusters of berries that turn a brilliant red in the fall and are shiny green the rest of the year. Whenever you spot this plant, heed the saying, "Leaves of three, let it be." If you should brush against it and develop a rash, redness, blisters, swelling, burning, or itching, it's advisable to remove contaminated clothing as soon as possible, wash the affected area of skin with soap and water, and if the rash is mild, apply calamine or other soothing lotion. I've found that applying wet compresses helps greatly, but if the reaction is extreme, contact your physician as soon as possible. When petted, dogs can transfer the oils from poison ivy onto your skin, so be sure to give Fido a bath after the hike, and refrain from petting dogs of other hikers on the trail.

Two other plants that can cause troublesome rashes include *poison sumac* and *poison oak*. Poison sumac grows as a bush or tree and has rows of two pointed leaflets opposite each other and a main leaflet at the top. *Poison oak* grows in swampy areas as a bush or vine and has three leaflets.

Mushrooms. Mushrooms are delicious and nutritious, but unless you know how to positively recognize mushrooms found in the woods, it can possibly be fatal to eat even one! Never allow your children to sample anything without absolutely knowing what it is. Available are several books on first aid and plant identification. It's a good idea to read and discuss this together so that everyone is aware of why it's so important not to nibble along the trail.

Hunting Season

Wear bright colors during hunting season. Hunting isn't allowed on Sunday, but check with local parks or the New Jersey Department of Environmental Protection for the dates that it is permitted.

Theft

It's a fact of life that thieves operate all over, even at deserted trailheads and campsites. Leave all valuables at home, and leave nothing inside the car to tempt a thief looking for a good day's haul. I usually just carry my driver's license and enough money for gas and tolls in my backpack.

I've listed some possible hazards, but if you use common sense, you'll find that hiking with kids is fun, free, and fulfilling. Go outdoors. Take your family with you and explore these suggested hiking trails. I promise you'll be on your way to an exciting journey.

Enjoy!

KEY TO SYMBOLS

Day hikes. These can be completed in a single day. While some trips allow camping, very few require it. But overnight camping is a great way to begin another hike the next morning.

Backpack trips. The length or difficulty of these hikes makes camping out either necessary or recommended for most families.

Easy trails. The relatively short, smooth, and gentle trails are suitable for small children, first-time hikers, or those yearning for a short, relaxing leg stretch.

Moderate trails. Most are 2 to 4 miles total distance and feature more than 500 feet of elevation gain. The trail may be rough and uneven. Hikers should wear lug-soled boots and carry the Ten Essentials.

Challenging trails. Often rough with considerable elevation gain or distance to travel, these are suitable for older or experienced children. Lug-soled boots and the Ten Essentials are standard equipment.

Hikable. The best times of year to hike each trail are indicated by the following symbols: flower (spring); sun (summer); leaf (fall); snowflake (winter).

Driving directions. These paragraphs guide you to the trailheads.

Turnarounds. Mostly along moderate trails, these are places where families can cut their hike short yet still have a satisfying outing. Turnarounds usually offer picnic opportunities, views, or special natural attractions.

Caution. Potential hazards—cliffs, stream or highway crossing, and the like—are marked where close supervision of children is strongly recommended.

Viewpoint. These are places with exceptional views.

Environmental close-ups. A special highlight worth stopping to examine.

Environmental cautions. A fragile, unique natural or historical feature.

A NOTE ABOUT SAFETY

Safety is an important concern in all outdoor activities. No guidebook can alert you to every hazard or anticipate the limitations of every reader. Therefore, the descriptions of roads, trails, routes, and natural features in this book are not representations that a particular place or excursion will be safe for your party. When you follow any of the routes described in this book, you assume responsibility for your own safety. Under normal conditions, such excursions require the usual attention to traffic, road and trail conditions, weather, terrain, the capabilities of your party, and other factors. Keeping informed on current conditions and exercising common sense are the keys to a safe, enjoyable outing.

The Mountaineers

1 MONUMENT TRAIL

Location ■ High Point State Park
County ■ Sussex
Type ■ Day hike or overnight camping
Difficulty ■ Moderate
Distance ■ 4.9 miles
Elevation gain ■ 300 feet
Hours ■ Dawn to dusk
Information ■ High Point State Park, 1480 State Route 23, Sussex 07461;
(973) 875-4800
Website ■ *www.njparksandforests.org*
Admission ■ Free; fee for parking, Memorial Day to Labor Day; fee for
camping

 Driving directions: From Colesville, in the northwest corner of the state, take NJ-23 north into High Point State Park. Just past the park office on the left, turn right and follow signs to the monument.

 You can see forever (or almost forever) if you hike through High Point State Park on a clear day. The road leads to a parking lot beside a 220-foot obelisk built to honor New Jersey's veterans. It stands 1803 feet above sea level—the highest point in New Jersey. When open, the 291-step climb to the top (fee) is definitely worth the effort, but save those vistas for the end of the hike. If you're too tired by the time you get to the monument, the view from the base is also fine for admiring the Delaware River, the Pocono and Catskill Mountains, the Wallkill River Valley, and farmland. The trail, a series of mini ups and downs along the Kittatinny Mountain ridge in the northwestern corner of the state, passes through dense woods, a cedar swamp, and along the bank of Lake Marcia—the highest lake in the state. Bring along a magnifying glass to examine sphagnum moss in the swamp and binoculars to view the hawks and vultures that frequent this area. Campsites with wooden tent platforms are available at Sawmill Lake, within the park, and, two cabins can be rented at Lake Steenykill, also within the park.

 Hiking boots and long pants are a good idea; where the trail narrows, you'll be brushing against shrubbery. Walk north away from the monument to the far end of the parking lot onto the Monument Trail, designated by a red and green circular blaze. The narrow, level trail is rocky, and at the ridge top there's a mixture of low-growing pitch pine and oak. Note how conditions at the higher elevations stunt the growth of the trees. As you begin a gradual climb at 0.2 mile, look to the left for an exceptional view of the Delaware River and Pennsylvania. For the remainder of the hike, you'll be

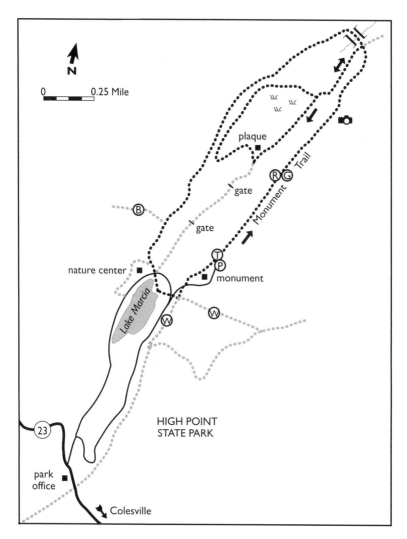

N

0   0.25 Mile

plaque

gate

Ⓡ Ⓖ

Monument Trail

gate

Ⓑ

Ⓣ
Ⓟ

nature center

monument

Ⓦ

Ⓦ

Lake Marcia

HIGH POINT
STATE PARK

㉓

park
office

Colesville

encountering slight ups and downs until the last segment, which is steep.

Being here in autumn is grand; besides the color change you can watch squirrels scurrying about looking for acorns. Descending at 0.3 mile is a bit difficult to negotiate, since some of the rocks along the trail are on a vertical tilt. A few yards ahead, you'll be crossing over a sea of boulders beneath beautiful red maple and mitten-shaped sassafras. Continue to the ridge at 0.5 mile, turning right onto a short, narrow path leading to an overlook with an exceptional view. When ready to proceed, return the way you came, again watching where you place your feet as you descend steeply into the woods. When the trail levels and you approach a wooden bridge at 0.9 mile, turn left before the bridge onto a wide, gravel-covered path. You are now walking through the Cedar Swamp, along a former carriage road. In a few yards, you'll encounter easy ups and downs as well as stands of tall rhododendron, some reaching 15 feet high. At approximately 1.2 miles, while still in the cedar swamp area, continue straight when the trail veers to the right. Soon, you'll enter an area with lush ferns that turn a brilliant yellow in fall. At the next road junction, just ahead, turn right. As you do, you'll see a memorial plaque dedicating this natural area to New Jersey State Senator John Dryden Kuser, a leading conservationist and son of Colonel Anthony Kuser and Susie Dryden Kuser. Colonel Kuser and his wife donated the land for this park and provided the funds to build the monument. In the swamp you'll find beautiful cedars as well as many beeches and chestnut oaks. To the right, just under 2 miles, you'll see sphagnum moss in the boggy area. And ahead, trees have sprouted up through the cracks in the boulders. Continue along the narrow boardwalk through a very wet area covered with sphagnum moss and the unusual wild calla plant, which is filled with red berries in fall. This is a great area to take out the magnifying glass, lie on the boardwalk, and study the interesting plants below. At the T where you originally entered the cedar swamp, turn left, and if you didn't notice the rhododendron the first time, you'll have another opportunity. Turn left when you reach Monument Trail once again, and cross over the wooden bridge. Interestingly, this trail was built by the Civilian Conservation Corps (CCC) in the 1930s, and the stone steps built into the trail ahead are evidence of the CCC's careful construction and craftsmanship. The trail begins to climb steeply at 3 miles, and the Delaware River appears to the right.

Descending through a mixed-wood forest along a narrow path, you'll encounter a few dips and rises until 3.9 miles, where the trail ascends steeply. Here the stone steps make climbing easier. On windy days the trees have a melody of their own as the limbs scrape each other and the leaves shake in the breeze. After huffing and puffing a bit, you'll see the monument to the left through the trees at 4 miles. At the junction with the road, turn left and follow the road. **Use caution;** an occasional car may come by. In a few yards, Lake Marcia will come into view on the right.

If you'd like to pause for a snack, pick a boulder for a natural chair. Continue on the Monument Trail along the shore of Lake Marcia. Soon the trail turns to the left away from the lake and ascends steeply over boulders. Watch your footing; some are loose. Cross the road, watching for cars, and cut through the woods again, but don't venture too far without having a blaze in sight. When the foliage is dense, they're difficult to see. The trail continues uphill through the woods and crosses a road again before reaching the monument and continuing to the parking area.

2 ABOVE LAKE RUTHERFORD

Location ■ High Point State Park
County ■ Sussex
Type ■ Day hike or overnight camping
Difficulty ■ Challenging
Distance ■ 5.2 miles
Elevation gain ■ 250 feet
Hours ■ Dawn to dusk
Information ■ High Point State Park, 1480, State Route 23, Sussex 07641;
(973) 875-4800
Website ■ *www.njparksandforests.org*
Admission ■ Free; fee for parking, Memorial Day to Labor Day; fee for
camping

Driving directions: From Colesville, in the northwest corner of the state, take NJ-23 north into High Point State Park. Just before the park office on the left, take a left onto a dirt road that leads directly to an unpaved trail parking lot.

You'll need sturdy shoes to negotiate thousands of rocks while exploring the southern portion of High Point State Park. The struggle along this section of the Appalachian Trail is worth the effort, because the views along the

Groundhogs are often spotted at High Point State Park.

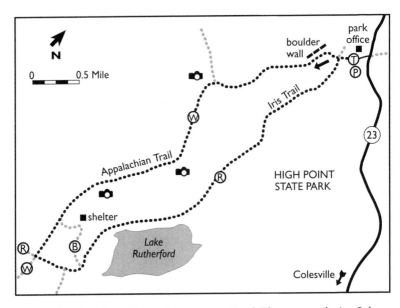

crest of the Kittatinny Mountains are sensational. If you come during July or August, plump blueberries are yours for the picking. Be certain to identify what goes into your mouth; there are some look-alikes that may be poisonous. In early morning or late afternoon, there's a good chance of spotting a groundhog as it makes its way along the rocky slopes in search of tender plants to eat. According to folklore dating from the sixteenth century, should the groundhog be frightened by its shadow when emerging from hibernation on February 2, it will head back underground, and spring will be delayed for another six weeks.

Facing the park office, enter a narrow trail located between two stone blocks, then turn left onto a trail marked by both white and yellow blazes. In 0.1 mile you'll see a red marker and a sign on the left indicating the terminus of the Iris Trail, while the yellow trail takes off to the right. Continue straight ahead, following the white blazes of the Appalachian Trail as it gradually climbs. At the T at 0.25 mile, in front of a wall of granite, turn left. From here, you'll be going up and down over rocks and boulders of all sizes and shapes. There's a lovely view of forest and mountain ridges to the west with Sawmill Pond in the foreground, at just over 1 mile.

The trail then turns eastward, leaving the ridge top. You'll descend on loose rocks that resemble a river of boulders and then scramble up again on a similar bed of granite. A steep rock outcrop appears shortly, and when you sit down to rest, observe the free show. At your feet ants scurry about every which way, carrying loads of food that weigh more than they do. Another 0.5 mile brings you to an overlook facing east, with a view of Lake Rutherford.

In a few yards, the view is even better; here you'll see why New Jersey is nicknamed the Garden State. The well-marked trail meanders along on high ground finally reaching a ledge with another beautiful vista to the east; **use caution** because there's a sharp drop-off.

A short distance farther, a sign and blue blazes indicate the way to an overnight shelter. Turn back the way you came and enjoy the vistas again on the way to your car.

If you'd like to lengthen the trip (by about a mile) and return on a different trail, continue south on the Appalachian Trail until it meets the Iris Trail, marked with red blazes. Turn left, following the Iris Trail past Lake Rutherford and eventually back to the start.

CULVER TOWER

Location ■ Stokes State Forest
County ■ Sussex
Type ■ Day hike or overnight camping
Difficulty ■ Challenging
Distance ■ 4.5 miles
Elevation gain ■ 600 feet
Hikable ■ Year-round
Hours ■ Dawn to dusk
Information ■ Stokes State Forest, 1 Coursen Road, Branchville 07826; (973) 948-3820
Website ■ www.njparksandforests.org
Admission ■ Free; fee for parking Memorial Day to Labor Day; fee for camping

Driving directions: From Newton, take US 206 north. Turn right on Coursen Road into Stokes State Forest, drive past the park office, take the next right, and continue for a short distance to the Stony Lake day-use area.

In the first century A.D., Publius Syrus wrote the maxim, "A rolling stone gathers no moss." Perhaps he was inspired by hiking trails similar to those in Stokes State Forest, where thousands of odd-shaped rocks are adorned with lush, green moss. Take in a fabulous view of Pennsylvania and the Delaware Water Gap from the mountain ridge traversed by the Appalachian Trail. Nearby stands the Culver fire tower, which is manned only when the risk of fires is high. Kids can hardly resist the temptation to climb the six flights of stairs leading to the top, but **caution** them to hold onto the railing; the winds are quite strong at this altitude.

In autumn this is a great place to watch the bird migration, so bring

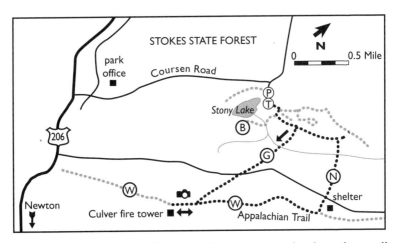

binoculars and a bird identification book. As you meander through a small portion of the 15,000 acres that make up Stokes State Forest, you'll see a great variety of trees and wildflowers. Plan on staying overnight; seventy-seven tent and trailer sites are available, as well as ten furnished cabins.

To begin this hike, look for a bulletin board with a trail map at the far end of the parking lot, toward the stone fence. Just behind this is a wide gravel path, which leads gradually uphill past light green, dark green, brown, and blue blazes. At the trail junction follow the dark green, brown, and blue markings. Chestnut oaks form a thick canopy overhead and, as the trail descends

slightly at 0.2 mile, continue straight on the dark green- and brown-blazed trail when the blue trail veers off to the right. An impressive hemlock grove soon appears.

Where the trail levels, a stone wall will be on the left. This once served as a boundary marker. At 0.5 mile, turn right, following the dark green-blazed Tower Trail, but watch your footing; rocks pop up everywhere. A lot of scrub oak and fern, along with moss-covered rocks, are found along this narrow section of trail. As the trail ascends steeply at 0.7 mile, you'll probably spot a lot of salamanders darting for cover at the sound of your footsteps.

Use caution crossing the road at 1.2 miles and while climbing the natural rock staircases. An open view to the west soon unfolds, giving you a preview of the magnificent vista at the crest of the ridge. Pay attention on this narrow, rocky section; there are some steep drop-off areas. The rocks can also be quite slippery after rain or from early morning dew. The top of the ridge

(1.5 miles) is a fine place to look out upon the Gap and surrounding farms, to view soaring vultures and hawks, or to relax and have lunch. Turn right onto the white-blazed Appalachian Trail, and walk 0.1 mile to the Culver fire tower. Climb the steps for a spectacular 360-degree panorama, but hold on to the railing in case there's a sudden gust of wind.

Heading north now on the Appalachian Trail, go past the junction with the Tower Trail. Follow this narrow, level path that has occasional views to the west. Turn left at the brown blazes at 2.8 miles, descending on the now wider but still rocky trail, which leads past a shelter. Stay with the brown blazes identifying the Stony Brook Trail. After crossing the road, use Mother Nature's rocks and tree roots to gain sure footing as the trail heads steeply downhill. Cross the stream at 3.1 miles,

The view of the surrounding countryside from Culver Tower is extraordinary.

where considerate hikers have placed rocks to protect against wet feet, and continue on to a wider section of trail fairly free of rocks. The trail is now less steep, with occasional ups and downs. Moss and lichens thrive in the shaded, damp forest, and a lovely grove of evergreens appears at 3.9 miles, with the scent of pine disappearing all too soon. The Stony Brook Trail also comes to an end. Turn left onto the wide, level Station Trail and follow it back to the Stony Lake area.

POCHUCK CREEK

Location ▪ Vernon Township
County ▪ Sussex
Type ▪ Day hike
Difficulty ▪ Easy
Distance ▪ 3 miles
Elevation gain ▪ Negligible
Hours ▪ Dawn to dusk
Information ▪ New York–New Jersey Trail Conference, 156 Ramapo Valley Road, Mahwah 07430; (201) 512-8348
Website ▪ www.nynjtc.org
Admission ▪ Free

Driving directions: Take NJ-94 north from Vernon and turn left at Maple Grange Road. Continue to Canal Road, turn right and proceed north to a

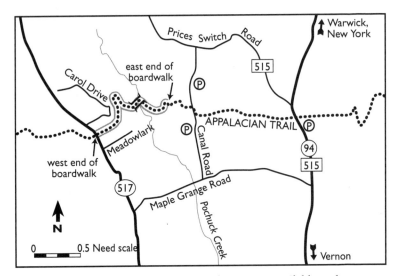

gate where parking is located. **Note:** Parking is not available at the western entrance to the boardwalk.

Plans to acquire the land necessary to build the Appalachian Scenic Trail mile-long boardwalk and a 110-foot suspension bridge began in 1978. In 2002, twenty-four years later, the work was completed—thanks to the hundreds of volunteers who donated approximately 9000 hours of time, talent, and sweat to this fantastic project that now joins part of the white-blazed Appalachian Trail between Pochuck and the Wawayanda Mountains. Today, hikers of all ages and abilities can enjoy this unique, scenic, and safe off-road alternative to the previous 2.2-mile narrow, winding—and sometimes hazardous—path along local CR 517. Classified as an Exceptional Resource Value Wetland, by the National Park Service, Pochuck consists of 240 acres and a 3000-foot-wide floodplain crisscrossed by tributaries. Actually, this is a non-delineated river with a 60-foot-wide stream channel that is capable of rising 6 feet or more during heavy rains, with a flow so fast that it can carry trees downstream! But there's no need to worry—for you'll be safe and dry during the entire hike—and depending on the season, you'll see excellent specimens of native and endangered plants and animals, plus the state's largest area of native cattails.

Arrive early to be guaranteed a space in the small parking area. After parking, walk north past a gate for about 500 feet. Cross the short bridge overlooking a creek where anglers can usually be found, and continue uphill following the rectangular-shaped white-blazes. The trail soon narrows to a dirt path strewn with some rocks and passes an area where the trees look a bit spooky due to their dead branches lower down.

After a curve in the trail, boulders appear on the right, followed by a low rock fence you'll have to step over carefully. In the spring the trees in this area put on a great show as their buds burst open. Still climbing gradually, watch for a ravine on the left before approaching another rock fence to step over. The boardwalk can now be seen in the distance. As you head downhill toward the boardwalk, look for an outstanding shagbark hickory on the right. Sporting compound leaves, 8 to 20 inches long, with only five leaflets, this beauty—named for its shaggy bark that curls away from the trunk at the edges—is noted for its toughness and was used for making spokes for wagon wheels. Nowadays its wood is favored for making ax handles and other tools. The hickory is also the preferred firewood in the production of hickory-smoked hams. Here, you'll find numerous wildflowers, including more may-apples, wild columbine, trillium, and violets.

Immediately after walking onto the snaking boardwalk, sit down on a bench that's been placed at the perfect spot for gazing out onto the huge meadow and enjoy the view. The suspension bridge follows and, if more than one person is on it, you'll definitely feel its sway as you look down to the water. Built in 1995, but not connected to the trail until boardwalk construction began in 1999, it consists of four 20-foot sections, a 15-foot center section, and two end sections totaling 110 feet. Made of wood planking cut into 648 pieces, 40-foot yellow pine transmission poles, crushed stone, poured concrete, various sizes of rebar, Tensar Geogrid spikes, lag screws, and wire cables. Each section consisted of sixty-four pieces that had to be cut, fitted, drilled, and connected—at the hands of volunteers. Volunteers on this and the boardwalk project included the New York–New Jersey Trail Conference (now the trail maintainer), Appalachian Trail Conference, National Park Service, New Jersey Division of Parks and Forests, Vernon Township Municipal Authorities, the consulting engineer firm of Purrell Associates, the Builders Association of North New Jersey, Jersey Central Power and Light, students from St. Benedicts Prep School and Vernon Public High School, members of St. Thomas Episcopal Church, and countless other dedicated individuals.

There are more benches ahead that invite you to take photographs, listen to the birds, wait for a turtle to swim by or spot one sunning itself on a log, or simply marvel at the boardwalk itself with its 8502 treadboards and 874 piers. As you hike farther, check out the cattails, plumed grasses, wildflowers, hemlock, laurel, firs, and five species of oak—red, white, black, scarlet, and chestnut—as well as yellow and black birch, sweet gum, sugar maple, rare yellow birch, and white pine. The mountain laurel and azalea bloom in spring. And, on occasion, you may spot a beaver, otter, porcupine, deer, black bear, various snakes (copperhead, black, and rattle), or a few of the more than two hundred species of birds that frequent the area, including ruffed grouse, broad-wing hawks, great horned owls, pileated woodpeckers, and towhees.

At approximately 1.4 miles, you'll reach the end of the boardwalk. Follow a level dirt path for a short distance before reaching CR 517, where you will turn around and retrace your steps to the parking area.

5 LAUREL POND

Location ▪	Wawayanda State Park
Counties ▪	Sussex and Passaic
Type ▪	Day hike or overnight camping
Difficulty ▪	Moderate
Distance ▪	4 miles
Elevation gain ▪	220 feet
Hours ▪	Dawn to dusk
Information ▪	Wawayanda State Park, 885 Warwick Turnpike, Hewitt 07421; (973) 853-4462
Website ▪	www.njparksandforests.org
Admission ▪	Free; fee for parking, Memorial Day to Labor Day; fee for camping

 Driving directions: Enter Wawayanda State Park on Warwick Turnpike, north of Upper Greenwood Lake. Drive to the boathouse and park. (See map on page 43.)

 This is black bear territory, so be **cautious** (see "Bears" in introduction)—although they'll usually scamper off as soon as they hear you. With the plentiful supply of berries and acorns these dense woods offer, the black bear grows from its birth weight of one pound to its adult weight of 300 pounds. Don't feel cheated if you don't spot a bear because there's a lot more to enjoy while hiking the beautiful trails within Wawayanda State Park.

 For openers, at the beginning of the hike there's a fantastic view of Wawayanda Lake, a crystal-clear body of

In some spots along the trail, hiking requires concentration.

water covering 255 acres. You'll also see the 40-foot-high remains of an iron furnace built in the nineteenth century; a cedar swamp; and Laurel Pond, which is both surface and spring-fed. The Wawayanda Lake dam empties directly into Laurel Pond. If you're here during warm weather, plan on taking a refreshing dip at the end of the hike. Or relax on the sandy beach and watch sailboats and canoes drift by while fishermen wait patiently for a bite.

Facing the lake, walk to your left along the shore. When you reach a trail with blue markings, walk straight ahead, going slightly uphill. Bear left at the fork. Just past the end of the lake, in 0.25 mile, are the remains of a charcoal blast furnace built by Oliver Ames and his sons in 1846. The initials "W. L. A" and the date, which his son William etched on the lintel on the main arch, are still visible, but ivy is slowly obscuring it. Iron ore was fired here at temperatures of 2000 degrees F, and the finished products, known as "pigs," were used to make shovels and railroad car wheels. Swords were added to the list during the Civil War.

In another 0.1 mile, cross a bridge bearing three yellow blazes on the right post; this identifies the Laurel Pond Trail. Adorned with an abundant supply of cattails, the pond is home to bullfrogs. During springtime the males sing their courting songs loud and clear. The southeast portion supports an impressive stand of hemlock, thought to be the only known virgin timber on the mountain. Continuing uphill, you'll see huge boulders hugging the side of the trail as well as shimmering silver pussy willows bursting open in early spring. In 0.5 mile there's a great overall view of the pond.

Stands of hemlock and rhododendron dot the hillside and add a touch of color to the grayish rock formations. At just under 1 mile you'll be on a dirt path with a gully to your left and towering hemlocks to your right. The aptly named Wingdam Trail, marked in blue, enters shortly thereafter. At this point turn right into the woods to return to the trailhead or continue southwest on the yellow trail. Continuing on the Laurel Pond Trail, you'll be walking with a rocky outcrop to your right and the gully to your left as you head downhill. You may want to take a break to look over the magnificent boulder field not far ahead. Once you enter hemlock territory, at 1.5 miles, the forest seems even quieter than before. Only an occasional chipmunk rummaging through the fallen leaves or a chickadee singing from a nearby tree breaks the hush.

The Laurel Pond Trail ends at the intersection with Cherry Ridge Road, a wide dirt path. Turn around here, keeping an eye out for the blue markings that soon appear with a double-yellow blaze at the junction. Turn left and follow the blue blazes uphill. Club moss abounds in between the massive boulders. Be careful as you step across the irregular-shaped rocks up ahead. Soon the trail levels off and becomes fairly free of obstructions. In early spring you'll probably hear the almost deafening high-pitched cry of the spring peeper, a small tree frog found only in the north and identified by an "X" on its back.

One of the highlights of this hike is the large dam on Wawayanda Lake that fills Laurel Pond below the giant boulders. Continue downhill; in 0.25 mile you'll be at the lakeshore once again. Turn left and follow the water's edge back to the start. By this time, you must be wondering where the name Wawayanda came from. According to Superintendent Bill Foley, although folklore depicts the word as coming from the Lenni-Lenape Indians and meaning "water on the mountain," it has no definable root in their language.

6 CEDAR SWAMP

Location ▪ Wawayanda State Park
Counties ▪ Sussex and Passaic
Type ▪ Day hike or overnight camping
Difficulty ▪ Easy
Distance ▪ 3.9 miles
Elevation gain ▪ 100 feet
Hours ▪ Dawn to dusk
Information ▪ Wawayanda State Park, 885 Warwick Turnpike, Hewitt 07421;
(973) 853-4462
Website ▪ *www.njparksandforests.org*
Admission ▪ Free; fee for parking, Memorial Day to Labor Day; fee for
camping

Driving directions: From the junction of Warwick Turnpike and Clinton Road at the south end of Upper Greenwood Lake, follow Warwick Turnpike north for 1 mile and turn left onto Banker Road. When the pavement ends, turn right onto the dirt road and follow it to the end. Park along the side of the road.

It's almost impossible to get lost because huge rhododendron thickets form a natural border along this trail. Sporting leathery dark green leaves throughout the year, with large pinkish purple flowers from late spring to early summer, these towering beauties also provide an ideal hiding place for wildlife. Here in Wawayanda State Park children and adults can appreciate and learn about the outdoors. Bring a sturdy bag so that little ones can collect interesting leaf specimens found along the trail, and encourage them to recognize the difference in tree shapes, perhaps starting with an oak and a hemlock. Paper and crayons are great for making rubbings. When you find tree bark with an interesting texture or see a leaf with an interesting shape, place a piece of paper over it, rub it with a crayon, and you'll have a permanent record. Although the rhododendron are glorious, you'll also pass

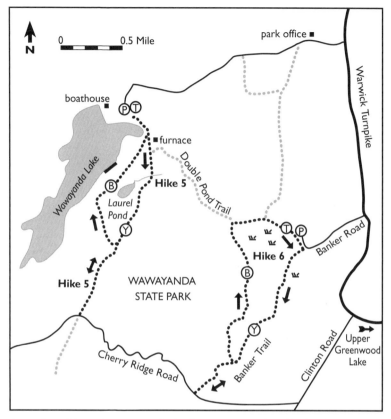

through a white cedar swamp, find sphagnum moss, hear bird calls, see frogs, and much more. Waterproof shoes are a good idea because sections of the trail may be wet or muddy.

Walk back on the dirt road the way you drove in. Before the blacktop road begins, in front of a horse farm at 0.2 mile, turn right onto Banker Trail, a wide dirt path with yellow blazes. In a few yards a pond appears on the left. Beware of the lush poison ivy here. Continue straight; cross the boardwalk and the short bridge over a swampy area that leads to a wet, heavily wooded area where rhododendron and hemlock make their first appearances. It's so junglelike in here that the sun never has a chance to shine through the brush. Watch out for the hundreds of tree roots that crisscross the trail in 0.3 mile, and in another 0.1 mile look for a huge bowl-shaped depression on the left. If you're here during late summer when the oaks are shedding their acorns, stop for a minute or two to listen to them hitting the ground. Hopefully, your head won't be in the way! Children are usually delighted to learn acorns

make great whistles. All they have to do is place both thumbs over the cap, leaving a tiny slit, and blow through the cavity to create a high-pitched sound.

Be on the lookout for a right turn at 0.75 mile. The trail soon climbs for a short distance, takes a slight dip, levels out before a steep 0.1-mile climb, and finally levels out again. The rhododendron suddenly disappear at this point and are replaced by graceful green hemlocks. At 1.5 miles swaying phragmites announce the swampy area, and in a short distance a T

This reindeer-shaped tree is excellent for making a rubbing.

and a tree with three yellow blazes mark the end of Banker Trail. Return the way you came. In 0.4 mile, just before the start of the blue-blazed Cedar Swamp Trail, look for impressive stands of rhododendron appearing on both sides of the trail. Turn left and follow the blue blazes.

The trail gradually climbs beneath a canopy of beech and hemlock, where many young trees have sprouted between boulders split by winter's constant freezing and thawing. Continue along this beautiful, wide trail that levels at 2.3 miles and is shaded by unbelievably high rhododendron. A large swamp appears 0.1 mile later; thanks to the efforts of considerate hikers, rocks and logs have been placed over most of the wet area, which is covered with sphagnum moss.

Walking over the long, meandering boardwalk that skirts through the cedar swamp, you'll see dozens of plants with heart-shaped leaves, called water arum or wild calla. In early summer lovely masses of greenish white unfold from the leaves; in late summer the masses ripen into red berries. When you reach the end of the Cedar Swamp Trail at 3.4 miles, make a sharp right and head east. A single yellow marker identifies the Double Pond Trail. Along the remaining 0.5 mile hike to your car, you may encounter deer quenching their thirst in the swampy areas that dot the area.

7 SURPRISE LAKE

Location ▪ West Milford
County ▪ Sussex
Type ▪ Day hike
Difficulty ▪ Challenging
Distance ▪ 3.5 miles
Elevation gain ▪ 650 feet
Hours ▪ Dawn to dusk
Information ▪ A. S. Hewitt State Park, c/o Wawayanda State Park, 885 Warwick Turnpike, Hewitt 07421; (973) 853-4462
Website ▪ www.njparksandforests.org
Admission ▪ Free

Driving directions: This hike begins on the western shore of Greenwood Lake within a few feet of the New York–New Jersey border. Drive north from West Milford on Lakeside Road. Public parking is on the west side of the road.

Just about everything a hiker could want can be found on this hike. For openers, there are fabulous vistas of Greenwood Lake that stretches out like a long finger and extends from New Jersey into New York State. The lake was created when German industrialist Peter Hasenclever built a dam at nearby Long Pond to provide power for the Ringwood ironworks. Today the

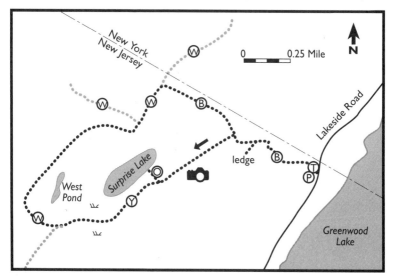

lake is jam-packed with boaters and fishermen. Although the trails on this hike are strewn with boulders and walking can be a bit difficult at times, there are plenty of opportunities for rest breaks. Besides the lake you'll pass a tiny pond and a small stream and walk under dark canopies of mature rhododendron.

 Sturdy shoes are recommended for negotiating the rocky trails. **Use caution** when walking on the ridges because the surface is uneven in many places.

Walk south 0.1 mile, turn right into the parking lot opposite a marina, and look for a double-blue blaze on a tree. Turn left to follow the blue blazes of the State Line Trail as you cross the gully and continue slightly uphill with the stream to the left. From this point, you'll have a number of minor ups and downs—and a few steep areas—while meandering through deep woods. Shortly you'll be climbing up a sea of boulders. After a heavy rain, tiny waterfalls drop down between these rocks, but you won't get your feet wet because there are a lot of boulders to walk on.

Markings aren't tightly spaced, so don't walk too far without making certain you're still on the trail by checking for blazes. If you don't see one, walk back to the last blaze and try to spot the one ahead. As you climb the steep trail, you'll have a firsthand look at the many white streaks of quartz in the rocks. In a short distance, you'll reach a horizontal wall of rock where trees have sprung up through the cracks. A blue blaze appears at 0.7 mile and a few feet farther is a double white square blaze painted on a boulder. At this point, you can take a ten-minute detour for a great view of Greenwood Lake by turning left and walking along the ridge. After enjoying the view and observing the hawks, walk back to the rock ledge where you originally saw the double-white square blaze and continue, climbing gradually. Turn left onto the yellow-blazed Ernest Walter Trail at 1 mile. Proceed uphill, steeply in places, over the boulders. The trail becomes so narrow in another 0.2 mile that the blueberry bushes seem to reach out to grab you. In a few feet you'll reach another view of Greenwood Lake, even more exceptional than the first. This is a good spot to rest, have a snack, and get the feeling of being "king of the mountain." It's easy to be in touch with nature atop the ridge while watching others below water-skiing and boating.

 When ready, continue ahead on the rock face. Usually there are hawks floating effortlessly overhead. Just when you think you've seen the prettiest view of the lake and surrounding countryside, there's an even better one ahead. From this viewpoint, you'll see an island smack in the middle of the lake on the New Jersey side. Look for the yellow blaze a short distance ahead and follow it into the woods, heading downhill on a narrow path. When you reach a triple-orange blaze, turn right to Surprise Lake. The real surprise is that you'll probably be all alone! Return to the yellow trail, which leads to a steep natural rock staircase and marvelous 15- to 20-foot-tall stands of rhododendron. Climbing down, you'll know what it feels like to be in a funnel because the trail seems to disappear in front of your eyes. Soft, damp moss covers the boulders, resembling the best carpet money can buy. The trail soon levels out and suddenly, at 1.5 miles, you enter almost total darkness— for another short stretch of rhododendron has overgrown the trail, providing a thick canopy. Where the boulders accumulate 0.2 mile ahead is often where feet begin to ache. These angular chunks of rock have frozen and thawed so many times that they've cracked,which explains why so many are standing sharply on end.

After crossing a bridge of boulders over a swampy area, climb steeply on the bare rock face. White blazes appear at the top; stay on the yellow trail leading into the woods. After a couple of minor ups and downs, you'll have to hold on to rocks and tree limbs once again to make it down into a narrow valley of rocks; sometimes a sitting position works best. The reward—and a fine place to catch your breath—is in a small glen that's wonderfully peaceful. Not many hikers can resist tossing leaves into the small stream or wetting bare feet.

Look to the right for a view of West Pond when you reach the mountain ridge. The yellow trail ends at 2.5 miles at a junction with the Appalachian Trail (white blazes). Head right, immediately climbing toward the edge of the ridge where there's an unobstructed view of the surrounding mountains. Turn right when you reach the blue blazes of the State Line Trail a short distance ahead. Continue following the blue markings back to the parking lot and your car.

8 HORSE POND MOUNTAIN

Location ■ Hewitt
County ■ Passaic
Type ■ Day hike
Difficulty ■ Moderate-challenging
Distance ■ 4.3 miles
Elevation gain ■ 400 feet
Hours ■ 8 A.M.–8 P.M.
Information ■ Norvin Green State Forest, c/o Ringwood State Park, 1304 Sloatsburg Road, Ringwood 07456; (973) 962-7031
Website ■ *www.njparksandforests.org*
Admission ■ Free

Driving directions: From Wanaque, drive north about 10 miles on CR 511 (Ringwood Avenue), staying with this road as the name changes to Greenwood Lake Turnpike. The parking area is on the left, opposite East

Shore Road, 0.5 mile after crossing Monksville Reservoir.

If you haven't been to this area for a while, you may be surprised to see the body of water that's suddenly appeared. It's the Monksville Reservoir, created in 1988 to serve northern New Jersey in times of drought. Because it fills the recreational needs of fishermen and boaters, it's now part of Monksville Recreation Area and Long Pond Ironworks State Park. The land surrounding the 500-acre reservoir also offers excellent trails and great lookouts for hikers. Sturdy hiking shoes are recommended because the trail leading to the top

Winter is a good time to spot birds along the trail as they stand out on the snow-covered ground and trees.

of Horse Pond Mountain is very rocky. There are two opportunities to appreciate the vastness of this 500-acre reservoir. The first is from the western shore, which is a closeup; the second, from an open area just below the summit, provides a panoramic view.

Walk south past an iron gate onto a wide gravel path marked with blue blazes. This is the northern terminus of the Hewitt-Butler Trail, an 18-mile-long mountain-hopper winding through the Skylands section of the state.

In a few yards, you'll walk through an extremely narrow pass that is an old railroad route. In earlier days this area was blessed with thriving iron-mine and smelting industries, which were particularly important during the Revolutionary War for the manufacture of armaments. Steep cliffs flank both sides of the trail; in winter, icicles may hang down from the sheer boulders. The ice, as it's heated by the sun, makes a soft, gurgling sound as it melts, reminiscent of a Japanese garden. Mostly level, the trail dips down and approaches the western shore of Monksville Reservoir. The opposite shore is so close that it makes the reservoir appear smaller than it really is. When you reach the top of the mountain, its true scale will be evident. Old tree trunks sitting in the water bear evidence of the recent flooding that resulted after the reservoir was filled with approximately 7 billion gallons of water.

The trail soon turns right into the woods and becomes narrow and rocky. As you climb past big boulders, you may catch the scent of sassafras. The soft pine needles underfoot in some places are a welcome alternative to the sharp rocks. There is a steep section over a huge rock wall at 0.7 mile. Continue

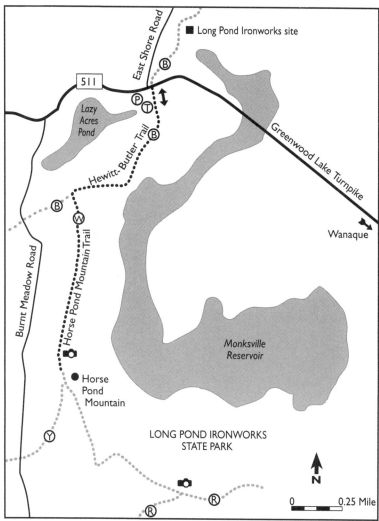

through a series of ups and downs, mostly ups, until you reach a junction with the white-blazed Horse Pond Mountain Trail at just under 1 mile. Leave the Hewitt-Butler Trail and turn left, following the white blazes. A gradual ascent along the ridge for about 1 mile leads to an overlook with a marvelous view of the reservoir and surrounding woods. This is an excellent place to have lunch and admire the scenery.

The top of Horse Pond Mountain, 0.2 mile farther south, awaits. While there is the satisfaction of having made it to the top, there unfortunately isn't a view from this spot. At this point you have two choices. One possibility (the one on which the mileage estimate is based) is to turn around and retrace your steps to the start. Or if you'd like to experience more of the same type of scenery, you might want to continue another mile to the southern end of the Horse Pond Mountain Trail, where you'll be rewarded by another panorama. This will add 2 miles and some elevation gain to your round trip.

Regardless of which option you choose, consider visiting the remains of Long Pond Ironworks north of Greenwood Lake Turnpike. Watch for fast-moving vehicles while crossing this road. Find the blue-blazed Sterling Ridge Trail, which crosses into New York State and follows a woods road to the ironworks site in 0.4 mile.

9 SHEPHERD LAKE

Location ▪ Ringwood State Park
County ▪ Passaic
Type ▪ Day hike
Difficulty ▪ Moderate-challenging
Distance ▪ 5 miles
Elevation gain ▪ 350 feet
Hours ▪ 8 A.M.–8 P.M.
Information ▪ Ringwood State Park, 1304 Sloatsburg Road, Ringwood 07456; (973) 962-7031
Website ▪ *www.njparksandforests.org*
Admission ▪ Free; fee for parking, Memorial Day to Labor Day

Driving directions: From CR 511 in the town of Ringwood, turn right onto Sloatsburg Road. Turn right again onto Morris Avenue to continue to the Skylands section of the park. Park in the "A" parking area, on the left side of the road.

Shepherd Lake, a 74-acre, spring-fed lake located in the heart of the Ramapo Mountains, is only one of the delights along this hike. While meandering through a tiny section of Ringwood State Park, you'll encounter a lot of wildlife. You'll also be within walking distance of Skylands Manor, a reproduction of the Jacobean mansions built in the English countryside four hundred years ago, and Skylands, the state's official botanical garden. Look up and you'll see tall, stately oak, maple, and beech. Look down and chances are you'll spot a rabbit or raccoon.

Plan on being on the trail early in the day; if the weather's warm, and if the lifeguards are on duty, you may opt for a refreshing swim after the hike. Or if you want to fish, trout, largemouth bass, sunfish, and pickerel are plentiful; a license is required.

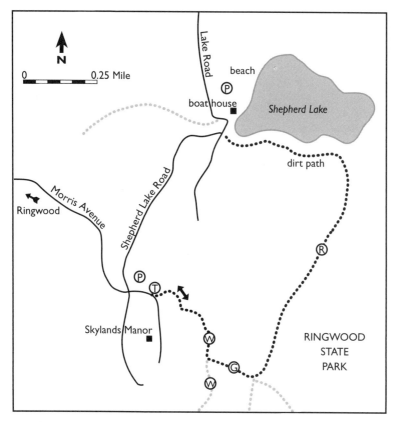

After leaving the parking area, walk left onto the entrance road, head east, and look for white blazes. Rows of crab apple trees, a feast for the eyes when they bloom in spring, appear on the right at 0.1 mile. Follow the white blazes, and turn left onto a grassy path that leads beneath a canopy of magnolias. You'll hear the music of a babbling brook before you see it on the left at 0.3 mile.

In a few feet, turn left at the triple green-on-white blaze. Wanaque Reservoir is visible to the right at 0.6 mile. In this next stretch columbine grows from the crevices. Reaching a height of 2 feet or more and blooming from March to April, this pretty wildflower bears a beautiful five-petaled blossom that grows face down like a lantern. Ancient herbalists used the juice of this plant to cure stomachaches.

The trail levels at the top of the ridge at 0.9 mile. Double red-and-green blazes signal a trail junction. Turn left onto the red trail. A huge rock wall is to your left where the trail levels, with marvelous vistas ahead. This is a good area to sit and enjoy a snack or simply admire the rolling hills and countryside. After a steep descent at 1.4 miles, the trail levels and leads to an area with large

This impressive eagle guards the entrance to Skylands and the beginning of the hike.

boulders that are perfect for sitting or climbing on. After a few ups and downs, the trail levels again and becomes very narrow at 1.8 miles. At 2 miles white birch appear and, shortly, Shepherd Lake comes into view. Turn left following the dirt path along the lakeshore. Skunk cabbage, one of the first plants to poke up through the snow, abounds in this wet area.

At 2.5 miles, you'll be opposite the boathouse and picnic area. A fine swimming beach is also nearby. After enjoying the scenery and activities at the lake, retrace your steps to Skylands Manor and your car.

10 GOVERNOR MOUNTAIN

Location ■ Ringwood
County ■ Passaic
Type ■ Day hike
Difficulty ■ Moderate-challenging
Distance ■ 2.3 miles
Elevation gain ■ 200 feet
Hours ■ 8 A.M.–8 P.M.
Information ■ Ringwood State Park, 1304 Sloatsburg Road, Ringwood 07456; (973) 962-7031
Website ■ www.njparksandforests.org
Admission ■ Free

Driving directions: Follow CR 511 north out of the town of Ringwood, bear right on Sloatsburg Road, and turn right again on Carletondale Road. About 0.5 mile down the road come to the Community Presbyterian Church parking lot on the right; ask permission to leave your car there.

No matter which season you choose to hike to the top of Governor Mountain, you'll have an exhilarating view of the countryside from a place locals refer to as "Suicide Ledge." Added rewards include a bountiful carpet of

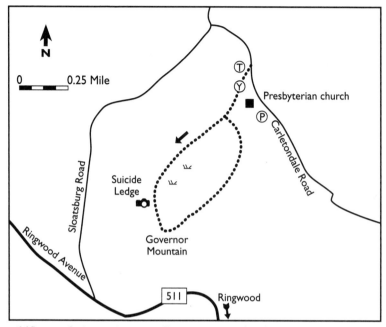

N

0   0.25 Mile

Presbyterian church

Carletondale Road

Sloatsburg Road

Suicide
Ledge

Ringwood Avenue

Governor
Mountain

511   Ringwood

wildflowers during spring, as well as towering red cedars. Sturdy hiking shoes are recommended for negotiating the steeper sections of trail.

Walk left (west) on Carletondale Road. Turn left onto the yellow-blazed Cooper Union Trail just past a fire hydrant (which faces large boulders on the opposite side of the road). Each fall the beeches, oaks, and maples towering overhead put on a show of vibrant yellows, browns, and reds. If the trees have already shed their leaves, watch out for holes between the rocks that the fallen leaves may be covering.

In a few yards you'll reach a tree with a split trunk shaped like a tuning fork. From this point proceed slightly uphill, crossing over the small stream. Children like to test their balancing skills on the narrow boards that have been placed here and, inevitably, one or two "accidentally" fall in. The narrow, rocky trail continues to gradually ascend through dense hemlock stands until the fork at 0.3 mile, where you'll bear right. A series of ups and downs follow before leveling 0.2 mile later. After another climb you'll reach a swampy area at 0.7 mile, a good place to create a game of hopping-over-the-rocks to avoid getting wet.

The ascent becomes steeper as you pass beautiful red cedars on the left. The trail soon levels and, at 1 mile, you'll have a magnificent view of Wanaque Reservoir. This huge, clear body of water has the capacity—100 million gallons—to supply several towns with water daily. From this point the trail descends steeply to the right, toward the reservoir; be careful as you

Views of surrounding countryside and the reservoir are exceptional from the trail.

walk along since there are patches of loose rocks. Another great view of the reservoir and countryside and a good place to stop for lunch is at Suicide Ledge, named for its straight drop.

When ready, continue along the edge of the ledge past large boulders. **Use caution** because this section can be slippery. In a few yards, head briefly uphill; the trail then descends steeply. Some of the smaller boulders in this area may also be slippery, so use care and go slowly. The most difficult part of the hike is now over.

The huge boulder (a glacial erratic deposited here by an ice sheet around 12,000 years ago) encountered at 1.7 miles is a perfect challenge for children, who can't resist climbing it. After passing this beauty, continue downhill steeply. Stay right at the trail junction, taking the original trail that passes the split tree trunk back to the starting point.

11 STONETOWN CIRCULAR

Location ▪ West Milford
County ▪ Passaic
Type ▪ Day hike
Difficulty ▪ Challenging
Distance ▪ 5 miles with car shuttle; 7 miles, round trip
Elevation gain ▪ 600 feet
Hours ▪ Dawn to dusk
Information ▪ Not available
Admission ▪ Free

Driving directions: From Ringwood Avenue north of Midvale, take West Brook Road across the Wanaque Reservoir and make the first right turn

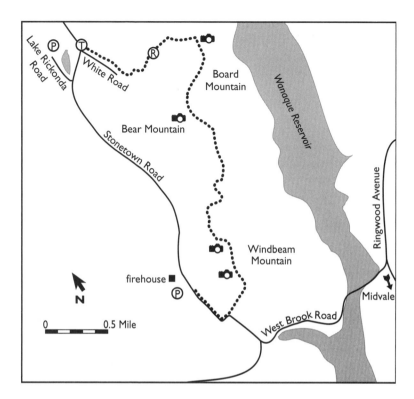

onto Stonetown Road. It's a little less than 1 mile to the firehouse on the left. Because of the length and difficulty of this hike, you may want to use a car shuttle. After asking permission to park, leave one car in the parking lot at the firehouse, and then drive the other car 2 miles north on Stonetown Road and turn left onto Lake Rickonda Road. Park at the end of the road.

Make certain you're in good shape before trying this hike. Several steep climbs are involved as well as one long descent that's sure to leave your legs quivering from the exertion. The effort is worth it, however, because the ridges along the Stonetown Circular Trail offer spectacular views of the Wyanokie Mountains, Wanaque Reservoir, Montville Reservoir, and miles of forest. Hiking over odd-shaped outcrops—and the opportunity to pick blueberries during summer—adds to the enjoyment of being alone in lush woodland. Carry a lot of water; on a hot day, you'll go through it quickly.

Walk along Lake Rickonda Road with the lake on the left. Turn left at the T on Stonetown Road and then right onto White Road at 0.5 mile (there is a double-red triangle blaze on a telephone pole), proceeding gradually uphill. Stately houses are to the left, shaded by a mix of maple, oak, and tulip trees.

At the double-red blaze at the end of the road, at 0.9 mile, turn left onto a wide, rocky trail. In a short distance look for a white arrow on a huge rock outcrop and head down into the gully. The only time the sun brightens this area is during fall and winter, after the leaves have fallen. Red blazes mark the trail, which makes a few turns in this section. At the double blaze (1.2 miles) turn left and watch your footing as you cross a field of boulders a few yards ahead. After crossing the creek at 1.4 miles, head steeply uphill. A magnifying glass will reveal how the club moss that's scattered among the cracks in the rocks resembles miniature pine trees.

Blueberry bushes soon appear, and at 1.7 miles the trail becomes narrow and level but then quickly ascends again. In a few minutes you reach the overlook atop Board Mountain, where there's a fine view of Wanaque Reservoir and the surrounding woods. Follow the trail up and down along some outcrops. Where the trail dips again, at 2.1 miles, a red cedar stands smack in the middle of the path. After a level section the red-blazed trail heads gradually upward again. The mountain laurel here is gorgeous, and in spring the blooms are especially grand. Another short, steep climb at 2.5 miles leads to a great view atop a wide, flat ridge on top of Bear Mountain, but during summer it may be obscured by foliage. Breathing in the aroma of fresh pine, you'll reach another vantage point facing the Wanaque Reservoir about 0.1 mile ahead. Be careful as you proceed downhill from here, as the grass hides some of the rocks and holes.

The blazes are far apart in this section, so don't go too far without making certain that you can still see the last one you passed. After a steep descent, the trail levels and continues over a series of boulders. At approximately 3 miles you'll find two trees that seem to be hugging each other. On closer examination, it's apparent that the birch and tulip have grown and merged into one trunk system.

From here there are several ups and downs, and at 4

Sitting on rock outcrops is a great way to appreciate the countryside and see the reservoirs atop Bear Mountain.

miles a steep climb will bring you to the crest of Windbeam Mountain with wonderful views to the west. Be very cautious when descending; the trail is very steep for several yards, but you can reach out to tree branches and trunks for support. After a dip, head uphill again. In a few yards, you'll reach another impressive westward overlook with water and forest below. From here, the going is pretty rough. Make sure to place your feet on solid rocks. A series of steps, made of logs and boulders, has been considerably placed to ease the way and prevent erosion, but the strain of holding back can be very tiring. At the junction with Stonetown Road, a triple-red blaze indicates the end of the trail. Turn right and continue 0.3 mile to the firehouse. If you are hiking the 7-mile loop, continue north from the firehouse for 2 miles until you reach Lake Rickonda Road and your car.

12 RAMAPO LAKE

Location ■ Ramapo Mountain State Forest
Counties ■ Passaic and Bergen
Type ■ Day hike
Difficulty ■ Moderate
Distance ■ 5.2 miles
Elevation gain ■ 220 feet
Hours ■ Dawn to dusk
Information ■ Ramapo Mountain State Forest, c/o Ringwood State Park, 1304 Sloatsburg Road, Ringwood 07456; (973) 962-7031
Website ■ www.njparksandforests.org
Admission ■ Free

Driving directions: From I-287, take exit 57 (Oakland) and follow Skyline Drive north to a parking lot on the left opposite the Camp Tamarack sign.

While hiking Ramapo Lake's perimeter, you might see muskrat, which Dutch settlers referred to as the "rote," or rat. About the size of a cat, this furry brown mammal makes a roundish house of cattails and grasses in the water and can sometimes be seen prowling around the water's edge for turtles, fish, and various water plants. For a short period, you'll be hiking the historic Cannonball Trail, a secret route through the Ramapo Mountains that was used during the Revolutionary War to transport cannonballs that had been cast in local furnaces.

To begin this hike go past a gate and head southwest along a wide, flat fire road. Huge boulders, rich in iron ore and dating back millions of years, appear at 0.25 mile. Continue straight ahead and in a few minutes you'll reach a mysterious circular stone tower with antennas sticking out. Descending

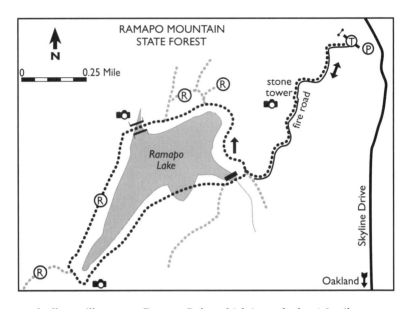

gradually you'll soon see Ramapo Lake, which is reached at 1.3 miles.

Turn right onto the level path that circles the lake. Colored blazes will occasionally be visible as other trails join in and then leave your path as you continue along the shore. You'll find huge stands of sassafras on the way to a tiny waterfall at 1.6 miles. This is an excellent spot to wet a bandana, fish a bit if you've brought a rod, and admire the scenery. Occasionally a frog will signal its presence by a "plunk, plunk" banjolike song, or a dragonfly—commonly called a "darning needle"—will plop down on a plant, resting between flights and searching for a tasty gnat or fly. At the fork at 1.7 miles, bear left and continue to the bridge at 2 miles, where you'll have an exceptional overall view of the lake. Again bear left along the lakeshore when the road forks just ahead. You'll have another beautiful view of the lake at 3.4 miles, where the surrounding boulders make an excellent place to sit or climb. From here there are slight ups and downs; stay with the gravel road as it continues the entire way around the lake. A bit past

Canada geese are frequent visitors to Ramapo Lake.

the dam at about 4 miles, look to the right for the fire road that leads back to the parking lot. If you miss it, you may wind up circling the lake again.

 ERSKINE LOOKOUT

Location ▪ Ramapo Mountain State Forest
Counties ▪ Passaic and Bergen
Type ▪ Day hike
Difficulty ▪ Challenging
Distance ▪ 7.7 miles
Elevation gain ▪ 300 feet
Hours ▪ Dawn to dusk
Information ▪ Ramapo Mountain State Forest, c/o Ringwood State Park, 1304 Sloatsburg Road, Ringwood 07456
Website ▪ www.njparksandforests.org
Admission ▪ Free

Driving directions: From I-287, take exit 57 (Oakland) and follow Skyline Drive north to a parking lot on the left opposite the Camp Tamarack sign.

The Cannonball Trail was the secret route used by the Continental Army for transporting munitions cast at Pompton Furnace. The trail takes you atop the ridges of the Ramapo Mountains, where you'll stand beside a huge boulder, known as an erratic, that was transported here by glaciers thousands of years ago. Your destination is Erskine Lookout with a terrific view of Lake Erskine and Wanaque Reservoir. An abundance of blueberries to chomp on during late summer is an added bonus, but be certain of what you're eating. Long pants are in order for this hike; because the trail isn't used too often, you may be scratched by overgrown blueberry bushes or overhanging poison ivy.

Begin the hike by crossing Skyline Drive (watch for oncoming traffic) and follow the yellow blazes of the Hoeferlin Trail, named to honor mapmaker and trailblazer William Hoeferlin. After a short climb you'll see a sign pointing left to a shelter used by Native Americans. Archeologists have found hundreds of artifacts within the 6-by-12-foot stone formation that was once used by hunters for shelter. Explore the shelter now or continue the steep climb among the boulders. In a few spots you'll have to place your hands in crevices and grab onto trees to gain leverage. The trail soon levels, but the rest of the way—as you're surrounded by blueberry bushes and stands of mountain laurel, tall oaks, and beech trees—has gradual ups and downs. At 0.5 mile the trail turns; bear right at the double-yellow blaze. When the Cannonball Trail (indicated by a white *C* on a red circle) joins with the yellow-blazed Hoeferlin Trail,

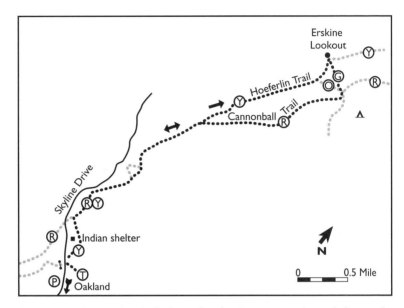

the route widens and is fairly free of rocks. Continue and turn left into the open at the double-red blaze at 1 mile. After walking a few feet along the road, turn right into the woods again onto a rocky, narrow trail heading uphill.

After a little over 0.5 mile through deep woods and then over boulders, double blazes indicate that the trails go their separate ways; follow the yellow markings on a narrow path through a fairly rugged but scenic area. Stick with the Hoeferlin Trail when triple-red blazes appear at 2.7 miles. After some easy walking over flat boulders, odd-shaped boulders are underfoot for the next 0.25 mile. From a certain angle the large, round erratic at 3.3 miles looks like a baseball suspended in air, but it's actually supported by smaller

rocks. Continue straight as orange blazes appear on the right at 3.6 miles; you arrive at Erskine Lookout, the high point of this hike. The view is extensive, with Wanaque Reservoir serving as a backdrop for Erskine Lake. The lake was named for Robert Erskine, a Scottish engineer who was brought to the area in 1771 to help the town of Ringwood solve problems it was having with its iron operations. As a result he helped Ringwood to become one of the most successful ironworks. In 1777 he was appointed general surveyor by George Washington. Erskine also worked on the first complete maps of northern New Jersey and southern New York.

To return to the trailhead, follow the arrow leading to the green trail and wind your way downhill 0.5 mile through ash, hickory, and black birch and past a scout camp's lean-tos. Turn right (4.5 miles) at the double-red blazed T where the Cannonball Trail meets the green-blazed trail. The trail is wide here but quite rocky as it gradually goes up and down hills. Soon you'll

Huffing and puffing—and even pushing—can't budge the glacial erratics found along the Cannonball Trail.

encounter a field of boulders. Be aware that fallen leaves may hide holes between the rocks. Continue southwest, retracing your original route as the Hoeferlin Trail joins the Cannonball Trail from the right.

14 RAMAPO RESERVATION

Location ■	Ramapo Valley County Reservation
County ■	Bergen
Type ■	Day hike
Difficulty ■	Moderate
Distance ■	5 miles
Elevation gain ■	600 feet
Hours ■	Dawn to half an hour after sunset
Information ■	Ramapo Valley County Reservation, 584 Valley Road, Mahwah 07430; (201) 825-1388 or 201-327-3500
Website ■	www.co.bergen.nj.us/parks/Parks/Ramapo/htm
Admission ■	Free; fee for camping permit

Driving directions: From Oakland, take NJ-202 north about 5 miles. The entrance to the reservation is on the left.

Ramapo Valley County Reservation boasts more than two hundred species of birds, but there's more here than the songs of warblers, mockingbirds, and woodpeckers. There are also the cool, shaded hillsides and ridges filled with majestic trees—flowering dogwood, mountain laurel, and pink azalea. The hike, with many ups and downs, leads past numerous scenic spots including Scarlet Oak Pond, the Ramapo River, and the MacMillan Reservoir. Originally purchased from the Native Americans in 1700, this land had been the site of a farm, a gristmill, sawmill, and a bronze foundry, before being purchased with state and federal funding by the Bergen County Park Commission in 1972. Sturdy shoes are best for negotiating this rocky terrain.

From the parking lot, head into the woods and look for the silver-blazed trail (lids from tin cans that are used as blazes on this trail). A plaque on a boulder commemorates where New York City hotel owner A. R. Darling built a mansion and operated a dairy farm in 1864.

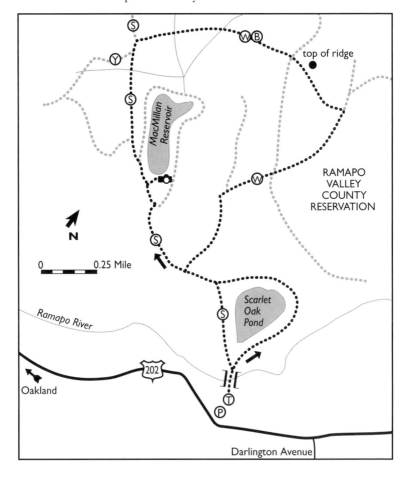

Toads can frequently be found on the rocks skirting the trail.

Continue over two bridges and turn right at Scarlet Oak Pond. With the pond on the left, the level, wide trail passes the Ramapo River to the right.

At 0.4 mile, bear left at the fork, following the trail along the pond in sight of a meadow laden with wildflowers from early spring through fall. Queen Anne's lace, standing straight as a soldier, was named for its pretty blossoms that resemble a queen's headdress. According to legend the deep purple floret in the center of this lacy flower is a drop of blood from a queen's finger. You'll also find Joe-Pye weed here; it's especially beautiful in late August when it sports a cluster of tiny pinkish purple flowers. Supposedly named for an Indian medicine man who used the plant to cure typhoid fever, Joe-Pye weed was chewed by young Indian men who believed it would bring them good luck before a date.

Turn right at the junction with the silver trail and walk uphill following the tin markers. Shortly you'll cross over two concrete bridges. After the second one, where boulders of every size and shape lie in the stream, swing left and continue uphill at the double-silver blaze. After the third bridge at 1.3 miles bear right onto a side trail for a sweeping view of MacMillan Reservoir. Return to the main trail and continue, climbing along the west side of the reservoir, where the water is nicely framed by surrounding forest. After passing the junction of the yellow and silver trails at 1.4 miles, the trail gradually descends and is rocky for another 0.5 mile.

Turn right into the woods at the triple-white blaze and follow the white and blue blazes. This section is a bit rough because of loose rocks, but it gets easier as it ascends again at approximately 2 miles. After a few ups and downs, take a sharp right to head uphill. The large, flat rocks at 3 miles make perfect seats for resting. Turn right near the top of the ridge. The trail goes through an open field, heading downhill once again on a wide, grassy trail surrounded with many wildflowers. Turn right at 3.4 miles onto the white-blazed trail. The path is level for a while. At 3.9 miles, where you see double-silver and white blazes, bear left to head downhill. There is a confusing number of side trails in this area, many of them marked with tin-can blazes, so be careful to stay on course.

Continue on the rocky trail until you reach the silver-blazed trail and turn left, pass Scarlet Oak Pond and cross the bridges over the Ramapo River, and return to the parking lot.

15 TERRACE POND

Location ▪ Hewitt

Counties ▪ Sussex and Passaic

Type ▪ Day hike

Difficulty ▪ Moderate; challenging if alternate is taken

Distance ▪ 5 miles; 5.5 miles, if alternate is taken

Elevation gain ▪ 340 feet

Hours ▪ Dawn to dusk

Information ▪ Wawayanda State Park, 883 Warwick Turnpike, Hewitt 07421; (973) 853-4462

Website ▪ *www.njparkandforests.org*

Admission ▪ Permit required; $4 for Newark residents, $8 for others. Apply in person at Newark Watershed Conservation and Development Corporation (NWCDC), 223 Echo Lake Road, Newfoundland 07435; (973) 697-2850 (Monday–Saturday, 8 A.M.–4 P.M.); or NWCDC, 40 Clinton Street, 4th floor, Newark 07102, (973) 622-4521 (Monday–Friday, 9 A.M.–5 P.M.).

 Driving directions: From NJ-23 in Newfoundland, drive 6 miles north on Clinton Road to a small parking area on the right (east) side of the road (across from a row of large boulders).

Getting to Terrace Pond is half the fun of this hike, but be forewarned: kids can't resist stopping dozens of times along the way to launch leaf boats down a brook, climb huge boulders, or admire the tiny waterfalls. At several points along the trail, you'll have a good chance of finding the rare, pink

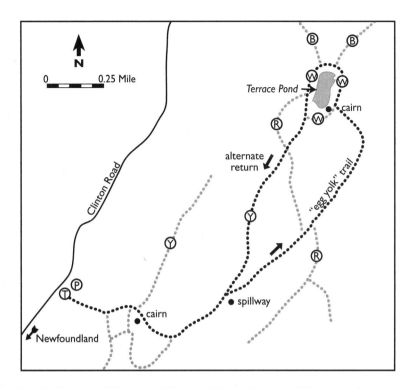

lady's slipper, and if you're hiking in May or June you'll be treated to the vibrant blooms of wildflowers. Hold out for lunch until you reach the granite ledge overlooking the pond, where you can gaze down upon this sparkling jewel. Plan on starting early so you can spend a lot of time enjoying Terrace Pond, which is one of the loveliest places in northern New Jersey. Although the trail is easy most of the way, sturdy shoes are recommended for negotiating a few of the rocky, sometimes slippery, areas.

The trail begins a few yards south of the parking area. Follow a wide, unmarked, rocky road that heads east, and take the first woods road to the left at 0.3 mile. Continue uphill another 0.2 mile and bear right at the Y onto a wide, yellow-blazed trail, the Terrace Pond South Trail. Observe this intersection carefully as you'll be returning the same way, and it's easy to miss. There should be a cairn (column of rocks) to mark this junction. The trail in this area is wide and level, and many of the surrounding trees have been defoliated by gypsy moths. With a magnifying glass you can examine their egg cases left on the limbs and tree trunks, or in early spring you can watch as thousands of gypsy moths emerge from their egg cases.

The spillways at the 1-mile point are good spots to linger for a moment. A few yards ahead huge boulders form a wall on the right. Here, a new trail with a blaze resembling an egg yolk—a yellow circle on a white background—appears. Take this trail; gradually, you'll climb past more rock walls.

At 2 miles, turn left and begin carefully climbing the ridge. (**Caution:** There's a sharp drop-off on the left where the trail narrows.) Follow the trail as it turns left and reaches its highest point atop a rocky ledge at 2.2 miles. Here you'll feel on top of the world as the wind blows through your hair. Turn right onto the white trail, indicated by blazes on the rocks. Continue descending steeply for 0.3 mile to the pond. It's possible to explore the shoreline by following the trail that encircles the pond.

To return, retrace your route. Be careful not to miss the beginning of the egg yolk trail at 2.6 miles; it's marked by a rock cairn on top of the boulders, with three egg yolk blazes a few feet behind. Another rock cairn at 4.5 miles signals the intersection with the unmarked woods trail that you took on the way in. Continue straight ahead on this trail at the cairn instead of following the yellow trail to the right. Then turn right again to the starting point.

Note: A recommended alternative circles the pond and returns by another route. This adds 0.5 mile and is also more strenuous, but the views and

A hiker enjoying the view of Terrace Pond

local scenery make the extra strain worthwhile. Follow the white trail as it circles the pond in a counterclockwise direction. Blue blazes soon join in. The trail is wet in spots, and there are some boulders to clamber over. Beautiful stands of mountain laurel set off views of the pond. Stay to the left as blue blazes head off to the right, and continue following the pond. Arrive at the yellow-blazed Terrace Pond South Trail, and follow it southward as it leads over several ridges and eventually brings you to the junction with the egg yolk trail. Continue and keep an eye out for the cairn identifying the unmarked trail you came in on. Continue straight as the yellow blazes turn right, then turn right at the T toward the starting point.

16 BUCKABEAR POND

Location ■ Pequannock Watershed
County ■ Passaic
Type ■ Day hike
Difficulty ■ Moderate
Distance ■ 4.6 miles
Elevation gain ■ 200 feet
Hours ■ Dawn to dusk
Information ■ Newark Watershed Conservation Development Corporation (NWCDC), 223 Echo Lake Road, Newfoundland 07435; (973) 697-2850
Website ■ Not available
Admission ■ Permit required (see Hike 15 for contact information for NWCDC)

Driving directions: From NJ-23 in Newfoundland, drive north 1.2 miles on Clinton Road and turn left onto unmarked Schoolhouse Cove Road. (The remains of Clinton Furnace are off the right side of Clinton Road just before the turnoff.) Continue 1 mile, turn right onto another dirt road, and drive 0.1 mile to the parking lot on the right. Stop at the Pequannock Watershed (223 Echo Lake Road, off NJ-23 south of Clinton Road) to pick up a trail map and purchase your parking permit.

Early afternoon is the best time to enjoy exquisite views of Clinton Reservoir and the final destination, Buckabear Pond. Don't be afraid to hike this trail in the winter when the slightest breeze pushes thin layers of ice toward the shore, creating melodious sounds. Attractions, in addition to a refreshing hike through a variety of trees, include an abundance of birds, lush mountain laurel, flowing brooks, and evidence of beaver activity. Wear sturdy shoes to avoid stubbing your toes on this extremely rocky trail. A tree identification book will enhance

your hike, especially in the winter when the trees have lost their leaves.

The trail begins at a tree marked with three white blazes to the left of the parking area. Clinton Reservoir soon comes into view. Continue along until the double-white blaze at 0.25 mile. Follow the blazes along the water's edge. Distinctive ironwood trees thrive in the moist, shady areas and can be identified by their twisting gray-and-blue-banded trunks and in spring by drooping clusters of stiff bracts. The tree with the yellowish sheen on its peeling bark is the yellow birch; its seed cones provide a steady diet for birds in winter.

Beavers are alive and well in this area—and fond of certain trees!

At 0.75 mile, just before the trail descends, look to the right for a tiny island shaded by evergreens. A brook crosses the trail in a few yards, and if the temperature is right, it's a fun spot in the winter to admire icicles. During

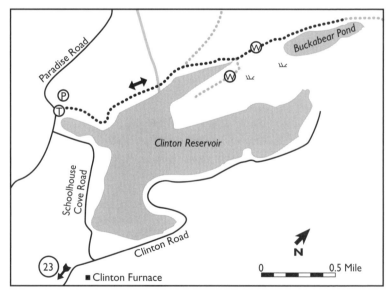

the rest of the year the sound of the tumbling water provides a calming melody. The trail now levels for a few yards before beginning a series of dips and climbs. At a trail junction marked by three white blazes, stick to the right, heading along the edge of the reservoir. Check out the trees along the water's edge just after this section. You may see beavers; fresh wood chips at the base of a tree are a dead giveaway that they're around, as are the branches they've gathered to dam the water.

Leave the reservoir behind as you approach the shoreline of Buckbear Pond. What looks like the remains of a rusty tractor appears at 2.3 miles and just ahead is the perfect spot to admire Buckabear Pond. A wide, flat boulder provides a natural seat for a picnic lunch or a rest. Turn back after enjoying the view.

17 BEARFORT MOUNTAIN LOOKOUT

Location ▪ Newark Watershed
County ▪ Passaic
Type ▪ Day hike
Difficulty ▪ Moderate
Distance ▪ 6 miles, round trip
Elevation gain ▪ 300 feet
Hours ▪ Seasonal, subject to change
Information ▪ Newark Watershed Conservation Development Corporation (NWCDC), 223 Echo Lake Road, Newfoundland 07435; (973) 697-2850
Website ▪ Not available
Admission ▪ Permit required (see Hike 15 for contact information for NWCDC)

Driving directions: From NJ-23 in Newfoundland, drive north 1.2 miles on Clinton Road. Bear right at the remains of Clinton Furnace on the right side of the road, and continue 0.8 mile.Park on the right at a small cutout bordered by two huge boulders. Stop at the Pequannock Watershed (223 Echo Lake Road, off NJ-23 south of Clinton Road) to pick up a trail map and to purchase your parking permit.

The destination of this hike is the Bearfort Mountain fire tower, where you're treated to panoramic views of The Highlands, some of the oldest rock formations in the Appalachian Range, and a variety of trees in addition to views of the New York City skyline. According to the National Historic Lookout Register, the original lookout on Bearfort Mountain was a wooden platform or tree lookout, circa 1880. In 1909 the Newark, New

Jersey, Watershed Department built an iron-frame tower, which was replaced with a 50-foot-tall wooden tower that burned down in 1932. A tree platform replaced it until 1934 when the current 68-foot-tall steel tower was erected. Open year-round, visitors are usually welcome when the tower is manned. When climbing to the top platform, be sure to hold on to little ones who may get excited and lose their footing on the steep steps. It's best to wear sturdy hiking shoes because there are countless boulders along the trail to the tower.

The hike, a joy in any season, is extra special in the spring, when the azaleas and other wildflowers, including yellow loosestrife and roundleaf sundew, are in bloom. During fall Mother Nature paints the leaves brilliant colors. One note of warning: Several trails intersect this area, so be alert at each junction. It's a good idea to keep your compass and map handy.

The beginning of the trail is unmarked. Go past a gate and head north, uphill, on a wide, rocky path flanked on the right by a stream. In 0.25 mile, on the right, you'll find stone steps and a stone wall. Once back on the main trail, continue straight to the first red and white blaze. This is a densely wooded area where there is shade on even the hottest summer's day. After passing a pond on the right, the trail curves left and leads to an open area. Cross this section, head left, and bear right at the Y at 0.6 mile. In a few yards on the left you'll encounter

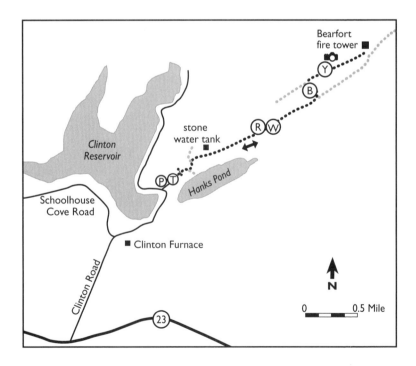

a large stone structure. If you look for an entrance, you won't find one because it's a water tank that was built in the late 1800s to supply water to a castle farther south via a pipe and springhouse. The castle, which belonged to New York clothing manufacturer Richard Cross, was disassembled a few years ago.

Ahead are giant boulders perfect for climbing. This spot is a favorite hangout of woodpeckers and songbirds. A gradual climb begins at 0.9 mile, and after some level areas the trail steepens for about 0.25 mile. Soon you'll be walk-

Hikers are treated to a panoramic view upon reaching the fire tower.

ing atop boulders, and at 1.5 miles there may be a tiny waterfall formed by the runoff from a swampy area. You'll face a challenge a few yards ahead at a rock outcrop formed by glacial erractics. It's fun to explore but be careful; the rock can be slippery, and the narrow ledge drops off to the left. When you've crossed the gully at the blue connector trail at 1.7 miles, pause at the other side to search the shady nooks around the rocks. From April through July, you'll find a delicate lantern-shaped wildflower known as columbine. Use a magnifying glass to examine its flower, which can be red, yellow, blue, or purple and hangs down as the petals grow backward in tubular spurs. In her book, *Wildflower Folklore*, Laura Martin writes that according to ancient superstition, "Lions ate columbine in the spring to revive their strength."

Leaving the boulders behind, you'll be treated to the wonderful aroma of pine as you enter deep woods at 1.8 miles. The trail soon swings left, descending steeply for a few yards. Turn left at the blue-blazed junction; mountain laurel is profuse along this narrow section. In 0.25 mile turn right at the yellow blaze and climb gradually while surrounded by pines. At 2.5 miles, you'll be in an open area with more boulders and a fantastic view of the Clinton Reservoir. Keep going. The best is yet to come!

Turn right at the next trail junction and head toward the fire tower. Before enjoying the 360-degree view, you might want to rest or have lunch at one of the picnic tables. Retrace your steps when ready to return.

18 OSIO ROCK

Location ▪ Norvin Green State Forest
County ▪ Passaic
Type ▪ Day hike
Difficulty ▪ Moderate-challenging
Distance ▪ 2.5 miles
Elevation gain ▪ 400 feet
Hours ▪ Dawn to dusk
Information ▪ Norvin Green State Forest, c/o Ringwood State Park, 1304 Sloatsburg Road, Ringwood 07456; (973) 962-7031
Website ▪ *www.njparksandforests.org*
Admission ▪ Free

 Driving directions: Drive west on Glen Wild Road from Bloomingdale. After entering Norvin Green State Forest, park in the lot on the right side of the road.

Seeing the sunset from Osio Rock is memorable, but completing the hike in darkness can be tricky unless you're adventurous—or there's a full moon—and you bring along flashlights and spare batteries for everyone. A cell phone

Large boulders on the way to Osio Rock

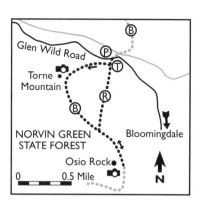

can make all the difference in an emergency but only if it works. Remember, if you don't know exactly where you are, you won't be able to transmit that information. A handheld Global Positioning System (GPS) can help, but if you're in a dense wooded area, it won't be able to detect your position. Everything has its benefits as well as drawbacks, and that's why it's important to keep blazes in sight. Even in full daylight hiking here among the boulders is sometimes rough, but the exceptional views throughout the hike repay the effort. Sturdy shoes are a must and a walking stick will come in handy.

Cross Glen Wild Road to the trailhead for the blue-blazed Hewitt-Butler Trail, which ascends a short hill, weaves around, and arrives at the junction with the red-blazed Torne Trail. The trail is very close to the road before heading in a southwest direction to ascend Torne Mountain. When you pause for a breather along this narrow, rocky trail, turn around for a fantastic view of unspoiled forest. At the first ridge, at approximately 0.5 mile, you'll be rewarded with another exceptional 360-degree view stretching endlessly into the distance. The few houses and tiny lakes are almost hidden from view by dense forest and hills. In spring, you can see colorful masses of rhododendron. Moss covers the trail in many spots and can sometimes be slippery. Watch your footing as you walk over the boulders on this ridge.

Beautiful woods and lakes appear far below. The trail descends gradually, and you'll shortly be on a flat boulder peering down at mountain ridges to the south. At 1 mile you'll be descending steeply, probably sliding on your butt and using your hands for support as I did for a few yards before climbing again. Continue straight ahead, still following the blue blazes. Look for the junction where red blazes appear on the left, as this marks the return route. Continue uphill to the huge boulder atop the next ridge at 1.4 miles. This is a good place to turn back if you're tired, but Osio Rock is only a few minutes farther and well worth the extra effort. Once you reach the high point at Osio Rock, there are impressive views to the east and west.

When ready, retrace your steps. At 2 miles you'll descend into a small gulch before turning right onto the red-blazed Torne Trail. Here, kids may need a boost since this section of trail begins by climbing up a large boulder and heading uphill for a short distance. The trail gradually descends and levels off; you'll be a few yards from the end of the trail when it drops again. Turn right. Follow the blue blazes to the right toward the road and return to the parking area.

19 WYANOKIE MINI-CIRCULAR

Location ▪ Norvin Green State Forest
County ▪ Passaic
Type ▪ Day hike
Difficulty ▪ Challenging
Distance ▪ 3.7 miles
Elevation gain ▪ 550 feet
Hours ▪ Dawn to dusk
Information ▪ Norvin Green State Forest, c/o Ringwood Park, Box 1304, Ringwood 07456; (973) 962-7031
Website ▪ *www.njparksandforests.org*
Admission ▪ Free

 Driving directions: From Wanaque, take Ringwood Avenue (CR 511) north of Midvale, turn left on West Brook Road, and left again at the sign for Snake Den Road. Park at the Weis Ecology Center (150 Snake Den Road; (973) 835-2160).

This trail through dense woods and the Wyanokies heads into Norvin Green State Forest, a hilly wilderness oasis. A couple of steep ascents and descents are involved, but the payoffs are the lovely views, a variety of trees, and inviting streams to rest beside. Norvin Green is a popular family hiking location thanks to the efforts of the Green Mountain Club in blazing these trails in the 1920s and the care extended today by the Weis Ecology Center and the New York–New Jersey Trail Conference. Well-marked trails crisscross the hills and reach several peaks with extensive views of green forest. Plan on starting out early in the day so you can take time to visit the Roomy Iron Mine, a leftover from days long gone when the ironworks industry thrived in the area. Roomy Iron Mine, considered by the staff at the Weis Ecology Center to be safe to explore, has a low entrance, so you'll have to crawl a couple of feet before reaching a large circular room open to the sky. A 5-foot-high tunnel leads to a

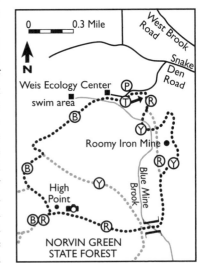

Norvin Green State Forest offers a variety of views and lovely trees.

passageway about 60 feet long, and here you'll need a flashlight. The ground is wet, so walk with caution.

Walk east for 0.1 mile to pick up the red-blazed Wyanokie Circular Trail, which passes in between a few houses. All signs of civilization are soon left behind as the trail enters a grove of hemlocks. The temperature can be several degrees cooler in these woods on hot summer days. Turn right at the beginning of the yellow-blazed Mine Trail. The route leads over two small ridges, crosses Blue Mine Brook, turns left sharply, and soon crosses the brook again. The rocks in the water look picture-perfect, and the sound of the water is pleasant as it falls down a steep chute. At a huge boulder, you'll cross the red-blazed trail before heading uphill to an open area with a pleasant panorama, a sample of what lies ahead.

Follow the yellow blazes as they turn south. After some gentle meandering, the trail dips down and twists to the right in front of the entrance to the Roomy Iron Mine. Although water slowly drips from the rock ceiling and collects in tiny pools, this is one of the few abandoned mines in the area not flooded with water. Speak softly so as not to disturb any of the cave critters, such as the bats that hibernate here during winter months. When you are finished exploring, continue on the Mine Trail; turn left where red and yellow blazes meet.

Blue Mine Brook, at 1.4 miles, is a great place to wet a bandana or sit and listen to the latest bird concert. From this point, you'll be walking close to another stream. At a wooden bridge erected by hardworking members of the New York–New Jersey Trail Conference, you may wish to turn around. If not, proceed straight, going up and down slight hills until a steep climb to the top of the ridge begins. The tall tulip trees in this area were prized by the Native Americans because the sturdy trunks were the perfect shape for canoes.

Follow the red-blazed trail to High Point and enjoy a 360-degree view, one of the best to be found in the region. To the east is Wanaque Reservoir—the largest reservoir in the state—with New York City's skyline in the distance beyond. In every other direction you can see lush green forests, and if you're lucky you'll spot hawks soaring effortlessly on thermals.

From High Point continue west for 0.1 mile, and turn right onto the blue-blazed Hewitt-Butler Trail. When the yellow-blazed trail joins in from the right, follow the blue and yellow blazes. Bare rock in this area can be slippery from the morning dew or rain. The trail follows the ridge past outstanding mountain laurel before descending to Blue Mine Brook and a canopy of tulip trees. Turn right when you reach the green-blazed trail that leads onto Snake Den Road. You'll have glimpses of a man-made, lovely, rock-framed swimming pool fed by a natural spring.

20 THREE MOUNTAIN PONDS

Location ■ Delaware Water Gap National Recreation Area
County ■ Sussex
Type ■ Day hike or overnight backpack
Difficulty ■ Moderate
Distance ■ 5 miles
Elevation gain ■ 350 feet
Hours ■ Dawn to dusk
Information ■ Kittatinny Point Visitor Center, Kittatinny Point, Columbia 07832; (908) 496-4458
Website ■ www.nps.gov/dewa
Admission ■ Free

Driving directions: From the town of Flatbrookville, near the junction of Warren and Sussex counties and the Delaware River, take Old Mine Road south for 0.6 mile and turn left on NJ-624, Blue Mountain Lakes Road (formerly Flatbrookville/Stillwater Road). The parking area is at the top of a hill in approximately 3 miles.

What you'll find on this hike is great diversity. Each body of water is unique, and along the rim of each of these fascinating habitats—Long Pine Pond, Crater Lake, and Hemlock Pond—lies another world teeming with life. Salamanders, frogs, insects, and aquatic plants are only a few of the delights waiting to be discovered. Pack a magnifying glass and look carefully when arriving at each pond. You may find snails clinging to the rushes and reeds. Or at Hemlock Pond, surrounded by a canopy of majestic hemlocks, you may catch sight of a beaver at work. There may even be a few deer nearby.

Most of the hike follows the Appalachian Trail, and backpackers may camp 1 mile north of Crater Lake off the white-blazed trail. Sturdy shoes will help protect against the many rocks encountered on the narrow path. An experimental weather station is set up in front of the parking lot, and a hand water pump (perfect for warming up muscles and filling canteens) can be found off to the right.

Walk a short distance to the parking lot on the left side of the road, and look for a narrow white-blazed trail leading north into the woods.

The first half of this hike is along a fairly level stretch of the Appalachian Trail. Much of the trail is beneath a canopy of oak, beech, birch, and hemlock with lovely stands of mountain laurel scattered here and there. At 1 mile the trail descends steeply, requiring a bit of sitting and sliding. Grab onto tree roots wherever possible because the boulders can be very slippery after a rain or when covered by leaves in the fall.

Long Pine Pond soon comes into view on the left. At the double blaze at 1.2 miles, detour a few yards to the edge of the pond. Fallen logs at the water's edge provide an ideal spot to sit and enjoy the view or to examine the lush carpet of sphagnum moss. Once back on the main trail, turn left and continue heading gradually downhill. After another 0.3 mile there is a steep section that leads over large rocks. When you reach the broad rock ledge at the top, look for Crater Lake on the right. Old logging roads crisscross the trail in a few yards. There's a wonderful view of the surrounding ridges where the trail levels at the top of this ledge. In another 0.1 mile, where boulders are piled up, turn right for another fabulous view of Crater Lake. From here you can climb down to the rim of the lake or continue on the main trail. If you're staying on the main trail, proceed slightly downhill as the trail widens until it

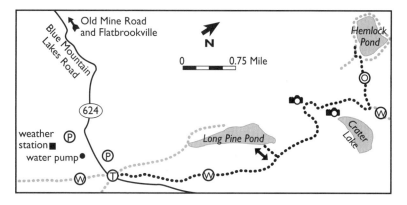

Children enjoy examining fungus growing on a tree trunk.

levels at 1.8 miles and another nice view of Crater Lake appears.

Continue uphill, and just after a left turn on the trail, turn left at the Hemlock Pond Trail post (2.1 miles) and follow orange blazes, which are sparse in some places. Hemlock Pond magically appears in the distance at 2.2 miles and is a hint of the reward to come. To reach the pond follow the narrow, rocky trail as it meanders steeply downhill, goes up and down for a bit, and finally levels out on a wide trail. (Pay attention to the path you've followed, as several trails converge in this area.) Head for the pond when it comes into view again. The logs at the water's edge are a great place for a snack or a moment of quiet reflection.

Return by the same route. On the way back, look for 3- to 4-foot-high tree trunks bearing the telltale toothmarks of beavers at work.

21 SWARTSWOOD

Location ■	Swartswood State Park
County ■	Sussex
Type ■	Day hike or overnight camping
Difficulty ■	Moderate
Distance ■	1.5 miles
Elevation gain ■	200 feet
Hours ■	Trails, dawn to dusk
Information ■	Swartswood State Park, P.O. Box 123, Swartswood 07877; (973) 383-5230
Website ■	*www.njparksandforests.org*
Admission ■	Free; fee for parking, Memorial Day to Labor Day; fee for camping

Driving directions: From I-80, take exit 25 to US 206 north to Newton. Take a left on Spring Street and another left onto CR 519. In about 0.5 mile, turn left onto Route 622. At the stop sign turn left onto CR 521. Parking is on the left.

Swartswood State Park, a recreational gem, is open year-round. Established in 1914 as New Jersey's first state park, the original acquisition was a 12 1/2-acre gift from George M. Emmans. He stipulated that it was to be used as a public park for everyone. Today the original land serves as the Emmans Grove Picnic Area. The park now consists of more than 700 acres of land and 600 acres of water. Swimmers enjoy the crystal clear lake formed by glaciers thousands of years ago, while lifeguards keep watch. The lake is also a sailor's dream, for it's perfect for launching sailboats, kayaks, and canoes, while anglers can try to catch bass, sunfish, catfish, walleye, perch, and

Swartswood Lake, used by anglers, swimmers and boaters, is especially appealing to hikers, who can view it from many vantage points.

pickerel. Best of all, the park is paradise for hikers. Trails include the 0.6-mile paved, level Duck Pond Multi-Use Trail that meanders through a forested area along Duck Pond and is sprinkled with interesting exhibits that provide information on the unique natural features found in the park. The trail also features a bird blind in a quiet area for viewing and is wheelchair accessible. It's ideal if you only want to take a short, easy hike or an excursion on roller blades or a skateboard. The moderately rated, white-blazed, 2.8-mile Spring Lake Trail, starting at the end of the Duck Pond Trail, follows natural hilly terrain through a secondary succession forest to secluded Spring Lake. Bear Claw Trail, marked with yellow blazes, is 0.8 mile and starts from the right of the kiosk in the Duck Pond parking area. It's rated easy to moderate and follows an earthen, hilly path. It ends where it meets the paved Duck Pond Trail, allowing hikers to combine the two trails for a full loop ending at the parking area.

I chose the exciting 1.5-mile Grist Mill Trail, a loop starting by the dam at the southernmost end of Swartswood Lake. Although the terrain is steep and rocky, it's well worth the effort.

After parking, walk over to Keen's Gristmill, built in the 1830s on the site of several earlier mills. The earliest mill, erected by Charles Rhodes and dating back to the Revolutionary War, was used to grind locally grown corn into meal. No one knows if a dam existed at that time, but when Rhodes died in 1799 the mill fell into disrepair and, according to a park brochure, was most likely abandoned. It is believed that the Keen family built the current mill around 1838—for that's the date cut into a cornerstone facing the Middleville-Swartswood Road. Word passed on through the years tells that the limestone for the mill was cut from exposed outcrops nearby. Blair Academy purchased the mill in the late 1880s and installed modern machinery that included a turbine in the basement with a large iron or steel shaft going up into the mill proper. This, in turn, operated the grinding stones and other various implements.

When ready, cross the bridge and take some time to admire the sweeping view of the water as it rushes over the dam. A nearby picnic table and benches overlook the lake. You'll probably have to pull yourself away from this picturesque spot to begin the hike. Walk straight onto the Grist Mill Trail following the yellow blazes within white rectangles. Gradually climbing, you'll quickly arrive at a huge, old tulip tree with a double trunk and thick branches reaching out farther than you can see. On the other side of

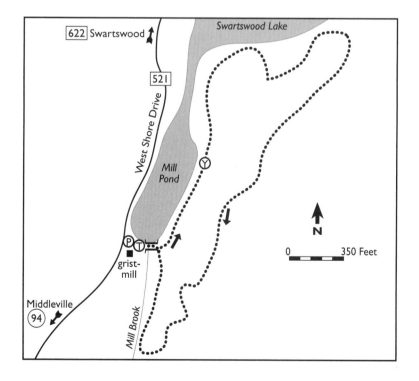

the tree are remains of an old rock fence. The narrow dirt trail descends gradually. During summer and fall, the trees, heavy with leaves, obscure the lake, but there are several open areas ahead where the views are great.

Cedar and hickories abound, and soon you'll be climbing steeply as the trail turns toward the lake, which is now in full view. Swans can sometimes be seen hanging around distant Snake Island. Shortly you'll find clearings where you can walk to the water's edge for a closer view of the island.

When you reach a red post sign indicating private property, take a sharp right at the double blaze. When you spot the next blaze, hike in the direction you just came, which will take you on a different part of the trail. A series of low, attractive stone fences follow the gradual ups and downs of the trail. When the lake appears on your right, the trail becomes steeper, followed by more ups and downs and stone fences. Ahead another climb is followed by a steep descent along a very narrow section. Clubmoss, found in damp places, makes a lovely showing in this area. Resembling tiny pine trees, these low-growing plants breed by spores and spread quickly. Amazingly, according to author Gerald Durrell in *A Practical Guide for the Amateur Naturalist*, these green flowerless land plants "are an ancient group which 250 million years ago included giant trees."

At 0.5 mile, the trail continues uphill very steeply, followed by an extremely steep descent. Continue by bearing left where the trail turns left, go over an interesting rock wall using **caution**—in autumn the fallen leaves may be slippery. You'll soon be rewarded by a sea of ferns, and from way up, you'll be looking down upon a beautiful stream. Its beauty and the sound of the water as it flows over boulders are certain to awaken all the senses. Watch your footing as you descend; the trail slants quite a bit. This is another excellent spot to choose a comfortable boulder to sit on, admire the scenery, and hear nothing but the stream below. When you get closer, you'll probably be tempted to float a leaf downstream or just relax and watch the water cascading over boulders of all shapes and sizes. The trail soon leads back to the parking area.

Note: If you plan on staying overnight, reserve one of the sixty-five tent and trailer sites. Available from April 1 through October 31, each site has a fire-ring, picnic table, and lantern holder. Flush toilets, showers, and laundry facilities are within walking distance, and trailer sanitary and water stations are nearby as well. Group campsites are available with a minimum occupancy of seven and maximum of twenty. The park has added six yurts to its campground offerings. A yurt is a circular tent built on a wooden frame with a concrete floor, a skylight, a lockable wood door, window screens with flaps, and two bunks which can sleep four people.

If you want to fish, bring your fishing gear and a license. Winter is a great time to be here, too, for there's still good hiking opportunities as well as ice skating, ice fishing, and cross-country skiing.

22 PAULINSKILL VALLEY TRAIL

Location ■ Newton
Counties ■ Sussex and Warren
Type ■ Day hike
Difficulty ■ Easy
Distance ■ 4 miles
Elevation gain ■ Negligible
Hours ■ Dawn to dusk
Information ■ Paulinskill Valley Trail Committee, P.O. Box 175, Andover 07821;
(908) 684-4820
Website ■ *http://www.pvtc-kvsp.org/*
Admission ■ Free

Driving directions: From Newton, take CR 519 north to CR 622 west and follow signs to Swartswood State Park. Park off the road on the left, opposite Junction Road. If you cross the bridge over Paulinskill Lake, you've gone too far.

It isn't difficult to imagine another era while hiking the abandoned New York, Susquehanna, and Western Railroad's flat, narrow, cinder-based trail. Trains transporting coal, milk, and other goods played an important role in boosting New Jersey's economy. But by 1962 trucking proved to be a more economical way to deliver merchandise, and a 27-mile-long section of track was removed. The City of Newark purchased the section for $22 million in 1962 with the intention of using it as a water conduit connecting the proposed Tocks Island Dam Reservoir with the Newark Watershed in Pequannock.

When the project stalled, dozens of organizations began urging the state to acquire the property for recreational purposes, including hiking, biking, horseback riding, cross-country skiing, and fishing. A lot of discussion—and fighting—followed. In 1985 New Jersey's Department of Environmental Protection considered purchasing the trail, but furious landowners who wanted to repurchase each backyard section of the tract opposed the idea. A public Green Acres meeting was arranged. (Green Acres, a program begun in New Jersey in 1961, has funded the purchase of thousands of acres of open space, including recreational facilities through bond issues. However, the Green Acres committee opposed this trail.) A small group of trail advocates then formed an ad hoc group known as the Paulinskill Valley Trail Committee. Len Frank was appointed chairman and waged a battle for public ownership of the trail for seven years.

With only $1000 in seed money, Frank and the committee went to work on the principal of bringing people out into wilderness and open spaces and getting them involved in education and conservation activities. Soon the committee began conducting hikes on the property and gained the support of the

Sierra Club. The committee's efforts didn't stop there. They raised money by bringing maps, pictures, pamphlets, and petitions to public events, and sold tee shirts, caps, mugs, and $10 annual memberships to supplement their funds. In the end the committee's hard work and determination paid off. When Chuck Haytaian became state Speaker of the House, he told of the trail's benefits to the public, and the battle was won in 1992.

Paulinskill Valley Trail—named by the Paulinskill Valley Trail Committee—became part of the New Jersey State Park system—and the 2-mile-long section of trail described in this hike goes through Kittatinny Valley State Park. Today outdoor enthusiasts have permanent access to its 27 miles. Telegraph poles and occasional railroad ties remain on both sides of the trail as well as a great variety of trees, 560 species of birds, and lovely wildflowers. You may also spot beaver, deer, muskrat, mink, and other wildlife.

Walk southwest from the parking area into the woods, and bear right at the fork at 0.2 mile. The concrete slab to the right supported a bridge that carried trains over CR 622. A bit farther ahead the trail dips between two ridges and at 0.5 mile, when the land drops off to the right, you'll see a lovely forested hill on the left. Paulinskill Lake appears on the right at about 0.75 mile.

If you're here in summer, you'll feel cool while gazing upon the water beneath a thick canopy of oak and maple that shades the path. You may pass riders on horseback or hear water-skiers occasionally, but they won't be too distracting in these peaceful surroundings. At 1 mile the trail passes between huge slabs of

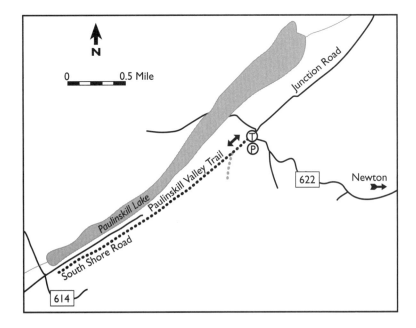

rock. Spend a few minutes exploring; young trees have sprouted in the cracks of the rock, and you'll notice horizontal layers of slate. A few yards farther you'll be treated to another view of the lake and shortly thereafter a few houses and log cabins appear along the bank below. The end of the lake comes into view at just under 2 miles, and if you look carefully you can spot the remains of the Swartswood Creamery and Ice House on the right. A barricade and pile of slate at a high point overlooking CR-614 mark the end of this section of the trail.

Return the way you came. On the way back, now that you've had time to admire the lake, you might want to identify some of the birds or search for old railroad spikes, mileage and whistle markers, cattle passes, battery boxes, or railroad ties hidden in the brush along the trail. When you reach the start of the hike, look up at the hill on the right where you can see the remains of the water tank that serviced steam engines. Taking the fork to the right leads up onto a small hill to the old railroad bed of the New York, Susquehanna, and Western Railroad.

Note: As of this writing, except for the completion of a few bridges, hikers can enjoy approximately 50 continuous miles on public trails through Sussex and Warren Counties by combining the Paulinskill Valley Trail with the 21.2-mile Sussex Branch Trail that begins at Waterloo Road, 1 mile west of US 206 in Byram. The trail joins the Paulinskill Valley Trail at Warbasse Junction and turns north of Newton before terminating farther north in Branchville.

Heading southwest through several towns, the 27-mile Paulinskill Trail joins the Appalachian Trail, plus other trails within the Delaware Water Gap National Recreation Area, near the Delaware River at the Columbia Lake Wildlife Management Area in Knowlton Township.

23 KITTATINNY VALLEY STATE PARK

Location ■	Kittatinny Valley State Park
County ■	Sussex
Type ■	Day hike
Difficulty ■	Easy
Distance ■	3.2 miles
Elevation gain ■	100 feet
Hours ■	Trails, dawn to dusk
Information ■	Kittatinny Valley State Park, P.O. Box 621, Andover 07821; (973) 786-6445
Website ■	www.njparksandforests.org
Admission ■	Free

Driving directions: From I-80, take US 206 north to Andover and turn right on Goodale Road. Turn right at the park entrance and continue to park headquarters.

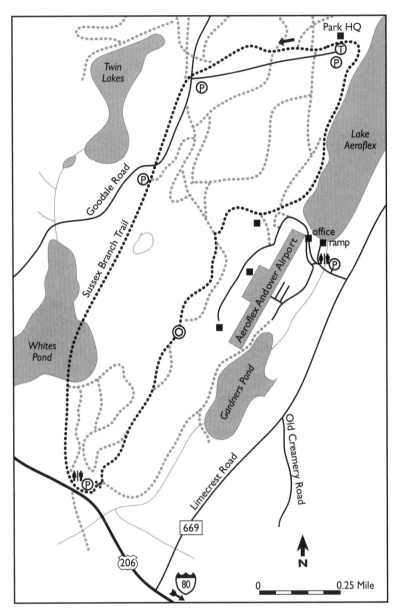

Whether you want to escape everyday stress or simply enjoy fishing, kayaking, mountain biking, and especially hiking, Kittatinny Valley State Park is the place to spend a morning, afternoon, or an entire day. Created in 1994, the 1692 scenic acres include Aeroflex-Andover Airport, Lake Aeroflex, several old logging trails as well as two rail trails. The 27-mile-long Paulinskill Valley Trail was once part of the New York, Susquehanna, and Western Railroad right-of-way that transported agricultural products and Pennsylvania coal to cities in eastern New Jersey as well as New York City. The 21-mile-long Sussex Branch Trail was a line of the Erie-Lackawanna Railroad that operated from the mid-1800s to the mid-1900s and transported iron ore, agricultural products, freight, and passengers. Hikers will enjoy meandering along densely wooded trails through valleys formed by glaciers and past limestone ridges beneath oak, sugar maple, tulip poplar, and hemlock as well as along wetland areas supporting a huge variety of plant and animal life.

Since things are different each time I visit, it's a good idea to start your day at park headquarters and ask if there are any trail changes or closures. The headquarters is in a huge white house to the left of the parking lot. The left section of the house was built as a farmhouse for Sarah Hill in 1825. When Fred Hussey purchased it in 1906, he added on to the house, built a horse barn, smoke house, and piggery, and expanded the farm. In 1957 the Aeroflex Corporation, of which he served as president, built the airport runway. Before leaving, stop by the small garden located in back of the house where beautiful plantings—among them bee balm, columbine, poppy, and peonies—draw dozens of butterflies.

When ready, walk past the house toward the parking lot and alongside some of the original buildings—an ice house, dairy and horse barns, and wood shed. In a short distance, turn right onto a gravel path that follows the edge of the woods. Eastern bluebird boxes have been placed in the open field, and on hot summer days, you'll be happy a canopy of tall trees is overhead. White snakeroot, which blooms in late summer, is one of the understory plants. Back in the days before milk processing, cows that ate it produced tainted milk, and since the plant is toxic, those who drank the milk would become quite ill. When Native American women realized what caused their "milk sickness," they warned others to pull the plant out of the fields or confine their cattle.

The understory is brilliant during fall when the yellow, white, and purple asters are in bloom. With a magnifying glass, you can see why this attractive plant is called a composite: each petal is a flower. As you continue on the trail, you'll be in what is known as an "edge habitat," where you'll witness both woods and meadow. In this area, it's easy to spot the Ailanthus, known as the tree of heaven because it seems to keep growing, in full sun, up to the sky. Springing up like a weed, its leaves are similar to the black walnut, but you can immediately tell the difference by checking the stem. Once the leaf node is broken, it leaves behind a small notch resembling a tooth, and although the stem appears to have twenty-three individual leaflets, it's really only one leaf!

A remnant left from a former Boy Scout camp, here from 1919 to 1954

Continue to a parking lot just inside the park entrance, cross Goodale Road, and immediately turn left onto a narrow section of the Sussex Branch Trail. Migrating birds, squirrels, rabbits, and chipmunks can sometimes be seen munching on the fruit of the wild cherry trees, and if you're here at the right time, you'll see the impressive seed clusters hanging from the Ailanthus trees on the right. Stay on the Sussex Branch Trail as it crosses Goodale Road. In August and September you'll see the red berries of the spicebush and through October the red, bristly stem of the wineberry produces purple berries.

The narrow cinderbase trail is bordered on both sides with virgin third-growth tulip, white ash, hemlock, hickory, and sugar maple. Long ago this area was cut completely—the first time for farms and the second and third times for the iron industry when trees were used to keep the iron furnaces burning. You'll know you're approaching Whites Pond when you hear spring peepers calling. This pond eventually will become a swamp as it's slowly being choked by lily pads. For the time being the pond is enjoyed by migrating birds, including terns and ducks, who stop by in early March.

Switch to a narrow trail coming up on the right for a closer look at the pond and, hopefully, wildlife. If you stand here for about fifteen minutes, you'll see almost every species of woodpecker, including the downy, hairy, and pileated. On the day I hiked this trail, I admired a pair of mute swans—mute because they don't make grunting sounds and when they fly their feathers make a pleasant whooshing sound. Check out the shrubs bordering the pond, especially the jewelweed. With early morning dew on the flower, it resembles a diamond and is often referred to as *touch-me-not* because when its seedpods are touched, they jump. Many people use this plant as a natural remedy for poison ivy, while migrating birds use it as a nutritious food source.

When ready, return to the Sussex Branch Trail and turn left when you reach US 206. In a few yards turn left again to pass through a wooden park gate. Continue into the woods onto an overgrown dirt trail. In a few yards, you'll come to the remains of a brick post, nearly hidden by weeds, and two magnificent old Japanese maple trees, remnants of a former homestead. After a short distance, an orange-blazed trail joins in and after a few ups and downs along the narrow path you'll reach a gravel road. Follow the right fork. When you reach a road junction, continue across a grassy area, with a flagpole to your left. Pick up a dirt trail alongside the lake, and turn left with the lake on the right. Lake Aeroflex—110 feet deep and 1 mile long—is one of New Jersey's deepest natural lakes. It dates back more than 10,000 years when glacial meltwaters filled it in. Lovely lily pads pop up near the bank, while tall Norway spruce are to the left. Eastern red cedar also makes a showing, with a lot of poison ivy growing beneath. The poison ivy is an important food source as well; the white berries are eaten by grouse and downy woodpeckers, especially during the migration period. When the leaves of the poison ivy drop, you can see the hairy stem, and during winter if you see a hairy rope climbing a tree, stay away. Remember, "Leaves of three, let it be." "Berries white, run at sight." "Hairy rope, don't be a dope!" Ahead you'll find an interpretive sign describing Camp Wawayanda in the 1940s. Although the buildings are long gone, some of the square cement blocks can still be seen to the left. Initially the camp was built in military style with two straight rows of cabins. Later the director of the camp initiated a village concept where the boys would be separated according to age so they could associate with their peers. A short distance away, the staircase on the right is also a remnant from the boy scout camp. Here they used a boat dock and had swimming races. Swimming is no longer allowed because of the depth of the lake and the safety issue; however, the remaining cement structure is a good platform for anglers.

While walking along, notice the angles in the shale that runs northeast to southwest. This is the way the glaciers came, and deep in the woods are small ridges of limestone. At the V bear left, and where the half-gravel, half-paved trail widens, with trees on the right and an open field on the left, you'll see park headquarters. On the way back to the parking lot, watch for Queen Anne's lace, known as bird's nest because it curls up in a cup shape and also known as white carrot because the root smells like a carrot. Why the purple spot in Queen Anne's lace? The story goes that when Queen Anne was knitting, she accidentally pricked her finger, and a drop of blood fell onto the lace!

Note: Bring a fishing rod and license and try your luck at reeling in large-mouth and smallmouth bass, pickerel, lake trout, brown trout, and rainbow trout. Or simply sit at one of the picnic tables beneath the gorgeous grove of spruce trees, enjoy a picnic lunch, and watch the boaters and planes flying very low over the lake as they take off from and land at the adjoining airport. Be aware that hunting is allowed in areas of the park; it's advisable to call the park office for dates, times, and locations. Hunting is not allowed on either the Paulinskill Valley Trail or the Sussex Branch Trail.

24 VAN CAMPEN GLEN

Location ▪ Delaware Water Gap National Recreation Area
County ▪ Warren
Type ▪ Day hike
Difficulty ▪ Moderate
Distance ▪ 2 miles
Elevation gain ▪ 200 feet
Hours ▪ Dawn to dusk
Information ▪ Park Headquarters, Delaware Water Gap National Recreation Area, Bushkill, PA 18324; (570) 588-2435, weekdays; (908) 496-4458, weekends
Website ▪ www.nps.gov/dewa
Admission ▪ Free

Driving directions: From the Kittatinny Point Visitor Center located along I-80 (westbound take New Jersey exit 1 and bear left 500 yards; eastbound take the first exit ramp after the Delaware River toll plaza and continue straight about 300 yards), take Old Mine Road north for 10 miles and turn right at the sign for Van Campen Glen (just past a sign for the Depew Recreation Site) and proceed to the parking area.

I've rarely seen other hikers on this short but challenging trail. Those who do hike the trail have a wonderful adventure, for they can enjoy the phenomenal beauty encountered every step of the way. Despite a couple of short climbs next to edges that drop off, the sight of Van Campen Brook's many exquisite cascades is well worth the effort. The temperature is several degrees cooler within the glen on hot summer days, and during fall the trees are a patchwork of color against the gray boulders. Have lunch or a snack before or after the hike in the picnic area adjacent to the parking area where you can see and listen to the melody of the brook and admire the outstanding shag bark hickory and hemlocks, or wait until you arrive at the upper waterfall, a musical as well

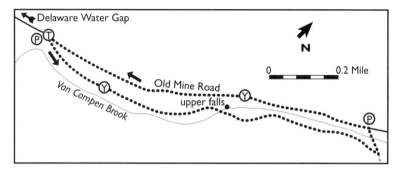

as visual treat. Sturdy shoes are essential for negotiating the damp, moss-covered rocks and logs.

Start by walking to the water's edge, and turn left to follow the narrow, rocky, yellow-blazed trail beside Van Campen Brook. Carefully negotiate the array of odd-shaped boulders and tree roots. As you make your way up and down, the brook is never far from view, and when you stop to catch your breath, you'll hear its melody as it flows on its way to the Delaware River. Walk slowly, take advantage of fallen logs across the trail to sit and enjoy the height of the trees, the sun shining through the canopy, and the beauty surrounding you.

You'll soon come to an enormous boulder resting in the middle of the path—another perfect spot for soaking in the exquisite tumbling cascades. Climb up the man-made rock staircase to get around the boulder. When you reach the top, you'll probably feel like king or queen of the mountain. As the trail gradually moves away from the brook, check out the ferns that thrive in these moist woods. The moss-covered rocks are extremely slippery in this area. In a few yards the trail levels and crosses a log bridge, where you'll have a grand view of a waterfall below and to the right. From this point there's a steep descent, mini-cascades tumbling over flat boulders, and foliage so lush during summer months the sun can barely peek through. Mushrooms are everywhere in the damp areas and after more ups and downs, you'll be higher above the water with a sheer drop on the right, so hold your children's hands and walk slowly. If you don't have a walking stick with you, the exposed tree roots are handy to hold on to, and in a few yards you'll be next to the water again. Trillium thrives along the bank during spring, and towering oaks, tulip trees, and evergreens are outstanding year-round.

At the double-yellow blaze, cross a bridge and turn left, with the river now on your left. Boulders along the way provide seats for admiring more waterfalls. The deafening roar of the water announces Van Campen's upper falls. Linger here for a while, dip your feet in the water, have a snack, and enjoy the breeze generated by the tumbling water. When you're ready, cross the bridge over the brook and climb the steps heading up to the top of the falls. Small children will probably need a boost because the steps are quite steep. Ahead is another bonus—water tumbling down through an impressive gorge. Keeping the water to your left and following the yellow blaze, you'll come to an incredible spot and pass where the flowing water has carved out a narrow path past impressive high granite walls.

Where the trail levels, there's a calm stretch of water providing another good spot to look around, admire the surroundings, float a leaf downstream, and study the boulders on both sides. Ahead, you'll be entertained by short sections of calm water followed by rushing water with small and larger waterfalls tumbling over boulders. You'll need some tricky maneuvers to get over tree roots and rocks, but the extra effort is rewarded with more cascades. After a few ups and downs dense foliage blocks the view, but not the sound, of the water. The water comes back into view in the distance, and when the trail widens and swings to the right, the river will be on the left.

 When you come to Old Mine Road, you have two options: turn left onto the road and continue to the parking lot, or turn around and retrace your steps. Although there are few cars on this road, walking back the way you came will give you another perspective on the beauty of the area, and it's safer because you won't have to worry about traffic. Should you decide to return on Old Mine Road, think about its history. Built by the Dutch in the mid-seventeenth century to transport ore from the Pahaquarry copper mine to Esopus (now Kingston) on the Hudson River, Old Mine Road was the first road built in the United States. You'll see the glen on the left far below the road. To return to the parking area, turn left a few yards after the downhill section begins.

25 DUNNFIELD CREEK CIRCULAR

Location ▪ Delaware Water Gap National Recreation Area
County ▪ Warren
Type ▪ Day hike or overnight camping
Difficulty ▪ Moderate
Distance ▪ 3.4 miles
Elevation gain ▪ 600 feet
Hours ▪ Dawn to dusk
Information ▪ Park Headquarters, Delaware Water Gap National Recreation Area, Bushkill, PA 18324; (570) 588-2435
Website ▪ www.nps.gov/dewa/
Admission ▪ Free

 Driving directions: From I-80 West, after the 3-mile marker at the sign for the rest area, park in the second parking lot just past the rest area. From Pennsylvania via I-80, after crossing the Delaware River, drive past the Kittatinny Point Visitor Center, and turn left to cross under the interstate. Turn left at the T and enter the parking lot.

More than 2.5 million people are drawn to the Delaware Water Gap National Recreation Area each year. Most go directly to the Kittatinny Point Visitor Center, where they can enjoy a leisurely picnic or views of the scenic Delaware River. Hikers, however, come for the peace of the surrounding woodland trails on the Kittatinny Ridge—best hiked on a weekday—and the sight of a huge boulder dating back 450 million years.

If you're planning to camp, there is no fee, but check in at the visitor center first. Backcountry camp-

The wooden bridge over Dunnfield Creek at the beginning of the trail.

ing is permitted only along the Appalachian Trail and only for hikers on extended trips of two or more days. It is limited to within 100 feet of the trail and more than 0.5 mile from the departure point. Campfires are prohibited.

On this loop hike, which includes a section of the famous Appalachian Trail, you're bound to see wildlife. You'll also see and hear Dunnfield Creek as it melodiously tumbles down on to the Delaware River. Each season offers a new delight. Spring ushers in new ferns; during summer the fragrance of honeysuckle fills the air and rhododendron put on a magnificent display; in fall the leaves turn, casting a bright glow against a backdrop of tall, green hemlocks; and in winter a sheet of ice covers the stream's pools, while a blanket of snow decorates the rocks.

To begin the hike, walk to the northern end of the parking lot and enter the woods on the Appalachian Trail, indicated by double-white blazes. Dunnfield Creek, on the left, with all sizes and shapes of boulders strewn along its bed, casts a special spell. The mating song of bullfrogs can be heard each spring, and the wooden bridge just ahead is a perfect place to pause and listen to the music of the creek as it makes its way past downed trees and boulders. Straight ahead you'll see trees crowding the edge of the creek. With their roots reaching into the water like giant toes, the trees suck up hundreds of gallons of water daily; ultimately, the water finds its way from the fine root hairs to the branches and leaves. There are also a lot of tree roots spread across the trail, so watch your footing.

After a gradual climb, bear right at the fork with the blue-blazed trail. As you continue uphill, you'll come across mini-waterfalls here and there cascading through cracks in the boulders. At the trail junction sign for Worthington State Forest, go slightly downhill onto the right fork at 0.3 mile to follow the blue-blazed trail that soon narrows. Cross the wooden bridge, and if it's been raining heavily, you'll see more tiny waterfalls. Continue going uphill, following the blue blazes. At the fork go left onto the red trail, which will soon take you past a swampy, level area, with the creek to the left and a hill to the right. Waterfalls appear one after the other now, and when you swing next to the creek again, you'll probably encounter a lot of

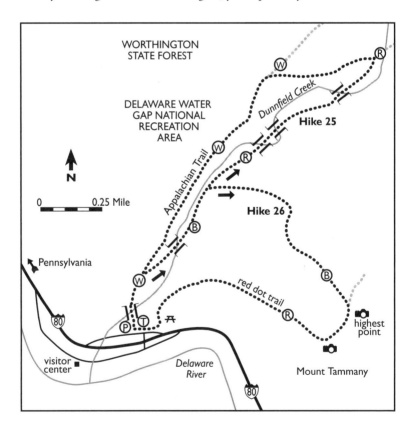

birds. The next bridge is at 0.7 mile, and another is just beyond it.

In a few yards you'll reach a large, downed tree—a perfect seat from which to observe birds flitting from limb to limb and bees gathering nectar from blooming shrubs. Head slightly uphill from here; the creek is now to the left. As you walk farther away from the creek, the trail levels but becomes quite rocky. At 1 mile, tall tulip trees loom overhead; the fifth bridge is at 1.1 miles. Continue slightly uphill, and at the T at 1.4 miles, where the red trail swings to the right, take the left fork onto the Holly Springs Trail. Go uphill for a few yards on the wide, rocky path, continuing straight as it becomes grassy and passes through a lovely field of ferns. At 1.9 miles the Appalachian Trail appears again. If you are going to camp, go right onto the white-blazed Appalachian Trail. If you're returning to the trailhead, turn left here, going downhill gradually on an extremely rocky path. Look out for loose rocks. The trail changes into a level dirt path at 2.2 miles and dips again in 0.25 mile before leveling. Dunnfield Creek comes into view once more to the left at 3 miles. Continue to the first bridge and the parking lot.

26 MOUNT TAMMANY

Location ■	Delaware Water Gap National Recreation Area
County ■	Warren
Type ■	Day hike
Difficulty ■	Challenging
Distance ■	4.3 miles
Elevation gain ■	1180 feet
Hours ■	Dawn to dusk
Information ■	Park Headquarters, Delaware Water Gap National Recreation Area, Bushkill, PA 18324; (570) 588-2435
Website ■	*www.nps.gov/dewa/*
Admission ■	Free

Driving directions: From I-80 West, after the 3-mile marker at the sign for the rest area, park in the second parking lot just past the rest area. From Pennsylvania via I-80, after crossing the Delaware River, drive past the Kittatinny Point Visitor Center, and turn left to cross under the interstate. Turn left at the T and enter the parking lot.

You'll huff and puff hiking up the steep, rocky trail to Mount Tammany's summit, but the reward is a spectacular view of the Delaware Water Gap, Mount Minsi, and surrounding farmland. Plan on frequent rest stops on the way up and be sure to carry ample water. During summer months, you might want to watch the water as it cascades through large boulders and fallen trees on its journey to the Delaware River.

Mount Tammany, located within the 70,000-acre Delaware Water Gap National Recreation Area, is part of the wooded mountain ridge known as the Kittatinnys—from a Native American word meaning "Big Mountain." At the top, a perfect spot to admire the Delaware River as it cuts through the mountains, you'll probably see turkey vultures and broad-winged hawks gliding on the wind currents.

According to geologists, when the flat-lying rocks below folded, erosion beveled them. Later uplift of the area caused the rivers and streams to cut downward. As the land rose, the main stream probably maintained its original course, thereby separating the valley into bands of resistant and nonresistant rock. Water then eroded the softer materials and passed around the harder rock of emerging ridges. The main stream eventually formed a ridge and the notches, or "water gaps," emerged.

Walk a few yards into the woods from the north side of the parking lot to the double-white blazes that mark the Appalachian Trail, and follow the trail across a small bridge. The path gradually ascends, paralleling Dunnfield Creek. At 0.3 mile, at a sign and map for Worthington Forest, the trail divides; take the right fork, following the blue blazes. Cross a second bridge at 0.7 mile; after heavy rains, there are usually mini-waterfalls tumbling over the rocks on the left. The trail climbs for 0.1 mile and then divides. Once again take the right fork and continue to follow the blue blazes as they lead relentlessly upward. Although the trail is steep, the lush stands of oak, hickory, and tulip provide pleasant distractions, and during late spring, masses of mountain laurel bloom near the top of the ridge. The Delaware River pops into sight at the trail's highest point, but the best view is less than

five minutes away. Turn right and follow the blue blazes to an open area. A short walk onto the large boulders of Mount Tammany reveals a magnificent panorama of the Delaware River and Mount Minsi in Pennsylvania. This spot, perhaps New Jersey's most scenic overlook, is a perfect place to eat lunch and watch canoeists paddling far below.

From here continue right onto a trail marked with a red circle on a white background. This rocky trail passes a magnificent stand of mountain laurel before starting its gradual descent. After 0.5 mile the going becomes slow and difficult as the trail drops rapidly over a steep rock face. **Use caution** when you reach this section and be sure you have a good foothold when climbing down the rock. In this area mountain ridges are visible in the distance and hemlocks tower overhead. You'll get another glimpse of the river before reaching the parking lot at the rest area. Walk past the picnic tables at the west end and follow a dirt path that climbs over a small ridge leading, in less than 0.2 mile, to a second parking area and your vehicle.

27 PINE SWAMP

Location ■ Mahlon Dickerson Reservation
County ■ Morris
Type ■ Day hike and overnight camping
Difficulty ■ Moderate
Distance ■ 3.8 miles
Elevation gain ■ 150 feet
Hours ■ Dawn to dusk
Information ■ Morris County Park Commission, 53 East Hanover Avenue, Morristown 07960; (973) 326-7600
Website ■ www.morrisparks.net
Admission ■ Free; fee for camping

Driving directions: From I-80 West, take exit 34B onto NJ-15 North. Drive 4 miles and exit at Weldon Road, following Weldon Road east 3 miles to the reservation entrance. Continue to the picnic area (second entrance on the left) and park.

A longtime resident of Morris County, Mahlon Dickerson (1770–1853) owned local iron mines, spoke several languages, and was a recognized botanist. Considering that he also served as governor, U.S. senator, and Secretary of the Navy, it's no wonder that the largest park in Morris County—Mahlon Dickerson Reservation—was named in his honor in 1967.

The trails within these 1500 wooded acres are situated along old logging roads where you'll have ample opportunity to see impressive stands of spruce, azalea, mountain laurel, and rhododendron. Although there aren't any views on the main part of this hike, a short detour at the end will bring you to an overlook with a view of Lake Hopatcong, 9 miles in the distance. At one point, you'll also be standing at the highest elevation in Morris County at 1395 feet above sea level. The park has facilities for overnight tent and trailer camping as well as a full schedule of events, including naturalist-led hikes and campfire demonstrations.

Walking north from the parking lot (away from Weldon Road), you'll pass an old-fashioned water pump on the left that's perfect for filling a canteen and showing younger children what fetching water in the good old days was like. To the right is a fitness cluster—this unique outdoor recreational facility was scientifically designed for conditioning the entire body through the use of stretching, strengthening, and cardiovascular movements.

Continue past the beautiful wooded picnic grove, following the Highlands

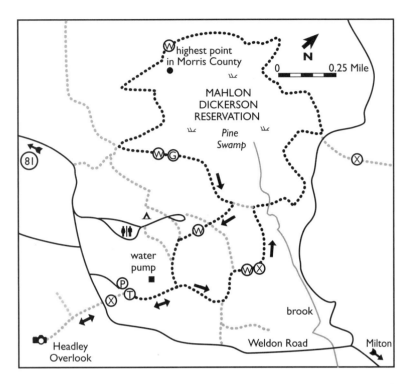

Trail, indicated by teal and white blazes. At the sign for the Pine Swamp Trail marked with white blazes at 0.3 mile, turn right to follow the wide gravel path that is level for a short distance before descending gradually. During summer months the dense canopy of oak, beech, and tulip trees provide shade, while autumn brings dazzling color as well as a shower of falling leaves. Not too many people can resist floating leaves downstream, so plan on a brief pause at the brook at 0.5 mile.

Follow the double-white blaze to the left, climbing gradually uphill past graceful tulip trees. If you're ready for another quick break, you might want to watch others practice rappelling on the huge boulders in this area.

From this point, there are many short ups and downs, At the junction you can go either way on the Pine Swamp Trail, which is a 3.6-mile loop, but turn right to continue following the teal and white blazes. The trail crosses a beautiful brook, a perfect place to listen to the music of the water as it swirls past a variety of odd-shaped rocks. There are also gorgeous stands of mountain laurel that put on quite a show during spring and provide a soothing green throughout the winter months. Stay with the white blazes as the teal-blazed Highlands Trail turns off to the right.

The trail makes several turns before entering the swamp for which it is named. After a moderate climb a sign on the left at 2.3 miles announces the highest point in Morris County, which unfortunately does not feature a view. Soon you'll come to three signs leading to the Pine Swamp Trail: one points the way you came, one leads to the camping area, and one points to the Boulder Trail. The camping area, which can be reached in a little more than a mile, is almost as popular with toads and garter snakes as it is with people! You'll want to bear left onto the green-and-white-blazed Boulder Trail, ascending gradually, with small boulders along the trail and huge ones here and there in the woods. At 3.2 miles, where the green and white blazes continue straight, turn right to follow the white blazes to the picnic area where you'll probably want to stop for a snack and a drink. When you're ready, continue along the trail to return to your car.

For an exceptional scenic view, follow the teal blazes south from the parking area, and **use caution** crossing Weldon Road. Turn left at the sign indicating Headley Overlook; a short walk will bring you to the 1300-foot overlook with a view that includes the northern section of Lake Hopatcong.

Turtles can often be spotted sunning themselves on logs at the edge of the brook.

28 HEDDEN COUNTY PARK

Location ■ Hedden County Park
County ■ Morris
Type ■ Day hike
Difficulty ■ Easy
Distance ■ 2.7 miles
Elevation gain ■ Negligible
Hours ■ Trails, dawn to dusk
Information ■ Morris County Park Commission, 53 East Hanover Avenue, Morristown, 07960; (973) 326-7600
Website ■ www.morrisparks.net
Admission ■ Free

Driving directions: From NJ-10 near Dover, go north on CR 513 and turn left at the first stop sign at Concord Road. Follow East Randolph Avenue to a small parking lot on the right side of the road.

Named for the Hedden family for their donation of 40 acres of land in 1963, Hedden Park officially opened in 1970. Through its land acquisition program, the park commission has increased its size to 380 acres. In addition

Watching and listening to the water cascading over large and small boulders is a joy.

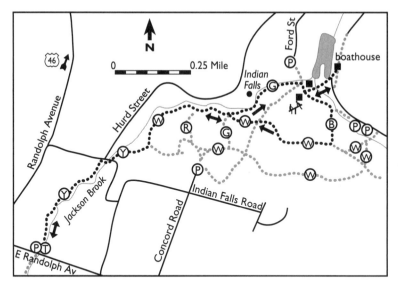

to well-maintained hiking trails, you'll find a pretty pond, fishing pier, boat rental facility, picnic areas, a large playing field, a Saturn playground, and ice skating during winter months.

Facing the woods, look for a trail sign to the right of the parking area, and begin on the yellow-blazed Jackson Brook Trail. From spring through fall, the first thing you'll notice are the dazzling wildflowers such as the goldenrod with clusters of small yellow-rayed blossoms and dainty purple asters displaying striking yellow centers. Asters, considered sacred by Greek and Roman deities, were thought to possess magical powers, and the leaves were burned to keep away evil spirits and drive off serpents. Today the aster is used as the floral emblem for September.

Almost immediately you'll come to the brook, to the right of the trail. Its melody, as it tumbles over large and small boulders, is enchanting as is its beauty. The trees provide a welcome canopy of shade on the hottest summer's day, and just ahead boulders as well as lush ferns abound.

In a short distance you'll see a lone house is on the opposite bank and, from this point, there's a gradual downhill section leading to a road. Cross it, turn right, go over the bridge and brook following the yellow blaze, and follow the iron guard rail. Where it ends, look carefully for a narrow opening on the left onto the trail again. With the brook now on the left, you'll encounter huge stands of Queen Anne's lace. Also known as wild carrot because of the smell of its root, this hairy-stemmed biennial wildflower that often resembles a bird's nest sports flat-topped flower clusters frequently with a single purple flower in the center. The trail ascends slightly at 0.5 mile. In a few yards, turn left onto the white-blazed Hedden Circular Trail; the brook is still on the left. Some steep spots follow for a short distance, but the trail quickly levels out along a narrow ledge that's surrounded by shrubs, trees, and ferns. Watch your step in this area, for you'll be about 20 feet above the brook, walking next to huge boulders, and encountering some loose rock. Slowly descend along the narrow ledge to a short level stretch before more ups and downs. If you're hiking during summer, the water will be hidden from view, but you'll still be able to hear it.

Bear left onto the green-blazed Indian Falls Trail. The brook reappears as you pass more boulders. You probably won't be able to resist sitting on one of the huge, flat boulders to admire the three tiny falls dropping into the brook's main pool. This is a stunning spot, especially if you're here during autumn around 4 P.M. when the sun is reflected in the water. The scene is exhilarating, and the area is so quiet that the sound of the birds singing, the squirrels scampering in the freshly fallen leaves, and the insects buzzing as they hover over the water is magical. Watch your footing as you continue.

 Detour at the sign for Indian Falls at 1 mile. Certainly not as huge as Niagara Falls, it is still a place you'll want to return to again and again. When you can pull yourself away from the beautiful scenery, retrace your steps to the green-blazed trail and continue straight. A parking lot and picnic grove appear on the opposite bank at 1.1 miles. Cross the bridge at 1.2 miles. To the right is a Saturn playground and to the left, a wide expanse of lawn. Turn right; when you reach the paved path, turn left, cross a bridge, pass the picnic area, and head toward the boathouse on the left. Spend some time at the pond watching the ducks and geese, and look for a beaver lodge at the edge of the pond just beyond the boathouse. Made of mud and sticks, it's reputed to be Morris County's most accessible beaver colony.

When you're ready to leave this pleasant area, turn left facing the pond and continue to the right of the parking lot, pass the map board, and retrace your route. Turn right at the picnic area keeping it on your left, and turn left at the T at the top of the paved trail. Gradually climbing, you'll hear the sound of a small waterfall beneath the bridge up ahead. It's worth the few extra yards to see it. Before the bridge, look on the right for a trail sign for the blue-blazed connector trail, turn left. This section is rugged with a lot of rocks to step over and a gradual uphill climb through dense woods. At the T at 1.8 miles, turn right to rejoin the white-blazed Hedden Circular Trail. Watch your step: the trail is mostly gravel with frequent boulders. Cross a stream at 2 miles as you walk uphill past lovely sassafras and tulip trees. You'll hear Jackson Brook just ahead at the junction with the green-blazed trail. Continue on the white-blazed trail and then the yellow-blazed trail to return to your car.

29 TRIPOD AND BEAR ROCKS

Location ▪	Pyramid Mountain Natural Historical Area
County ▪	Morris
Type ▪	Day hike
Difficulty ▪	Moderate
Distance ▪	3.3 miles
Elevation gain ▪	300 feet
Hours ▪	Trails, dawn to dusk; visitor center, 10 A.M.–4:30 P.M., Wednesday–Sunday
Information ▪	Pyramid Mountain Natural Historical Area, 472A Boonton Avenue, Boonton 07005; (973) 334-3130
Website ▪	www.morrisparks.net
Admission ▪	Free

Driving directions: From I-287, take exit 44 to Main Street in Boonton to Boonton Avenue (CR 511). Turn right onto Boonton Avenue and proceed northbound for 3.3 miles. Park at the visitor center, on the left.

This hike offers one pleasant surprise after another. Not only will you be passing through lush woods, but you'll have a fine view of New York City's skyline from the top of Pyramid Mountain. There's more icing on the cake with two excellent examples of glacial erratics—huge boulders believed to have been swept and deposited here by a glacial ice sheet around 12,000 years ago. Tripod Rock, balanced on tiny, ball-shaped rocks, is a 160-ton beauty, while Bear Rock casts a tremendous shadow upon the swampy area it monopolizes.

A hiker admires tripod rock.

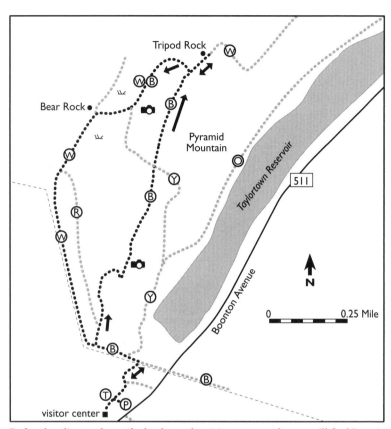

Before heading to the trail, check out the visitor center where you'll find Lenni-Lenape Indian artifacts, bird nests, and other interesting exhibits as well as Douglas Vorolieff, one of the nicest and most knowledgeable naturalists in the state. Don't forget to pick up a trail map while you're here. Sturdy shoes are recommended because the trail is rocky in many places.

Follow signs to the blue-blazed trail and turn left onto it. Cross the footbridge at 0.1 mile, and follow the short boardwalk over a brook. After a heavy rain, you might see a tiny waterfall in this area as you gradually ascend Pyramid Mountain. On the way up, you'll be surrounded by boulders and tall oaks. In 0.25 mile, you'll begin to ascend a rock staircase thought to be laid by a construction crew many years ago. To the right are two large ball-shaped boulders that look as though they may fall with the first strong breeze.

After passing a powerline tower, and at approximately 0.4 mile, bear right at a blue-blazed post, staying with the blue trail and climbing steeply through a mixed forest of beeches, oaks, tulip trees, and red maples. A lovely pond soon comes into view, and as the trail levels a bit ahead, you'll be treated to a fantastic view of New York City. During autumn, the trees in this area resemble an artist's palette.

The trail heads downhill at 0.9 mile, and at 1.3 miles, where blue blazes lead to the left, continue straight on a white-blazed trail that leads to Tripod Rock. This is a great spot to stop, rest, and try to figure out how the rock got here. You'll hear youngsters begging adults to hoist them onto the top of the rock as well as a lot of fellow hikers creeping beneath it. When finished, backtrack down the white trail and turn right at the double-white blaze heading up and then downhill. Be careful in the fall, when leaves obscure rocks on the trail.

When the trail levels out, you'll be in a swampy area where sphagnum moss thrives. A short distance ahead, the woods take on a distinct cathedral-like feeling late in the afternoon. After crossing a bridge over a tiny brook, you'll come to Bear Rock at 2 miles. Take your time to walk around and climb partway up. This is an excellent place to picnic and a good place to seek shelter should it suddenly start to rain. When ready, continue on the white trail through woods and under a row of powerlines. Continue through a clearing, with the woods on either side, followed by a short climb that quickly levels out again. To the left are small boulders perched on huge rock walls. The bedrock is a metamorphic rock called gneiss. After heading slightly downhill at 2.9 miles, you'll see another tower. Stay right at the junction with the Butler Montville Trail and follow the blue blazes east under powerlines. The trail soon leads down the rock steps and back to the parking lot.

30 TURKEY MOUNTAIN

Location ▪ Pyramid Mountain Natural Historical Area

County ▪ Morris

Type ▪ Day hike

Difficulty ▪ Challenging

Distance ▪ 4 miles

Elevation gain ▪ 340 feet

Hours ▪ Trails, dawn to dusk; visitor center, 10 A.M.–4:30 P.M., Wednesday–Sunday

Information ▪ Pyramid Mountain Visitor Center, 472A Boonton Avenue, Boonton 07005; (973) 334-3130

Website ▪ www.morrisparks.net

Admission ▪ Free

Driving directions: See Hike 29.

Try this hike in spring when the buds are bursting open or on a hot summer's day in almost total shade under a natural canopy of trees. Sturdy

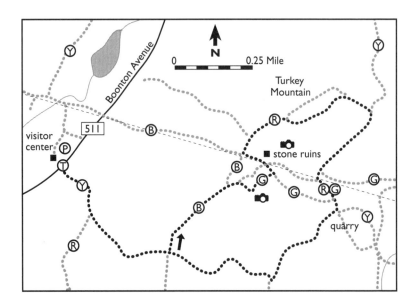

shoes are necessary for negotiating the endless boulders and slippery areas. Before starting the hike, stop in at the visitor center to pick up a map of the trails, check out the interesting exhibits, and ask for a calendar of events. The land you'll be hiking on was used as a hunting, fishing, and gathering site by Native Americans for more than ten thousand years. Many explorers followed, and evidence of their presence can be seen when walking past surveyor's stones and stone walls that marked homestead farms and woodlot boundaries.

From the parking lot, cross the road and take the yellow-blazed trail, a few feet to your right. It quickly passes an industrial park before meandering up and down through dense woods. Throughout the hike you'll find boulders of all sizes and shapes. You'll also find a lot of beech trees, recognizable by the smooth, shiny gray bark and large "toes" that seem to bury themselves in the earth.

At 0.6 mile, turn left onto the blue-blazed trail. After a rain you might have to jump across a narrow stream. As you begin a gradual climb, watch for the mitten-shaped leaves of the sassafras as well as oak trees. A bit farther ahead glacial erratics are scattered about. The blue trail turns left at 1 mile; pick up the green trail and continue straight. After an unmarked trail bears left, follow the green trail to the right, which leads to a beautiful view of Lake Valhalla. When you're ready, continue on the green trail to the remains of a stone house, built around 1910. A few feet ahead to the right is a terrific view of Manhattan's skyline. Turn left (west), at the powerline tower, onto the level, unmarked grassy trail, keeping the next tower in view. At the red trail marker (on a post), turn right into the woods, and while gradually heading uphill examine the in-

teresting tree trunks but watch out for protruding greenbriar.

After bearing right at the fork and lifting
your feet through high ferns and over boulders, a right turn will lead you to a huge boulder that's perfect for a rest break. The only
time you can appreciate the distant view is during winter after the leaves have fallen, but in
spring and summer months, you'll probably
see a pair of doves that have claimed this area.

*Check out the shrubs along
the trail; you may come
upon an unusual, beautiful
insect.*

Identified by a long pointed tail, long neck, and small head, these birds
emit a long, mournful cry that can be mistaken for an owl.

As you descend the red-blazed trail, Lake Valhalla comes into view. Watch
where you step; rocks are sometimes hidden by high grasses, and for 0.1 mile
the trail may be slippery. Be careful where it slants and falls away to the left.
The red and green trails meet at 2.8 miles. Follow the red-blazed trail
through more shrub brush, tall grasses, and forest to the T. This is the end of
the red trail, indicated by three red blazes. Turn right onto the yellow-blazed
trail, which is fairly wide and flat and almost devoid of rocks. In case you
miss walking on rocks, you'll encounter more as the road descends gradually
through lush forest. After passing a narrow stream at 4 miles, take the right
fork, following the yellow blazes steeply uphill. Continue straight when the
blue-blazed trail intersects, pass the industrial center, cross the road to the
visitor center, and return to the parking lot.

31 THE TOURNE

Location ■ Tourne Park
County ■ Morris
Type ■ Day hike
Difficulty ■ Moderate
Distance ■ 1.7 miles
Elevation gain ■ 327 feet
Hours ■ Trail, dawn to dusk
Information ■ Morris County Park Commission, 53 East Hanover Avenue,
Morristown 07960; (973) 326-7600
Website ■ www.morrisparks.net
Admission ■ Free

Driving directions: Traveling north on I-287, take exit 43 for Intervale
Road (Mountain Lakes). At the end of the ramp, turn left and cross over

These dense woods sport trees that seem to touch the sky!

I-287 to the traffic light. Turn right at the light onto Fanny Road. Proceed straight to the second stop sign. Turn right onto West Main Street. Bear left at the Y onto Powerville Road. Continue until the first road on the left, McCaffrey Lane. Turn left. You'll see the sign for Tourne Park.

Traveling south on I-287, take exit 45 for Myrtle Avenue to the T at the end of the exit ramp. Turn left onto Myrtle Avenue to the second traffic light. Turn right at the second traffic light onto Wonton Street. At the blinker light, turn left onto Boonton Avenue. Proceed downhill to the traffic light and turn right onto Main Street. Bear left at the fork and follow Main Street to West Main Street. Bear right at the Texaco Station, and turn right onto Powerville Road. Look for the Tourne Park entrance sign on the right and turn left onto McCafferty Lane to enter the park.

This rugged park is one of the Garden State's gems. Besides offering hiking trails traversing hills strewn with huge granite boulders, there are picnic sites, equestrian trails, ball fields, and in the winter, cross-country skiing. The park is also the only remaining undeveloped fragment of the Great Boonton Tract that was originally purchased by David Ogden. Ogden served as colonial attorney general of New Jersey in 1759. McCaffrey Lane, the main road leading into the park, was built in 1767 by his son Samuel Ogden to haul iron ore from the nearby Hibernia mines to his ironworks in Old Boonton, where he manufactured cannonballs for the Continental Army during the American Revolution. Much of this land was inherited and acquired by Clarence Addington DeCamp in the late 1850s. Using hand tools and levers, DeCamp built two roads leading to the top of the Tourne. Considered one of Morris County's first conservationists, DeCamp encouraged local residents to accompany him on hikes in the woods and fields. In 1958 the Morris County Park Commission wisely acquired the initial 219 acres from Logan Steele and

Dr. Lewis Hull and opened the park to the public in 1960.

After entering the park, the first parking area is for the Emile K. Hammond Wildflower Trail. If you've arrived during spring, this 1-mile trail is not only an excellent way to limber up, but it offers a dazzling array of wildflowers.

When ready, drive to the second parking lot adjoining a baseball field and a large meadow. The red-blazed DeCamp Trail leads to the top of the Tourne and starts on the right side of the road near the Overlook sign. Start the steep climb alongside the rope strung between posts. To the right at 0.2 mile are huge boulders forming a natural den. As you huff and puff your way uphill surrounded by impressive woods, you'll pass excellent places to spot deer early in the morning or late in the afternoon. The bench on the left just as the trail curves slightly to the right is a welcome sight as well as a good place to sit, have a drink, and take in the lush surroundings. Just ahead there's a tree with dozens of huge holes in its trunk that's still alive.

Most hikers can't resist sitting on a boulder shaped like a chair a few yards ahead. This is also the perfect place to look back and admire the woods—especially in September and October when they're adorned in spectacular color—and to listen to the flutter of leaves in the breeze and the song of a bird breaking the silence. Another bench soon awaits. Through an opening in the trees you can view the countryside, watch hawks soaring by, count the

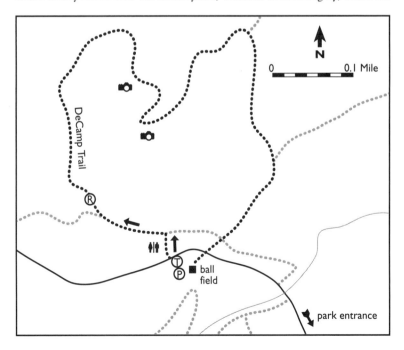

dozens of acorns at your feet, and understand why the area was named Tourne—derived from the Dutch word meaning "lookout" or "mountain." In September the juniper on your right at 0.6 mile is adorned with berries. The trail levels at this point, and a picnic table and benches await in the open, grassy area ahead. Walking downhill you'll come to a memorial adorned with American flags for the victims of the September 11 World Trade Center tragedy. In front of the memorial is an overlook shaded by a canopy of chestnut trees. From the memorial continue downhill and look for a narrow, unmarked, gravel side trail on the right at 0.9 mile. As this trail descends gradually through a valley of boulders surrounded by trees, you'll come to a good area to wait for wildlife. When ready, return to the main trail and continue downhill. Along the way you'll come to a rock bench and a spot where squirrels and chipmunks can sometimes be seen scurrying about. At 1.5 miles another bench in dense woods provides a view of a gully. The trail levels a bit in a few yards, and at 1.7 miles, you'll arrive at the parking lot.

32 HIGH MOUNTAIN

Location ▪ High Mountain Park Preserve
County ▪ Passaic
Type ▪ Day hike
Difficulty ▪ Challenging
Distance ▪ 5.1 miles
Elevation gain ▪ 500 feet
Hours ▪ Dawn to dusk
Information ▪ The Nature Conservancy, New Jersey Field Office, 200 Pottersville Road, Chester 07930; (908) 879-7262. Wayne Township Department of Parks; (973) 694-1800, ext. 3260
Website ▪ nature.org
Admission ▪ Free

Driving directions: From NJ-23, take the Wayne exit and proceed north on Alps Road approximately 2 miles to the traffic light at the intersection of Alps and Ratzer Roads. Take an extreme right onto Ratzer Road and proceed approximately 2 miles to the traffic light at the intersection of Ratzer Road and Hamburg Turnpike. After crossing the intersection, Ratzer becomes Pompton Road. Proceed about 200 yards to William Paterson University. Turn left through entry gate 1 and continue straight ahead to parking lot 6.

Early or late in the day, during any season, the climb to the barren, 879-

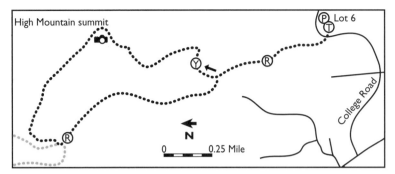

foot summit of High Mountain is worth the effort for the panoramic view—New York City's skyline, the graceful lines of the George Washington Bridge, and the surrounding Preakness Range of the Watchung Mountains. High Mountain Preserve—one of the largest tracts of forested land in the Piedmont region of northern New Jersey—was aptly named, for this bald, rocky knob is the highest in the area and consists of both woodlands and wetlands.

Managed by The Nature Conservancy, the preserve protects rare and threatened wildlife as well as a globally endangered basalt outcrop community. To date, 9 ecological communities and 380 plant species, including 18 rare plant species, have been identified here. According to The Nature Conservancy's literature, "several rock shelters in the area have been determined to be sites of pre-historic human habitation. During the American Revolution, high points along the ridge were used as signaling posts." Thanks to the New York–New Jersey Trail Conference, new hiking trails have been created and maintained here since the 1940s. Rarely will a furry creature venture too far from its warm burrow during winter months, but deer can be spotted year-round foraging for a bit of tasty bark. Even in warmer weather, it's a good idea to wear a hat to protect against the constant wind, and sturdy shoes will help guard against sore toes as you walk along the rocky trail.

From the parking lot, cross the road and look for red blazes marking a trail that heads north. Turn right at the intersection with the yellow trail. The large boulders in this area make great seats for relaxing and admiring the stands of beech, birch, and oak. At just under 1 mile, ascend again. The trail eventually levels and dips before climbing once more at 1.5 miles. Climbing steeply you'll be thankful that this natural area has been spared from development, for it is magnificent.

New York City's skyline appears to the east, below the crest of High Mountain. The foliage begins to disappear and the trail widens as you continue uphill next to stands of sumac. When you feel gusts of wind, you'll

Watch for the colorful berries and usual leaf pattern of the staghorn sumac.

know you're just a few yards from the summit of High Mountain. Here you'll be completely in the open; spend some time walking around and absorbing the beauty of the surrounding mountains, the towns below, and the skyline. When ready, scout a bit for the next blaze, which you'll find painted on a boulder. A bunch of trails converge at this spot, but with some searching you'll find yellow blazes leading down into the woods. Deer tracks are fairly common in this area. The descent soon becomes quite steep, so watch where you place your feet because fallen leaves tend to cover up holes.

After a few ups and downs, you'll hear cascading water, and at 2.5 miles you'll see a lovely brook. At the trail junction at 3 miles, turn left onto the red-blazed trail. This return route goes around High Mountain and is fairly level. The trail can be quite wet in places after winter melts or from spring rains, but it's wide enough to allow for easy detours around wet spots. After a grove of junipers at 3.6 miles, the trail descends and, 0.3 mile later, climbs gradually over large, bare rocks before leveling in a few yards. Follow the red trail back to the start.

33 PALISADES BOULDER FIELD

Location ■ Palisades Interstate Park
County ■ Bergen
Type ■ Day hike
Difficulty ■ Challenging
Distance ■ 5.5 miles
Elevation gain ■ 530 feet
Hours ■ Dawn to dusk
Information ■ Palisades Interstate Park Commission, P.O. Box 155, Alpine 07620; (201) 768-1360
Website ■ www.njpalisades.org
Admission ■ Free

Driving directions: Southbound from the Palisades Interstate Parkway, take exit 3 and park at State Line Lookout. Northbound from the Palisades Interstate Parkway, take the unnumbered exit opposite the southbound exit 3.

This awesome hike begins from the highest point of the New Jersey Palisades and steeply descends 530 feet to the Hudson River. Part of the trail is an obstacle course through a sea of boulders and part of it is a series of stone steps leading downward. Wear sturdy hiking shoes because some of the huge rocks are smooth and slippery—particularly when weather conditions are wet or icy.

Although this hike is strenuous in places, it's well worth any muscle aches you may have afterward, for the views beneath volcanically formed vertical columns are exceptional. No doubt, Italian explorer Giovanni de Verrazano was impressed when he discovered the Palisades in 1524, which he referred to as a "fence of stakes." Heavy quarrying once threatened this area, but when Congress established the Palisades Interstate Park Commission, the natural beauty of these basaltic cliffs was preserved for all to enjoy. The cliffs of the New Jersey section, whose present appearance dates back about 12,000 years to the Ice Age, have been named a National Historic Landmark and also a National Natural Landmark.

Starting at the State Line Lookout refreshment building, walk south along the entrance road you drove in on. At a tree marked with an aqua blaze and a sign warning "slopes are dangerous," turn left into the woods. You'll immediately see one of the cliffs and, to the left, an open area affording an exceptional view of the Palisades and the Hudson River.

Use caution walking down the steep stone steps. Even though counting the steps is fun, you'll need all the concentration you can muster to maintain your balance and to admire the rocky surroundings. Bear left at the

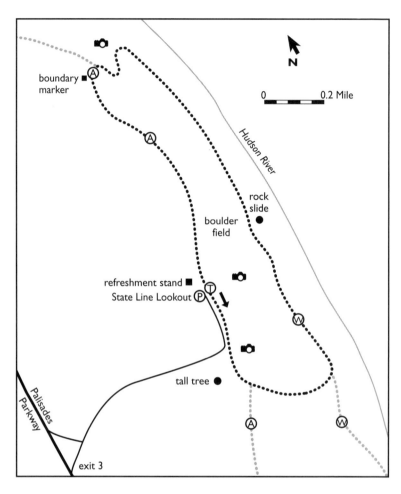

trail junction; be careful as you walk along the edge, which is unprotected and sometimes slippery. The steps just ahead will wind in and out along the edge of the cliff for 0.5 mile until you're level with the water. At this point, turn left (north) along the Shore Trail marked with white blazes.

After about 0.25 mile of easy walking along the shoreline, you'll have a fine view of a huge boulder called Indian Head peering down at you from the cliff. A short distance later, the trail leaves the shore and climbs steeply around the base of a large rock slide. Kids may have to use their hands and feet to climb over the larger boulders, but they'll love every minute of the challenge. When the trail levels, you might want to stop to regain your breath, have a drink "on the rocks," look up at the nearly vertical cliff face, or check out the passing boats.

As you continue you'll have a bird's-eye view of tulip trees and a rare view of their seed pods. Although the trail is nearly level, the climb over huge boulders seems endless at times. Pay attention to your footing, taking care not to get stuck in the deep cracks between boulders. You'll be happy you wore your hiking shoes as you clamber over smooth-faced rock surfaces. The rocks soon give way to a dirt trail, and rocks and dirt alternate until the trail levels off to follow the shoreline 0.5 mile to a picturesque waterfall amid the ruins of an ornamental garden from the turn of the twentieth century. From the waterfall, called Peanut Leap Cascade, follow the white-blazed trail as it again climbs steeply uphill by way of switchbacks, and then follows the stream that creates the waterfall. The white-blazed trail ends at its junction with the aqua-blazed Long Path. Turn left (south) on the Long Path, and then cross the stream over a series of wooden bridges. After 0.25 mile, the Long Path turns right (north) and ascends a steep series of stone steps toward the summit, where there are spectacular views of the Hudson. **Caution:** This section of trail along the cliff edge can be very slippery after a rain.

After another set of stairs, a New Jersey–New York boundary monument dating from 1882 is soon visible. Turn left to go slightly uphill, and after the trail levels an old road now closed to traffic joins in and returns you to the parking area.

34 LOST BROOK PRESERVE

Location ■ Tenafly Nature Center

County ■ Bergen

Type ■ Day hike

Difficulty ■ Easy

Distance ■ 4.25 miles

Elevation gain ■ 150 feet

Hours ■ Trails, dawn to dusk; visitor center, Monday, 1–5 P.M., Tuesday–Saturday, 9 A.M.–5 P.M., Sunday, 10 A.M.–5 P.M.; parking lot, Monday–Saturday, 9 A.M.–5 P.M., Sunday, 10 A.M.–5 P.M., after hours parking available along Hudson Avenue

Information ■ Tenafly Nature Center, 313 Hudson Avenue, Tenafly 07670; (201) 568-6093

Website ■ *www.tenaflynaturecenter.org*

Admission ■ Free

Driving directions: From US 9W in Tenafly, take East Clinton Avenue west, turn right on Engle Street, and right again on Hudson Avenue. Park at the Tenafly Nature Center.

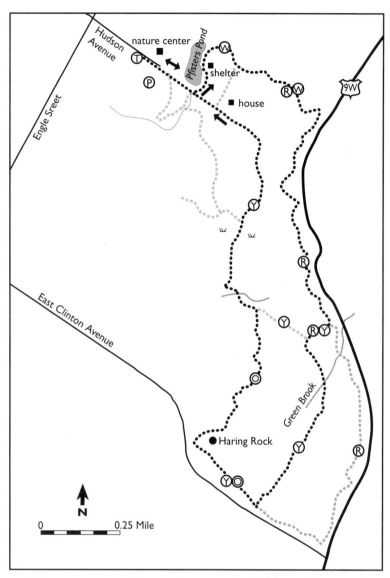

Before starting your hike, stop in at the Tenafly Nature Center to learn about the animals, birds, and insects of the adjoining woods. A naturalist is usually available to answer questions, and should you need additional information after the hike, you can return to browse through the library's collection of nature books.

The forest understory is aglow with wildflowers each spring, and there's an excellent possibility of spotting eastern painted turtles or wood ducks. On a sunny day be sure to scan Pfisters Pond for the northern ring-necked snake and the northern brown snake basking in the sun. Waterproof, sturdy shoes are recommended to protect feet against rocky and swampy areas. Food isn't allowed on the trail, but there is a picnic table adjacent to the parking area.

From the parking lot, head southeast along a wide, level dirt road past many spring-flowering plants. The Native Americans made good use of many of these plants, includ-

David, Kate, Zoe and Benjamin Zatz enjoy a break along the edge of Pfisters Pond.

ing the arrowwood, whose strong shoots made ideal arrow shafts, and the five-leaved wild geranium, valued as a tonic. You'll also find bittersweet, a deciduous shrub with leaves that turn yellow in the fall before dropping by mid-November. Bittersweet was once believed to cure bladder problems and kidney stones. After walking 0.1 mile, you'll come to a tiny gem known as Pfisters Pond. If you're here during summer, you'll see the spike-shaped flowers of the sweet pepperbush and the 1-inch flower clusters of the aquatic buttonbush.

Turn left at the far end of the pond onto a white-blazed trail where a boardwalk leads to an overlook shelter. This is an ideal vantage point from which to view the entire pond. Another boardwalk follows and meanders through a swampy area, with the pond to the left. When the trail veers away from the pond, you begin a gradual climb into the woods. From this point, there are a few gradual ups and downs. Turn left at a double-white triangle blaze at 0.5 mile, and follow the red and white blazes of the Bischoff Trail. These soon give way to red blazes of the Little-Chism Trail. The trail meanders through woods thick with lovely sweet gum trees, which litter the trail with their 1-inch-round seed capsules. Trail blazes are far apart in some sections, so to avoid losing the trail, be certain you know where the last blaze is before proceeding too far. In some places, blazes may appear on boulders rather than trees. There are swampy areas in this section of the preserve, and every so often a beautiful stand of mountain laurel appears. There are also occasional small boulder fields. Keep an eye out for the tall, straight tulip trees, and look for a majestic double-trunked specimen at 1.5 miles. Leaves from the previous fall litter the ground in places, covering holes in the ground and making walking tricky.

At the sign for D Spur, take a short detour and follow the red-and-yellow blaze passing through a field of ferns. A few yards ahead is a beautiful American beech, whose sandy brown leaves cling stubbornly in the dead of winter. It's a delight to watch the remaining leaves shimmer a bright golden color in the sun and shake with the slightest breeze.

At 1.9 miles turn left at the junction with the yellow-blazed Allison Trail. Just ahead is Green Brook, a delightful spot to pause for a drink or wait for passing deer. At 2.5 miles at a sign with a triple yellow-and-orange blaze, turn right onto the Seely Trail. The boardwalk over the brook ahead will keep your feet dry, and at 2.7 miles you'll reach Haring Rock, the largest glacial erratic in this area. Amazingly, the erratic wasn't left in the wake of a glacier but in the wake of development. Rather than dynamite it where it originally stood and where a building was to be erected, it was moved to its present location by a contractor. Turn right at the trail junction onto the orange-blazed Haring Rock Trail. The trail gradually descends. At the T turn left onto the yellow-blazed Allison Trail. This section of trail wanders past marshes and interesting rock formations. Take a left onto the dirt road at the triple-yellow blaze marking the trail's end. You'll pass a large, private house on the right as you head back to the parking area.

35 FLAT ROCK BROOK

Location ▪ Flat Rock Brook Nature Center
County ▪ Bergen
Type ▪ Day hike
Difficulty ▪ Easy
Distance ▪ 1.25 miles
Elevation gain ▪ 150 feet
Hours ▪ Trails, dawn to dusk; nature center, Tuesday–Friday, 9 A.M.–5 P.M., Saturday and Sunday 1–5 P.M., closed Mondays
Information ▪ Flat Rock Brook Nature Center, 443 Van Nostrand Avenue, Englewood 07631; (201) 567-1265
Website ▪ *www.flatrockbrook.org*
Admission ▪ Free

Driving directions: From I-95, exit at Broad Avenue, Englewood, and go north. Turn right at the traffic light on Van Nostrand Avenue and continue to the entrance of the park. See the center's website for more detailed directions and a map.

More than thirty years ago Englewood families volunteered their time to protect the city's open space while making the land available to everyone who enjoys the beauty of the natural world. They scraped graffiti from an abandoned stone quarry and cut 3.5 miles of trails through land with 180-million-year-old volcanic bedrock formations, wetlands, ponds, a cascading stream, meadows, quarry cliffs, and one of the last remnants of the Palisades forest. They also helped to design the building that houses a children's workshop, a greenhouse, and exhibits.

Visitors who hike the trails at Flat Rock Brook forget they're only a few miles from midtown Manhattan. The surrounding woods are so dense that you're guaranteed shade on the hottest day, and during any season you might spot a deer, raccoon, frog, and on rare occasions catch a glimpse of the secretive red fox. During spring a variety of wildflowers show off their dazzling colors. Walking the boardwalk a mere 0.1 mile affords a closeup look at jewelweed, in bloom from July through the first frost. Its bright yellow-orange flowers are thought to resemble jewels hanging on a necklace, and its nickname, touch-me-not, is appropriate because if touched when the fruit is mature, seeds

Dipping a hiking stick into the pond at Flat Rock Brook Park is especially fun in autumn when it's filled with colorful leaves.

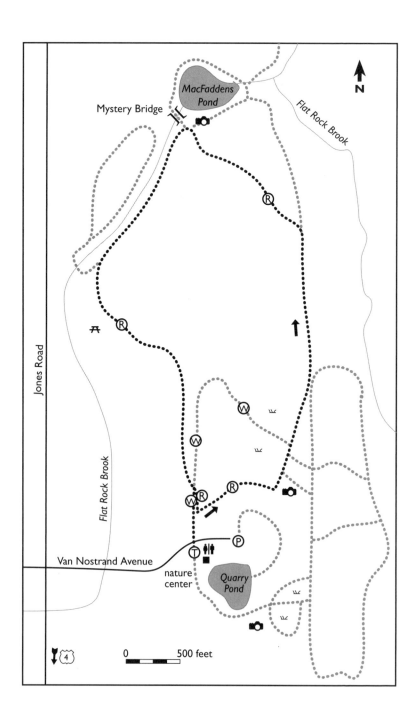

shoot out! The boardwalk guides you through the Backyard Habitat for Wildlife, two demonstration gardens of native plants selected to be both ornamental and useful to wildlife. The Gazebo Garden illustrates a particular design for a backyard area, and the Quarry Meadow displays a wide variety of plants available for habitat use. As you walk along the boardwalk, look up at the stone cliffs, the site of a former stone quarry.

When the nature center is open, check out the exhibits or attend a nature program. Water, restrooms, and free trail maps are available inside.

Start across the entrance road from the nature center entrance, and walk uphill on the white-blazed trail, where sweet gums and tulip trees tower overhead. At the trail junction, make a sharp right turn onto the red-blazed trail proceeding through a meadow and turning left into more woods before climbing to an overlook that provides a fabulous view of the valley to the south and west and the Watchung Mountains in the distance. Follow the trail as it veers left, and when the white trail joins in, continue straight on the trail with red-and-white blazes. A pond and the Flat Rock Brook appear in 0.5 mile.

According to local legend, a lady wanted her lover to build a bridge here. Although he wanted to, he never had the time. After she died he came back and built what is known as the Mystery Bridge, because no one saw it under construction. Standing in the center of the bridge, watch the water as it falls over the dam. On the opposite side of the bridge you'll find a flat ledge—a perfect viewing platform for surveying the pond and ducks.

Continue southwest on the red trail. The park's namesake, Flat Rock Brook, is on your right. At 0.6 mile, as you descend steep steps, you'll hear the melodious gurgling sound of water falling over the dam. This area is so delightful that children may be reluctant to continue preferring instead to sit, watch, and listen, and perhaps hop around on the flat rocks. But **use caution**, because the rocks can be quite slippery. Descend the steep staircase ahead and follow the red blazes as you leave the water for a short while. Just when you're beginning to miss it, the water returns, and with it, hundreds of rocks and boulders. Ahead, there are more gradual climbs and steep steps to negotiate.

At the T, turn left following the sign to the nature center or continue straight ahead to a picnic area along Jones Road where you'll find a seasonal restroom and a wonderful playground for children. To return to the nature center from the picnic area, retrace your steps to the red trail and turn right. As you climb, you'll see beautiful sweet gums in this damp area. Soon you'll be climbing steeply, stepping over tree roots, and heading over a long bridge followed by a few short ones to assure you'll keep your feet high and dry during wet weather. At the double-red blaze, bear right slightly. The trail levels out before climbing gradually again, and then the nature center building comes into view. When you see the sign for the picnic area and nature center again on the white-blazed trail, follow it back to the parking area.

36 MILLS RESERVATION

Location ▪ Mills Reservation
County ▪ Essex
Type ▪ Day hike
Difficulty ▪ Easy
Distance ▪ 2 miles
Elevation gain ▪ 100 feet
Hours ▪ Dawn to dusk
Information ▪ Essex County Department of Parks, 115 Clifton Avenue,
Newark 07104; (973) 268-3500
Website ▪ *www.essexcountynj.org*
Admission ▪ Free

 Driving directions: From Cedar Grove, drive south on Ridge Road, turn east onto Reservoir Drive, and then right onto Normal Avenue. Go 0.25 mile to the parking lot on the right.

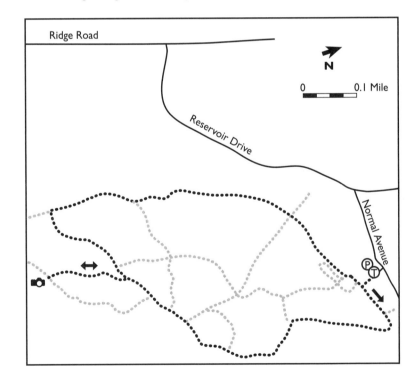

Sassafras reflects a recent rain.

Mythology tells of giants, demons, and dragons lurking deep in the heart of the woods. However, people have also found safety, food, and shelter in the forest. The same holds true today, thanks to a donation of 119 acres of woodland by the Davella Mills Foundation in 1954, and later additions that brought the total to 157 acres, hikers can enjoy peace and quiet on these trails despite the fact that the reservation is located between the crowded suburbs of Cedar Grove and Upper Montclair.

The high point of the hike is an overlook affording an excellent view of Manhattan, Staten Island, and Newark. During migration in spring and fall, chances are good that you'll spot several of the fourteen species of birds as they glide on the wind currents.

Leaving the parking lot, walk uphill on the gravel trail and turn left at the fork. The trail heads slightly downhill at 0.4 mile for about 0.25 mile. Turn left at the fork to leave the loop trail at 0.7 mile. **Use caution;** there are some steep drops along these cliffs. Oak and hickory are dominant, with a good showing of birch, tulip, and beech throughout this area. You'll reach the observation point and the remains of an old stone foundation at 0.9 mile. If you've brought binoculars, they'll come in handy for peering at hawks, the tiny American kestrel, or even a bald eagle.

When ready, return to the loop trail. At the fork, turn left and head downhill. The red oaks growing here were highly valued in the early 1800s by the local leather industry for the tannic acid in their bark. Turn right at the **T**. Continue straight on the gravel trail that leads uphill at 1.7 miles, but soon levels out. Hair cap moss, found throughout this area, may be curled up if the weather's been dry, but sprinkle a little water on it and watch it unfold. At 1.9 miles return to the **T** where you first joined the loop trail, turn left, and continue back to the parking lot.

37 FOUR BRIDGES

Location ▪	Lewis Morris County Park
County ▪	Morris
Type ▪	Day hike
Difficulty ▪	Moderate
Distance ▪	1.6 miles
Elevation gain ▪	120 feet
Hours ▪	Dawn to dusk
Information ▪	Morris County Park Commission, 53 East Hanover Avenue, Morristown 07960; (973) 326-7600
Website ▪	*www.morrisparks.net*
Admission ▪	Free

Driving directions: From I-287 South, take exit 35. Turn right and at the light turn right onto NJ-124 West (South Street). Continue straight, go around the green. Turn right at the light onto CR 510 West (Washington Street). The park entrance is on the left. Go to the Mendham Overlook Parking Lot.

From I-287 North, take exit 35 (South Street/Madison Avenue). At the light at the end of the ramp, turn left onto South Street. Follow signs for NJ-124 West to Morristown, to the green, and follow directions above.

If you enjoy the sound of water tumbling over rocks and admiring a beautiful stream, you'll love the Four Bridges hike at Lewis Morris County Park. Along this meandering densely wooded trail, you'll actually cross five bridges over babbling brooks, although the trail is named Four Bridges! No doubt, you'll also spot squirrels, chipmunks, and if you're lucky, a deer or bear.

Named for the first governor of New Jersey, the park—the first in the Morris County Park System—opened in 1958. At that time, it consisted of 350 acres; today it has grown to 1154 acres. Miles of hiking trails await visitors, but there is much more for the outdoor enthusiast in this vast park, including equestrian trails, swimming, boating, fishing, softball fields, a parcourse fitness circuit, sledding and ski touring, a Saturn playground, picnic sites, and a group camping area. You'll return again and again, especially for the excellent hiking opportunities.

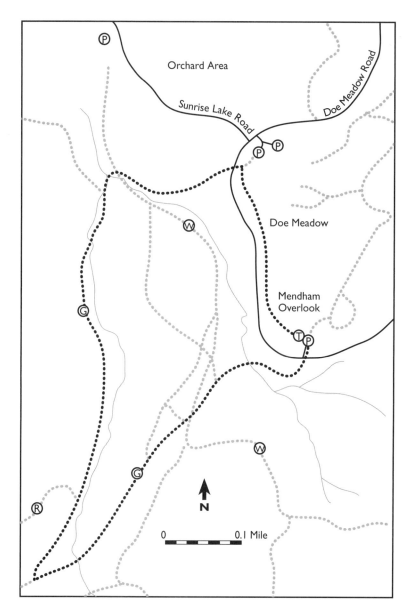

From the Mendham Overlook parking lot, walk to the main road and look for the trailhead midway down a grassy hill on the right side of the road. Follow the green blazes. Here and elsewhere on the trail you'll be surrounded by a variety of trees, including oak, beech, birch, and sweet gum. If you come during fall

and find acorns at your feet, you'll know oaks are above. In the fall, a mature oak tree can shed approximately a quarter of a million leaves!

Caution: Watch where you step while descending, especially after a rain when fallen leaves and tree roots can be slippery. At this point, you'll be walking parallel to the park's main road, descending gradually, with shrubs and trees creating a fine barrier. When the trail curves away from the road at 0.1 mile, a vast green lawn appears on the right just before the trail crosses a dirt road.

The bridges along this trail make excellent rest stops to admire the scenery.

Continue straight, following the green blaze. Here, the trail is mostly level, with a couple of gradual climbs. A sign for the Four Bridges Trail is at 0.3 mile.

Use caution as you cross the road. On the other side, look for a boulder with a green blaze painted on it. Because the trail is a bit difficult to find in this area, walk slowly until you spot another blaze. If you don't spot the next blaze, walk back to the last one and have another look. Descending steeply, you'll soon hear the sound of water, and a ravine will appear on the left at 0.4 mile. Beech trees—a gorgeous yellow in the fall—are abundant in this area. In a few yards, you'll be standing next to a babbling brook and the first bridge. Stay a while and listen to the beautiful melody as the water tumbles over the rocks. After crossing the bridge, turn right at the junction with Patriots' Path and continue on the green trail. A small pond appears on the right, and the second bridge is only a few yards ahead. Again, the sound of the water is enchanting. When ready, cross the bridge, bear left, and cross the third bridge. The brook is now on the right as the trail gradually ascends.

At 0.5 mile cross the fourth bridge, and continue uphill; the brook is now on the left. Ignore the next bridge, which goes to the left, and continue straight, staying on the level section of trail with the brook on the left. Also ignore the orange-blazed trail in a few yards. Continue straight following the green blazes. In this area the mix of evergreens mingled with the sweet gum, beech, and birch is dazzling, especially in the fall.

Crossing the fifth and longest bridge at 0.9 mile is especially exciting because you'll be above the rushing water with a bird's-eye view of any fish passing by. Turn left at the double blaze immediately after crossing the bridge. A nearby bench is the perfect place to rest, bird-watch, have a snack, or simply admire the surroundings.

During summer months, the meadow at 1.1 miles is ablaze with wildflowers. Follow the double-green blaze to the right, descending gradually. Step over a narrow brook, and with it now on the right side, look for the green blaze and follow it to the double-green blaze. Turn left, continue steeply uphill, and return to the parking lot.

38 LOANTAKA RESERVATION

Location ▪	Loantaka Brook Reservation
County ▪	Morris
Type ▪	Day hike
Difficulty ▪	Easy
Distance ▪	3.5 miles
Elevation gain ▪	Negligible
Hours ▪	Dawn to dusk
Information ▪	Morris County Park Commission, 53 East Hanover Avenue, P.O. Box 1295, Morristown 07962; (973) 326-7600
Website ▪	www.morrisparks.net
Admission ▪	Free

Driving directions: From I-287, exit at NJ-24 in Morristown, head east on South Street, and then turn left on Spring Valley Road and left again on Loantaka Way to a parking area on the left.

This hike is especially enjoyable for children of all ages and includes a short, low bridge that crosses over a shallow stream. But be forewarned: You may have to pause for a few minutes while someone tries to wet a bandana or pose for a photo. Used by hikers, bikers, and rollerbladers, the main trail is paved and mostly level as it meanders through a narrow strip of woodland that's particularly pleasing during autumn when fallen leaves create a golden carpet. Hungry ducks and Canada geese wait for a handout at Kitchell Pond, but it's best to only admire them because they tend to bite. The adjacent unpaved bridle trail, also open to hikers, is a great place to see beautiful horses—but remember to move to the side when they pass. Before leaving, allow your children to enjoy the Saturn playground.

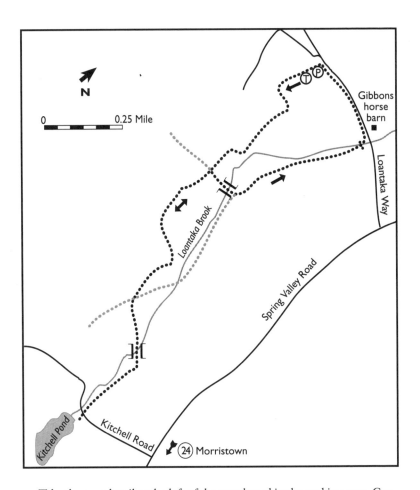

Take the paved trail at the left of the map board in the parking area. Continue straight ahead at the crossing. At 0.5 mile you'll cross a small bridge over the first of several streams. Skunk cabbage, named for its offensive odor, is abundant in the wet areas. Because it produces heat as it grows, it's one of the first wildflowers to poke its coiled bright green spathe through the ground and even pops up through snow.

The trail continues through woods, with no significant elevation change. Cross the short bridge over Loantaka Brook at 1.25 miles. At 1.5 miles **use caution** when crossing Kitchell Road to reach Kitchell Pond.

Allow time for exploration of the pond and the area accessed by a small foot- bridge before returning the way you came. At 2.7 miles turn right at the trail junction. Along the way you'll encounter the shagbark hickory, which was used

Can you guess which critter made these holes in the trunk of the tree?

for the spokes in yesteryear's wagon wheels and today's ax handles. As the name implies, this tree has loose bark standing out from the trunk. Deer are a common sight in this area, especially late in the day.

After crossing through a safety gate, turn left and continue along the road for about 0.25 mile to the parking lot. **Caution:** Keep to the extreme left side of the road to avoid oncoming traffic. To the right is the Gibbons horse barn, circa 1834, built by William Gibbons to house his thoroughbred racehorses, including Fashion, once known as the Queen of the American Turf.

39 GREAT SWAMP

Location ■ Great Swamp National Wildlife Refuge
County ■ Morris
Type ■ Day hike
Difficulty ■ Easy
Distance ■ 2.5 miles
Elevation gain ■ Negligible
Hours ■ Dawn to dusk
Information ■ Refuge Manager, Great Swamp National Wildlife Refuge, 152 Pleasant Plains Road, Basking Ridge 07920; (973) 425-1222
Website ■ greatswamp.fws.gov/
Admission ■ Free

Driving directions: From Madison, take Green Village Road southwest toward Green Village. Turn left on Meyersville Road, drive to the end of the road and park.

When English investors purchased 30,000 acres of land from the Delaware Indians in 1708 for a barrel of rum, four pistols, fifteen kettles, thirty

A boardwalk keeps this hiker high and dry through swamp and cattails.

pounds sterling, and other miscellaneous items, they probably went away laughing. But the Native Americans felt pretty good too, knowing that a good portion of the land sold was under water! Settlements quickly sprung up, and during the Revolutionary War, wood was collected from the upland areas for making wagon wheels. After draining the marshlands in 1844, foul meadow hay became the major cash crop. When farming was no longer profitable, the land was abandoned, and it slowly reverted to woods and swampland.

All was quiet until 1959, when the threat of building a jet port in the area known as the Great Swamp aroused concern. Raising more than a million dollars, groups of local citizens purchased 3000 acres and donated it to the U.S. Department of the Interior. This donation formed the nucleus of the Great Swamp National Wildlife Refuge, and in 1968 Congress designated the area as part of the National Wilderness Preservation System. Through the years, additional acres have been added. More than 244 species of birds have been spotted in the refuge as well as a variety of mammals. While traversing the woodland and cattail marsh, imagine how this area was created 25,000 years ago when the Wisconsin Glacier stopped abruptly on its way south. As it melted, long ridges of sand and gravel were left behind, blocking the outlet of an ancient river basin. Eventually, a huge lake formed, although it was drained when the retreating glacier created a second outlet. What remained were marshes and swamp.

Waterproof shoes or boots are advisable. Fall and winter are the best

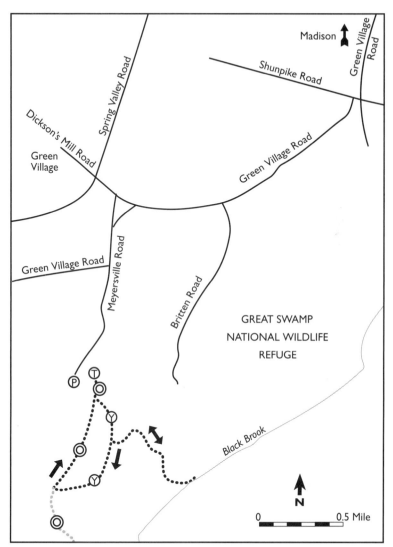

Madison

Shunpike Road

Green Village Road

Spring Valley Road

Dickson's Mill Road

Green Village

Green Village Road

Green Village Road

Meyersville Road

Britten Road

GREAT SWAMP
NATIONAL WILDLIFE
REFUGE

Black Brook

N

0   0.5 Mile

seasons to visit, when ground is firmer and insects are gone.

Walk through the fence opening in front of the parking area to a trail marked by orange blazes. When you come to a short boardwalk, you might hear the throaty song of red-winged blackbirds or the tapping of downy woodpeckers. At 0.2 mile turn left onto a yellow-blazed trail. Almost immediately, you'll see a carpet of club moss, a green flowerless plant that thrives in this damp environment. With a magnifying glass, look at its finely toothed leaves and spores.

At 0.5 mile a double blaze indicates that the trail divides; bear left and walk southeast. If you pause a couple of minutes at one of the rotting logs, you'll find a lot of wildlife and plants. Salamanders like the moist areas underneath logs, while deer mice and squirrels prefer the cozier interiors of logs for raising their families.

At 0.9 mile take a left to visit Black Brook, a fine place to find ducks and Canada geese. Return to the main trail and the double-yellow blaze at 1.4 miles, turn left and walk southwest. Cattails surround the boardwalk at 1.8 miles. Native Americans had many uses for this freshwater plant: They ate the young shoots, wove its leaves into mats, dipped the seed heads in fat to make torches, and used the fluffy seeds for quilt stuffing and insulation.

Turn right at the T a short distance ahead and walk northeast on the orange-blazed trail. (For a longer walk, turn left instead and then return.) Tall spruces appear just ahead; leave the trail for a few minutes to wander among them. When ready, return to the trail and continue back to the parking area.

⁴⁰ JOCKEY HOLLOW RAMBLE

Location ■ Morristown National Historical Park
County ■ Morris
Type ■ Day hike
Difficulty ■ Moderate
Distance ■ 4.5 miles
Elevation gain ■ 250 feet
Hours ■ Trails, 8 A.M. to sunset; visitor center, 9 A.M.–5 P.M., closed Thanksgiving, Christmas, and New Year's Day
Information ■ Morristown National Historical Park, 30 Washington Place, Morristown 07960; (973) 539-2016
Website ■ www.nps.gov/morr/
Admission ■ Fee; free with Golden Age, Golden Access, Golden Eagle, or National Parks Pass

Driving directions: From NJ-202 north of Basking Ridge, take Tempe Wick Road west and follow signs to parking for the Jockey Hollow Visitor Center.

George Washington's troops couldn't appreciate this magnificent scenery—not while doing military drills or sleeping overnight in freezing temperatures. The bitter winter of 1779–80 was enough to make any man miserable, and many of the 10,000 soldiers who were camped here perished for lack of food and clothing and the unrelenting blizzards. Hiking on a subzero day may give you some idea of what they went through, but warm clothing, sturdy shoes,

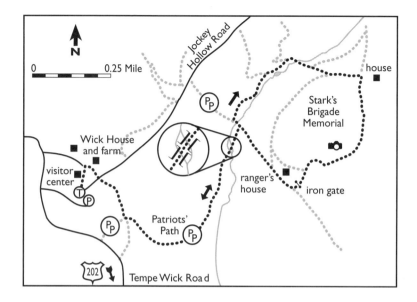

and trail mix makes a big difference. So does having the time to enjoy the solitude, the flora and fauna, and the sights and sound of a meandering stream. Plan on exploring Wick House (circa 1750) after the hike. Docents describe how Henry Wick prospered by logging and farming his 800 acres of timberland and open fields and how the house was used by Maj. Gen. Arthur St. Clair, while he served as commander of the Pennsylvania Line during the Revolutionary War.

Before starting the hike, pick up a free trail map at the visitor center. With map in hand, exit from the rear of the visitor center, follow a wide, grassy path leading toward the Wick farm, and turn right at the split-rail fence. After crossing a blacktop road (watch for oncoming traffic), continue through the woods on a narrower, grassy trail. You'll pass a couple of signs explaining the historical events that occurred here; at the trail sign at 0.25 mile, turn left onto Patriots' Path, designated by a blaze incorporating a winding river within a white circle. This area is a birdwatcher's paradise, largely due to the tall tulip trees that provide a generous seed supply. The trail becomes a series of ups and downs at 0.5 mile. On the ridge you'll hear the sound of water; look down into the narrow gorge on the right to see the stream you'll eventually be walking next to.

Look for beeches mixed in with oaks, birches, and ashes. Beeches sport a light gray trunk, 3- to 6-inch-long sharp-toothed leaves, and thick toes at its base. John James Audubon thought so much of this tree that he used its bough as a background for his famous painting *Passenger Pigeon*. At the sign for the Primrose and Grand Loop Trails, at 1 mile, go straight on the Grand Loop Trail. Cross over a wooden bridge. The next wooden bridge, a short distance ahead, is a great place to stop and admire the small stream as it meanders along. Continue straight, then turn left at the T at 1.3 miles, staying on Patriots' Path for a short while. After this, stay right at the next four trail intersections.

The first right turn comes up quickly and is marked by a double-yellow blaze at 1.4 miles. After climbing slightly, turn right again when the New York Brigade Trail signpost appears. In a couple of minutes you'll reach a small pond, which was a sheet of ice when we arrived in February. Turn right at the Mount Kemple Loop Trail post and again at the Y, following signs to Mount Kemple Loop Trail. When you reach the loop, turn left, following it in a clockwise direction.

After a gradual climb, you'll see the first sign of civilization—a house. Walk behind it, find the trail again, and right after the trail levels, you'll come to a memorial dedicated to Stark's Brigade. During the Revolution this slope afforded a perfect view of the valley and the Watchung Mountains; however, a mistake by the patrol could prove fatal, because it was difficult to distinguish between a patriot and a Tory. Patrolling this area of the Watchung Mountains was referred to as duty "on the line."

After descending from the memorial, turn left at the signpost for Camp Road Trail. Turn right at the T and walk through an iron gate. Thick vines nearby have gotten a stranglehold on many of the trees. Go past the ranger's house, turn left before a wooden bridge at 3.3 miles, and return the way you came on Patriots' Path. Turn right at a signpost for the Wick House and the visitor center.

41   PATRIOTS' PATH

Location ▪ Morristown National Historical Park
County ▪ Morris
Type ▪ Day hike
Difficulty ▪ Moderate
Distance ▪ 5 miles
Elevation gain ▪ 300 feet
Hours ▪ Trails, 8 A.M. to sunset; visitor center, 9 A.M.–5 P.M., closed Thanksgiving, Christmas, and New Year's Day
Information ▪ Morristown National Historical Park, 30 Washington Place, Morristown 07960; (973) 539-2016
Website ▪ www.morrisparks.net
Admission ▪ Fee; free with Golden Age, Golden Access, Golden Eagle, or National Parks Pass

 Driving directions: From NJ-202 north of Basking Ridge, take Tempe Wick Road west and follow signs to the visitor center.

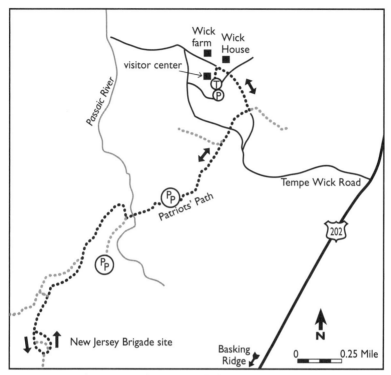

In 1966 Helen C. Fenske proposed the creation of a corridor to link parklands and historic sites from Mendham Township to Morristown. A name was needed, and historian/writer John T. Cunningham came up with Patriots' Path, which is fitting because you'll be following in the footsteps of Gen. George Washington and his Continental Army as you go through Jockey Hollow, inside Morristown National Historical Park. If you prefer solitude, visit during the week. The trail leads past where the troops camped, and one of their stone hearths still remains. After your hike, stop in at Wick House to learn how Henry Wick worked his 800 acres of timberland and open field, until the army felled the trees to build huts and fuel fires to keep the men warm during the coldest winter recorded in the eighteenth century.

Exit from the rear of the visitor center, follow the wide, grassy path leading toward the Wick farm, and turn right at the split-rail fence. After crossing a blacktop road (watch for oncoming traffic), continue through the woods on a narrower, grassy trail. Near the trail junction you'll pass a couple of signs explaining the historical events that occurred here during the bitter winter of 1779–80. At the trail junction sign at 0.25 mile, turn right onto Patriots' Path, which is designated by a blaze incorporating a winding river within a white circle. Head downhill on the rocky path.

Cross Tempe Wick Road and watch for passing cars. Shortly, you'll cross a wooden bridge over a stream flanked with boulders, ferns, and more skunk cabbage. A downed tree here can serve as a bench if you'd like to enjoy the peaceful surroundings before the long uphill climb ahead. At 0.9 mile you'll descend gradually, passing a field of low green weeds. As the trail narrows and meanders through hundreds of trees, you'll hear songbirds chattering, and if you're lucky you'll spot one of the resident owls.

Pause on the bridge spanning the Passaic River to watch the waters flowing past boulders and downed trees. Then cross the river, turn right, and continue uphill. At the top of the hill, at just under 2 miles, turn left to follow the sign for the New Jersey Brigade site. The level path gradually ascends again. Stay left at the trail junction sign at 2.1 miles, proceeding gradually downhill. At the next trail junction at 2.6 miles, turn left to go slightly uphill to the brigade site, where the troops endured bitter weather and a lack of food and clothing. From here, continue uphill a short distance to see the remains of a hearth left over from one of the soldier's huts. In 1780 twelve hundred huts, standing two feet apart, were built in Jockey Hollow. The huts stood 14 by 16 feet square and $6^1/2$ feet high. By the time the troops moved on, 800 acres of trees had been destroyed in the surrounding area.

Dense woods and cool streams make for a delightful hike year-round.

From the brigade site, climb steeply to the **T** junction with Patriots' Path at 3.2 miles, turn right, and return to the start.

42 DOGWOOD TRAIL

Location ■	Scherman-Hoffman Sanctuaries
County ■	Somerset
Type ■	Day hike
Difficulty ■	Easy
Distance ■	2.1 miles
Elevation gain ■	260 feet
Hours ■	Trails, daily to 5 P.M.; nature center, Tuesday–Saturday, 9 A.M.–5 P.M., Sunday, noon–5 P.M., closed Monday and holidays (Note: When the nature center is closed, park in the lower parking lot on Hardscrabble Road.)
Information ■	Scherman-Hoffman Sanctuaries, 11 Hardscrabble Road, Bernardsville 07924; (908) 766-5787
Website ■	www.njaudubon.org
Admission ■	Free

Driving directions: Take NJ-287 (north or south) to exit 30B, Basking Ridge. Take the westbound exit and continue through the traffic light at NJ-202. The road becomes Childs Road. Go 0.2 mile and bear right at the fork onto Hardscrabble Road, continue north for about 1 mile, and turn right at the parking lot sign.

The ridges and valleys in this area, formed approximately 600 million years ago, were just what Gen. George Washington was looking for. Because the ridges didn't have any natural passes, the enemy could be spotted in the distance, which gave the troops plenty of advance warning. Today, this hike leads through lush woods and an old farm field loaded with butterflies, wildflowers, and woodchucks as well as along the banks of the Passaic River. Deer, especially active an hour before sunset, are abundant.

This hike takes a couple of hours

Numerous tulip trees can be seen along the trail; occasionally a perfect leaf falls to the ground.

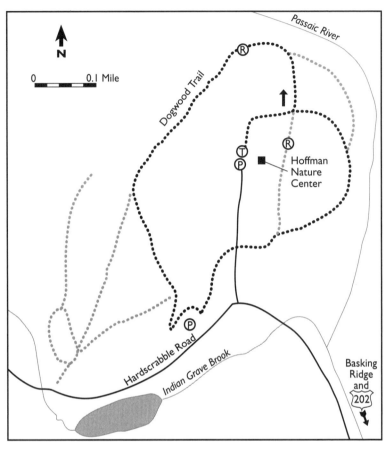

 to complete, depending on how many times the kids are tempted to peek beneath fallen logs or climb onto boulders. Begin on the Field Loop Trail, next to the Hoffman Nature Center. The trail descends slightly for 0.2 mile until it reaches a junction; turn left onto the red-blazed Dogwood Trail, which gradually climbs passing through thick stands of beech, birch, oak, tulip, and maple. At approximately 0.75 mile, turn left at the top of the ridge and continue following the red blazes as the trail descends past rock formations. **Caution:** When you reach the enormous sinkhole, walk single file; the leaves can be slippery and it's a long way down. A quarter mile farther look for the "elephant rock." When this tree was young, it was forced to grow around the rock and now is shaped like an elephant's trunk.

At 1.25 miles when you'll reach the lower parking lot on Hardscrabble Road, turn left and continue climbing again until you cross a road. Go straight on the Field Loop Trail. Butterflies favor this area and can often be spotted

among the black-eyed Susans and goldenrods. You'll hear and see a lot of birds and will pass side trails leading to the Passaic River—a great place for the kids to watch for birds and deer.

Continue uphill to return to the parking lot. Before leaving, stop in at the Hoffman Nature Center to see the many interesting exhibits and wonderful gift selection.

43 MOUNT HOPE HISTORICAL PARK

Location ■	Mount Hope Historical Park
County ■	Morris
Type ■	Day hike
Difficulty ■	Moderate
Distance ■	2 miles
Elevation gain ■	Approximately 200 feet
Hours ■	Dawn to dusk
Information ■	Morris County Park Commission, 53 East Hanover Avenue, Morristown 07960; (973) 326-7600
Website ■	*www.morrisparks.net*
Admission ■	Free

Driving directions: From I-80 East, take exit 35, and turn left onto Mount Hope Avenue. Proceed 0.5 mile to Richard Mine Road and turn left. Follow this 0.7 mile to Coburn Road and turn right. Coburn Road becomes Teabo Road. The entrance to the park is 0.7 mile on the left. From I-80 West, take exit 35B directly onto Mount Hope Avenue and proceed as above.

Mount Hope Historical Park lies within a narrow band of very old rock rich with mineral deposits. Mining began here as early as 1710 and in the late 1700s the land that now makes up the historical park was part of a 6271-acre property known as the Mount Hope Tract, which encompassed more than twenty active mining locations. John Jacob Faesch developed the tract in 1772, with each mine owned by one or more companies. One of the oldest iron mining areas in Colonial America, Mount Hope and surrounding Rockaway Township provided more than half of the iron ore extracted from the state until 1958. The state's richest mines—the Richard, the Allen, and the Tboe—were located at Mount Hope. Not all the mines are marked, so look carefully for large, deep depressions, known as subsidence pits, and find all that remains visible of the shafts, adits, and slopes that yielded what the Native Americans called *Succasunny*, or black stone— magnetite iron ore.

From the parking lot and adjacent picnic area, look for a trail sign that

Hikers spotting deep depressions can find all that remains visible of the shafts and slopes that yielded magnetite ore.

leads to a narrow, level, cinder rock trail. The trail begins past a steel gate amid a mass of goldenrod, which blooms with gorgeous yellow flowers from late June to October and was used in ancient times to stop the flow of blood from wounds. The trail gradually ascends. At the T turn left.

Continue uphill, bearing left where two trails meet. Birch and maple trees add to the beauty of the area, but watch your step because large rocks are underfoot as well as vividly colored leaves if you're here during autumn. At 0.2 mile you'll encounter a sign stating, "No hiking; Federal Property" indicating the U.S. Picatinny Arsenal terrain. Turn left, still ascending gradually, onto the red-blazed trail. From here, there are a lot of gradual ups and downs with huge boulders alongside the trail. On the left at 0.25 mile you'll find a series of depressions. Many can be identified by the rocks that have been dug out and piled next to the vast holes, and a few have trees that have sprouted up over the years.

The remains of the Teabo 2 mine lies in one of the huge depressions. According to park literature, Teabo 2 was 460 feet deep in 1880. By 1883 it was abandoned and access to ore from the Richard Vein was obtained through Teabo 3 and 4. At full capacity, 20,000 tons of ore was mined here annually. The fencing surrounding a section of this pit is made from a hoisting cable that was unwound to serve this new purpose.

Bear right at the fork, where the red-blazed trail gradually climbs. The trail is very narrow here, but it levels quickly and during summer months the oak canopy is much appreciated since the temperature is at least ten degrees cooler in the shade. You'll spot sassafras, sporting mitten-shaped leaves. Oil from its roots is used to flavor root beer and various medicines. After descending you'll come to a junction with the orange trail, which loops through the western side of the park. Turn left, and left again at the next trail junction to continue following the red-blazed trail. You'll find more depressions on the left. At 1.7 miles when you reach the signs for the Allen Tunnel on the right and Smoke Stack Shaft on the left, check the surrounding area carefully. This shaft was excavated in the 1850s to provide ventilation for the

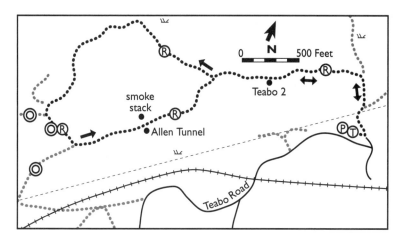

Allen Tunnel, which served as a major expansion for the Allen Mine. By 1855 it became the mine's primary access and extended 600 feet northward from Teabo Road into the ore body. From Teabo Road, officials note, it is still possible today to see the ruins of the Allen Tunnel.

After a quick climb the rocky trail levels off in an area where young and old trees blend together. A number of smaller pits can be seen alongside the trail. After the trail levels, and before you reach the steel gate, turn right to reach the parking lot.

44 DEER PARK LAKE

Location ■	Allamuchy Mountain State Park
Counties ■	Sussex and Warren
Type ■	Day hike or overnight camping
Difficulty ■	Easy to moderate
Distance ■	2.5 miles
Elevation gain ■	140 feet
Hours ■	Dawn to dusk except when snowfall is heavy; gate at Lot 1 is closed after the first heavy snowfall
Information ■	Allamuchy Mountain State Park, Stephens Section, Hackettstown 07840; (908) 852-3790
Website ■	www.njparksandforests.org
Admission ■	Free

Driving directions: From I-80, take exit 19 and drive south toward Hackettstown on CR 517. After passing a large building, take the first left

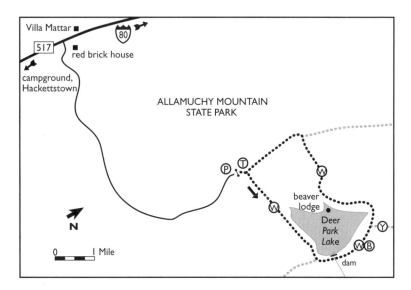

at a post next to a brick house. Proceed 2.3 miles to parking lot 2 at the end of the dirt road.

When you visit the north shore of Deer Park Lake, you may not see the broad-tailed beaver, the largest rodent in North America. But you will see its cone-shaped house and dozens of gnawed tree stumps. You'll also enjoy circling this charming lake, which sits in the serene wilderness of Allamuchy Mountain State Park. Spring and fall are the best times of year to visit, while winter is great for exploring on snowshoes and cross-country skis.

To begin the hike, cross under the gate at the end of the road and bear right along a level, wide trail marked with a white blaze. Ferns dominate beneath a canopy of beech, tulips, and oaks. The pond comes into view after 0.75 mile, and during summer and fall you'll be rewarded by the sight of water lilies floating in the clear, blue water. Proceed along the bank, turn left, and cross the concrete dam on the eastern shore toward the green oasis of evergreens, red maples, and sassafras. This is an excellent area for lunch or for children to skip pebbles across the water. A large fallen tree makes the perfect bench from which to view resident ducks and Canada geese.

From here the blue-and-white-blazed trail climbs gradually. The open field 0.25 mile ahead is filled with colorful wildflowers in spring, summer, and fall; farther on, to the left, are mounds of black rock. After a yellow-blazed trail comes in on the right, follow the trail as it hugs the north shore. Watch for signs of beaver activity. Children delight in discovering the beaver lodge at 1.7 miles and examining the rodents' tooth marks on the remaining stumps. Walking on from this point, the pond disappears from sight and the trail enters another wooded area where the dominant tree is the red cedar. This is the highest

Trees provide a cool canopy on the hottest day.

point on the trail. Turn left at the **T** to head downhill on the white-blazed trail. Continue straight ahead until you reach the gate you originally crossed under.

Note: Camping for trailers and tents is available from April 1 to October 31 at the Stephens Section of the park, located 2 miles north of Hackettstown on Willow Grove-Waterloo Road.

45 JENNY JUMP

Location ▪	Jenny Jump State Forest
County ▪	Warren
Type ▪	Day hike or overnight camping
Difficulty ▪	Easy
Distance ▪	3 miles
Elevation gain ▪	280 feet
Hours ▪	Dawn to dusk
Information ▪	Jenny Jump State Forest, Box 150, Hope 07844; (908) 459-4366
Website ▪	www.njparksandforests.org
Admission ▪	Free; fee for camping

Driving directions: From NJ-80, take the Hope exit and drive south on CR 521. In the center of Hope, turn left on CR 519 north, and follow signs to Jenny Jump State Forest.

A hiker admires a glacial erratic found along the Summit Trail.

Legend has it that a girl named Jenny was so engrossed picking berries at the crest of the mountain ridge that she didn't hear Indians with raised tomahawks creeping toward her. Her father, standing below, saw what was happening and yelled, "Jump, Jenny, jump!" She did—and, unfortunately, was killed by the fall. At least that's what Swedish missionary Sven Roseen wrote in his diary in 1747 to explain how Jenny Jump Mountain was named. The Minsi Indians are long gone from the area, although it's doubtful that they ever menaced Jenny at all. Situated about 12 miles southeast of the Delaware Water Gap, 1090-foot Jenny Jump boasts excellent vistas of the Kittatinny Mountain Ridge, with sweeping expanses of farmland below. If you plan to stay overnight, there are two group sites, six shelters, and sixteen campsites suitable for tents or trailers. Stop at the park office for a map before driving to the first parking lot.

Head uphill from the trail sign on the Swamp and Summit Trails. At the double-white blaze, turn right onto a wide, grassy trail that gradually continues uphill to a narrow trail marked by red and white blazes. After bearing right at the fork, you'll find yourself beneath a canopy of hemlocks surrounded by huge boulders. The Kittatinny Mountain Ridge then comes into view, and where the trail veers left at the double-white blaze at 0.4 mile, head straight toward the single-white blaze. Lush green farmland is below and to the right.

At 0.5 mile, where a double-white blaze indicates the Swamp Trail heading downhill, proceed straight and go uphill along the Summit Trail. A rest is always welcome after a climb, and you'll have your pick of natural rock seats.

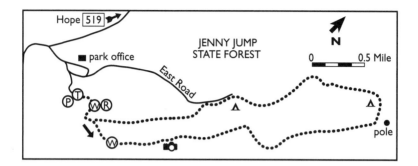

When you've recovered, continue on to an open area along a ridge where the views get even better. The trail becomes extremely rocky at this point, with several easy ups and downs. Soon you'll descend again, and then start a long climb at 1 mile for about 0.25 mile. The rest of the hike is a piece of cake.

Turn left at the pointed pole at 1.7 miles. When you reach group campsite B, swing left onto an oil-and-stone-surfaced trail. Campsites are large and roomy, and in addition to each facing a nice view, new modern toilet facilities have recently been installed. Nearby stands one of the largest rocks in the park—a leftover from the Ice Age.

Continue past campsite 11. At the sign for the Swamp Trail; turn right to pass through a lovely grove of evergreens. At the double-white blaze, bear right and continue to the parking lot.

46 PEQUEST

Location ▪ Pequest Wildlife Management Area
County ▪ Warren
Type ▪ Day hike
Difficulty ▪ Easy
Distance ▪ 1.7 miles
Elevation gain ▪ Negligible
Hours ▪ Trail, dawn to dusk; education center, 10 A.M.–4 P.M., closed holidays
Information ▪ Pequest Trout Hatchery and Natural Resource Education Center, 605 Pequest Road, Oxford 07863; (908) 637-4125
Website ▪ www.njfishandwildlife.org
Admission ▪ Free

Driving directions: From the junction with NJ-31, take NJ-46 east and follow signs to Pequest Trout Hatchery, which is located 9 miles west of Hackettstown.

Map showing trails from the Pequest Trout Hatchery. Labels include "exit from Pequest Trout Hatchery," "tall tree," "kiln remains," "Pequest Road," markers B, Y, T, P, and several R markers. Scale bar: 0 to 0.2 Mile, with N compass arrow.

Go through the main parking area and turn right on Pequest Road. Turn left on the gravel drive and park in the small space next to the kiln.

Hiking here is a golden opportunity for teaching children about natural resources and proving to them that corn doesn't come from a can but is grown in row after row of open fields. During the growing season you'll be hiking next to cornstalks more than 6 feet tall, but resist the temptation to pick an ear. Not only is it illegal to pick or destroy vegetation on this land, but this particular corn is good only for cattle. Come during spring, summer, or fall, when the pastures are ablaze with colorful wildflowers and butterflies. And winter is the perfect time for examining bark to identify trees in these serene woods, where lichens thrive on fallen logs and rocks.

After the hike visit the Pequest Trout Hatchery and Natural Resource Education Center, where approximately 600,000 brown, rainbow, and brook trout are raised annually as stock for the state's waterways. A self-guided tour leads to the nursery building and an observation deck overlooking concrete raceways, where trout are kept until they're large enough to be released. Inside the center, try your skill at the hands-on exhibits. If you bring a fishing rod, keep in mind that between late May and early October only artificial lures and flies are allowed along the special trout conservation stretch. A fishing license and trout stamp are required for those over fourteen years of age, except during the annual "Free Fishing Days" in June.

Until the 1930s the kiln near the trailhead was used to heat chunks of limestone into a powdery substance. Farmers fertilized their fields with the powdered lime, which also balanced the pH factor of the soil. Lime is still used by farmers today to reduce the acidity of their soil, but this type of kiln is no longer in use. To your left is the first of many cornfields encountered along this hike.

Walk slightly uphill for a few yards, following the red blazes. This narrow trail, surrounded by scrub brush, levels before it widens into a grassy path. Turn right at the T and look for the huge black walnut tree. Just past the tree, make a quick left. The trail is wider now, flanked on both sides by a variety of trees and a low wall made of rocks that farmers cleared from the surrounding land. The rusty patches seen on some of the stones show they contain iron. At this point, the trail ascends slightly. You're soon in the open, and from here you'll be darting in and out of the woods for a while. Views of rolling hills appear in the distance, with cornstalks surrounding you in the summer months. At the junction with the blue trail on the left at 0.3 mile, continue straight on the red trail. The red trail bears left, with an open field to the right and low shrubs to the left. A small man-made pond that attracts a tremendous amount of wildlife is at 0.4 mile. If you haven't spotted any of the local residents—deer, chipmunks, and groundhogs—check the tracks and droppings at the edge of the pond for signs of them. And look for the dragonflies that often hover like tiny helicopters over the pond.

Look carefully and you may spot the cardinal flower growing alongside the trail.

As the red trail veers to the right just past the pond, continue straight to the yellow trail. Dozens of cattails stand in the marshy area to the right as the trail, grassy now, continues with a lot of short ups and downs. The open field to the right is a favorite hangout for butterflies and honeybees. The honeybee, New Jersey's state insect, is a valu-able component of the food chain as it pollinates crops within the Garden State. Pause here for a while to listen to the honeybees buzzing and watch as they busily transfer pollen they've collected from the fields to hives they've built in overhead tree branch notches. You'll soon enter woods, and as you climb up the rocky, narrow trail, watch for the lush ferns that grow in this low-light area.

Reach a field and climb over a low rock wall on your way toward the power lines, where a nice view of the countryside awaits. Bear right under the powerlines at 0.75 mile. To the west are pretty vistas; as you descend, farms appear in the distance. The trail parallels the powerlines for a short distance, with woods on the right. Exercise care; this section of the trail is dirt with loose rock. Cedars, the first trees to take over when open fields begin filling in, are to the right. When the trail levels at just over 1 mile, take a right to follow the yellow trail back into the woods along the wide, flat, grassy trail. Woodchucks may run across the trail when they hear you approach. Wildflowers also abound in this section.

When you reach the junction of the red and yellow trails at 1.25 miles, proceed straight to the red trail. At 1.5 miles the open field affords a good mountain vista as the trail bears right. Turn left at the red arrow, where the trail is flanked by low rock walls. When you pass the black walnut tree, turn right then make a quick left to return to the parking area.

47 MERRILL CREEK

Location ■ Merrill Creek Reservoir
County ■ Warren
Type ■ Day hike
Difficulty ■ Moderate
Distance ■ 3.5 miles
Elevation gain ■ 100 feet
Hours ■ Trails, dawn to dusk; visitor center, 8:30 A.M.–4:30 P.M., except holidays
Information ■ Merrill Creek Reservoir, 34 Merrill Creek Road, Washington 07882; (908) 454-1213
Website ■ www.merrillcreek.net
Admission ■ Free

Driving directions: From Phillipsburg, take NJ-57 east. In 4.6 miles, turn left onto Montana Road and make two left turns, onto Richline Road and then again onto Montana Road. Follow signs to the Merrill Creek Reservoir Visitor Center.

Swimming isn't allowed in the Merrill Creek Reservoir, but hikers can visually soak in every ounce of the 650-acre body of water. The water presents an exciting yet calming effect. While hiking, you'll be surrounded by more than 2000 acres of forest and fields. The birding is excellent in spring and fall because migratory birds favor this area, and an observation blind is located in a protected cove along one of the trails. Plan on stopping in at the visitor center before the hike, where you'll learn why and how the reservoir was situated atop Scott Mountain, and how water is channeled into and released from it. According to naturalist Jane Bullis, "Water to fill the reservoir is pumped from the Delaware River during times when the river flow is high." The water is carried underground through a 3.5-mile-long pipeline. Conversely, when the river is low, water can be released from the reservoir

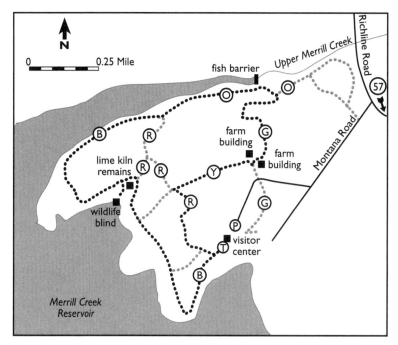

through that pipe. The water is used by seven utility companies in their generating facilities located along the Delaware River.

The reservoir is stocked with trout, large- and smallmouth bass, and a variety of game fish. If you plan on fishing, a license is required. Or if you have energy to spare, hike the 5.5-mile-long perimeter trail along the reservoir; it has one section that involves a steep climb.

After admiring the exquisite view of the reservoir and surrounding woods from the visitor center, head for the gravel path on the side of the building that leads into the woods. The trail soon becomes rocky and narrow. At the fork with red and blue blazes, bear left onto the blue-blazed Shoreline Trail, which follows the perimeter of the reservoir. While gradually descending toward the reservoir, you'll be walking through dense woods of oak, tulip, and sassafras. The reservoir first appears to the left when the trail levels out in 0.25 mile. Continue to the water's edge, where you can appreciate the vastness of this man-made water basin.

When ready, walk slightly uphill away from the water. Soon the reservoir comes into view again where the trail levels. Proceed along the bank past a spruce grove at 0.5 mile. As the reservoir disappears from view, you'll cross two boardwalks situated over a bog at 0.7 mile. Foundations of former farm buildings owned by the Cather family are in evidence as are the rock boundary walls.

Woods surrounding Merrill Creek Reservoir

As you near a fork where the blue and red trails merge, bear left, continuing on the blue-blazed trail. At this point, look for the remains of a lime kiln. Farmers transported limestone from deep in the valley to the top of the mountain, where they had a good draft and a lot of trees to provide fuel for the kiln. They then used the pulverized by-product to fertilize and balance the pH of their soil.

Turn left at the sign for a side trek to the wildlife observation blind at 0.9 mile. There is a good chance of spotting deer and birds in this area. Return to the main trail, turn left, and after another 0.3 mile, you'll be out in the open with a sweeping view of the reservoir ahead. The concrete building across the water is the 200-foot-high inlet-outlet tower used to control water flow. Asters and other wildflowers grow profusely in this area.

After climbing a short hill, you'll immediately descend into the woods again. At 1.4 miles, hundreds of dead trees stand submerged. After the reservoir basin was scoured out, it was stocked with fish and the trees were intentionally flooded. It is hoped that better aquatic life will abound after the trees decay. The trail is extremely rocky and difficult to negotiate for about 0.5 mile, but it's also quite interesting, with sweeping vistas of the reservoir and the sounds of birds as they fly close by.

After a few mini ups and downs, you'll reach a T. Turn left onto the orange-blazed Creek Trail at 1.9 miles. The route proceeds over low, wet areas through deep woods, following Upper Merrill Creek and the northeast arm of the reservoir. In fall the color of the leaves is dazzling! At the map post at 2.3 miles, turn right onto the green-blazed Orchard Trail and continue through some rocky areas under lush trees and shrubs. The trail leaves the forest and enters an abandoned orchard, part of the old Beers farm. Follow this trail as it changes to gravel past the Beers's old stone storage building and through a large field. Turn right onto the level, yellow-blazed Historic Farmstead Trail at 2.7 miles. It soon changes into a dirt path. At the junction, turn left onto the red-blazed Timber Trail, which passes impressive pine plantations and hardwood forests in various stages. When you come into the open again, you'll spot a corner of the reservoir with the visitor center a short distance ahead.

48 SCHOOLEYS MOUNTAIN

Location ▪ Schooleys Mountain Park
County ▪ Morris
Type ▪ Day hike
Difficulty ▪ Moderate-challenging
Distance ▪ 1.2 miles
Elevation gain ▪ 200 feet
Hours ▪ Trails, dawn to dusk
Information ▪ Morris County Park Commission, 53 East Hanover Avenue, Morris Township 07960; (973) 326-7600
Website ▪ *www.morrisparks.net*
Admission ▪ Free

Driving directions: From the junction of NJ-24 and US 206 in Chester, take NJ-24 west to the center of Long Valley and turn right. Continue on NJ-24 West and proceed up Schooleys Mountain past the Municipal Building. Turn right onto Camp Washington Road, turn right onto East Springtown Road, and turn right again into the park.

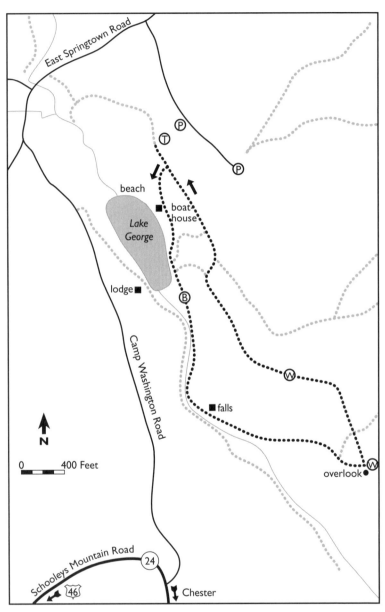

This hike is a treat, not just for the fabulous views and lush woods within Schooleys Mountain County Park, but for the year-round recreational opportunities: fishing, bridle trails, rowboat and paddle boat rental, ice skating on an 8-acre lake, a play area, picnic grove, a 470-foot floating bridge, a natural amphitheater where summer concerts are held, a group shelter for picnickers, and the Schooleys Mountain Park Lodge—available for corporate and private rental for meetings or parties. Originally purchased by the Morristown YMCA in 1923 and acquired by the Morris County Park Commission in 1968, the 797-acre park officially opened in 1974. The park was named for the Schooley family, immigrants from Germany, who owned land in this area in the late 1700s. During the late nineteenth and early twentieth centuries, visitors traveled to Schooleys Mountain by stagecoach and rail to take a dip in the pure-water spas. From the 1920s through the 1950s, children enjoyed summer camp here. Today the park attracts young and old, especially hikers who love the woods, the countless boulders, and the melodious sound of cascading water.

Park in the first parking lot, walk to the bulletin board, and head toward the pond, passing a picnic area and grove of beautiful red maples. Continue to the left of the boathouse, onto the wide gravel path, with the water on the right. In a few yards, you'll come to a junction and a sign leading to the Fallen Waters Trail; the Falls Trail (0.3 mile); and the Overlook Trail (0.5 miles). Take the blue-blazed Fallen Waters Trail, and continue downhill along a rocky dirt path. No doubt you'll be as amazed as I was to see the towering boulders. At 0.2 mile water cascading over rocks emits a lovely melody, while straight ahead huge boulders and mini-waterfalls tumble into another of the brook's natural pools. A short distance ahead, a boulder resembling a throne appears, and as you meander up and down while listening to the water's charming melody, you'll step over small rocks while major-sized boulders are to the right and left.

After the trail bears left at a trail sign adjacent to a yellow birch tree, it ascends gradually. With the brook on your right, sugar maples and yellow birch appear just as the trail becomes very rocky with more ups and downs. Watch your step in this area because you'll be walking over small boulders. A fantastic rock formation resembling a rooftop looms overhead, and as you walk beneath it check out the boulder-strewn ridges on the left. The water will be roaring as you turn a bit to the left following the blue blazes, and although it may seem that the trail will follow straight down over massive boulders, it doesn't. Continue to the left of the fallen tree, making your way down a staircase of natural boulders. Almost as soon as you start descending, a pretty waterfall can be seen and heard as it tumbles over large rocks. At this point you'll no longer hear the birds singing, for the sound of the water overtakes everything. This is an absolutely marvelous spot to cool off during hot summer days, but **use caution:** Poison ivy abounds in this area and not only grows alongside the trail but up tree trunks, so watch where you place your hands for balance.

Magnificent twin waterfalls suddenly appear, and almost immediately the trail levels and the only obstacles are tree roots. Shade provides relief in this area on the sunniest days, and water provides relief on the hottest days—just dip your bandana into the water and wrap it around your neck. At 0.6 mile, you'll either have to creep under or scamper over a downed tree. When you

The multiple cascades and waterfalls along this hike make it an incredible joy.

come to a private property sign on the right, continue left as the trail climbs steeply. At this point, you'll be far from the brook, although you can still hear it.

 A huge pile of boulders makes a great place to sit and rest after successfully climbing uphill thus far. At the top of the Falling Waters Trail watch for a short side trail that leads to an overlook affording a fabulous view of farmland far below. Even more interesting are the trees in this area. Growing out of giant-sized boulders, they're shaped like the letters V and H. One tree's trunk even resembles a chair! The countless boulders at this overlook make excellent seats, so relax before going farther. Return to the main trail and a sign that points to the Quarry Stone Path, which continues straight ahead; the Grand Loop Trail, a distance of 0.3 mile; or the white-blazed Patriots' Path Parking Area, 0.6 mile. I chose the latter. Although you won't be able to see the brook through the dense foliage in this area, you'll hear the welcome sound of water coming from the left. When you reach a toilet, take the right fork, turn left in a few yards where the trail levels, and proceed to the parking lot.

HACKLEBARNEY

Location ▪ Hacklebarney State Park

County ▪ Morris

Type ▪ Day hike

Difficulty ▪ Easy

Distance ▪ 3 miles

Elevation gain ▪ 220 feet

Hours ▪ Trails open 8 A.M., closing times vary; call for hours

Information ▪ Hacklebarney State Park, c/o Voorhees State Park, 119
Hacklebarney Road, Long Valley 07853; (908) 638-6969

Website ▪ *www.morrisparks.net*

Admission ▪ Free

Driving directions: Take US 206 to Chester, drive west on NJ-24/513 and follow signs to the park entrance.

This is a kid's paradise! Our first trip here was in the dead of winter, when the tips of large boulders poked through a blanket of freshly fallen snow. Our boys couldn't resist scampering from one boulder to another and, to tell the truth, neither could we. Situated along the Black River in a gorge of unusual beauty, Hacklebarney State Park lies primarily in a glacial valley. According to legend, it acquired its strange name from a local iron mine worker who persisted in heckling a foreman named Barney Tracey. Over time "heckle" Barney became "hacklebarney." Sturdy shoes are recommended.

Take the trail from the parking area, turn left, and walk down the deep stone steps just beyond the restrooms to Trout Brook and the first picnic area. Hiking will probably be slow going because children always want to stop and toss rocks into the brook or spend time splashing near the waterfall. **Caution:** Urge them to be careful; the rocks near the waterfall are quite slippery. Once you're back on the trail, look for trees that have sprouted in cavities of other fallen trees. Known as "nurse logs," these decaying trees provide nutrients and foundation for new growth.

Hemlocks are abundant in this 574-acre park because they're able to survive in deep shade. During spring Jack-in-the-pulpit thrives in the moist wooded areas near the river. Native Americans used the root to treat headaches. Also growing here is jewelweed, whose flowers reflect light and resemble tiny jewels after a rainfall. Some people claim the juice in the stem cures poison ivy when mashed and rubbed on the skin. The trail meanders downhill to the Black River. Plan on lingering near the water, where the giant rocks lining the bank are an opportunity for adventure for any child. In no time at all, the kids will be climbing on them, captivated by the fast-flowing river and fascinated by the many detours it takes around the rocks. Again, **use caution**; these rocks are so high and uneven that a slip and fall could be quite serious.

Follow the trail, keeping the river to your left. After crossing the second bridge, the trail ascends, curving away from the river and leading up a steep hill, past a playground, restrooms, and back to the parking area.

Note: Bring a fishing rod and your fishing license; the river is stocked annually with trout.

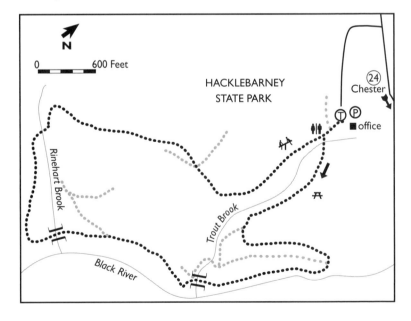

50 VOORHEES STATE PARK

Location ▪ Voorhees State Park
County ▪ Hunterdon
Type ▪ Day hike or overnight camping
Difficulty ▪ Moderate-challenging
Distance ▪ 2 miles
Elevation gain ▪ 150 feet
Hours ▪ Dawn to dusk
Information ▪ Voorhees State Park, 251 County Road, Route 513, Glen Gardner 08825; (908) 638-6969
Website ▪ *www.njparksandforests.org*
Admission ▪ Free; fee for camping

Driving directions: From north New Jersey, take I-78 west to exit 17; merge with NJ-31 North. At the second traffic light, turn right onto CR 513 North through High Bridge and follow signs to the park. From western New Jersey, take I-78 east to exit 16, cross I-78 to the traffic light. Proceed through the light and at the stop sign, turn left, merging onto NJ-31 North. At the second light on NJ-31 North, turn right onto CR 513 through High Bridge and follow signs to the park.

During the Depression thousands of people were unemployed with no hope of finding a job—that is until Franklin Roosevelt created the Civilian Conservation Corp (CCC). By planting trees, constructing shelters and picnic sites, and blazing trails through parks, hundreds of people were able to make money to feed themselves and their families. Voorhees is one of the places members of the CCC camped while building trails. Thanks to their efforts, hikers of all ages and abilities have a choice of several trails ranging from wide and graveled to rocky and steep. All except the Cross Park Trail and the Parcourse Circuit are multiuse and frequented by hikers, joggers, and mountain bikers.

Voorhees State Park also boasts an observatory. Built in 1965 by the New Jersey Astronomical Association (NJAA) on land leased from the state, it houses a 26-inch Newtonian reflector telescope, one of the largest privately owned telescopes in New Jersey. After the hike, spend the evening exploring the night sky by attending one of the skywatching programs offered year-round by the NJAA; call (908) 638-8500 for dates and times.

Camping here is a pleasure for there are fifty tent and trailer sites—surrounded by lush woods—with fire rings and picnic tables, modern toilets, and showers. Group campsites are also available. For reservations, contact the park.

Park at the Hoppock Grove parking lot, the first parking lot on the right after passing the office. Walk along the road a few yards to the right, and turn left at a sign pointing to the Hill Acres Trail and the Brookside Trail. Take the right fork following the red-blazed Brookside Trail. Almost immediately the trail turns left into the woods. In a few yards you'll have to decide whether to scramble over a huge downed tree or squeeze through a narrow side opening and walk around it. Children have more fun climbing over it! Stay right with the Brookside Trail at the next trail junction at 0.2 mile.

Even on the hottest summer's day, you'll feel cool hiking here because the trees provide a lot of shade. Along this section of trail, which is hard-packed dirt, you'll hear birds chirping as they hang out in and around the oak and tulip trees. Every so often, unmarked trails appear on the right; ignore them and continue following red blazes as the trial ascends and descends.

After crossing a narrow stream you'll come to a deep ravine on the left. You'll also see and hear Willoughby Brook as the water tumbles over various-sized boulders and emits a wonderful melody. A bench is situated at a perfect spot to relax and admire the brook and surroundings. In the wetter areas ferns form the understory from spring through fall, while the skunk cabbage that pops up as early as February thrives until late fall. Occasionally, you'll come upon stands of mayapples; these beautiful plants resemble tiny umbrellas.

Carefully cross a road at 1 mile to the green-blazed Tanglewood Trail. Follow it, ascending and descending once again along a trail strewn with rocks and uplifted tree roots. Cross an open grassy area bearing to the right

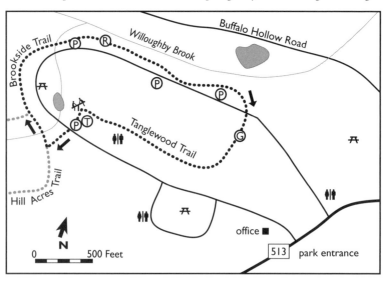

onto a narrow trail. When you reach the playground and picnic area, turn left at the swings, walk up the steps, and proceed to the parking area.

51 ROUND VALLEY

Location ▪ Round Valley Recreation Area
County ▪ Hunterdon
Type ▪ Day hike or overnight backpacking
Difficulty ▪ Moderate
Distance ▪ 2.4 miles
Elevation gain ▪ Negligible
Hours ▪ 8 A.M. to dark
Information ▪ Round Valley Recreation Area, 1220 Lebanon-Stanton Road, Lebanon 08833; (908) 236-6355
Website ▪ *www.njparksandforests.org*
Admission ▪ Free; fee for parking, Memorial Day to Labor Day; fee for camping

Driving directions: From I-78 West, take exit 20A (US 22 West) and fol- low the signs to the park entrance. From I-78 East, take exit 18 (US 22 East) and follow signs to the park.

Round Valley Reservoir didn't exist before 1958. What did exist was a natural horseshoe-shaped valley nestled in the rolling hills of Hunterdon County. Hardly anyone gave a thought to this hole in the ground—until it was filled with 55 billion gallons of water. Today, besides providing drinking water for the surrounding area, the 70-foot-deep reservoir is used by anglers, who are hooked on the smallmouth bass, sunfish, and rainbow trout, as well as by boaters, scuba divers, swimmers, and picnickers. A year-round treasure, the reservoir also attracts winter enthusiasts who love ice sports, cross-country skiing, snowshoeing, and sledding. For hikers, the recreation area offers trails ranging from very easy to moderate: the 9-mile Cushetunk Trail leads to a wilderness campground only accessible by foot or by boat. The 0.5-mile Family Hike and Bike Trail offers fine views of the reservoir. And the Pine Tree/Shore Line Trails have a combined mileage of 2.4 miles with marvelous closeup views of the reservoir and wooded areas. The Pine Tree Trail is my favorite. It's reserved only for hiking, skiing, and snowshoeing, and from it you can easily switch over to the Shore Line Trail, also reserved only for foot travel.

From the parking lot, limber up by taking a short stroll down to the dock for an overall view of the reservoir. Before or after the hike, plan on fishing (a fishing license is required) or paddling your canoe or kayak in the crystal clear water. Only campers can launch in this area, but park personnel can direct you to other launch sites.

When ready, walk up the hill on the same road you drove in on, and look for the green-blazed Pine Tree Trail on the right. Ascend on a rocky, dirt path wide enough for two. Although stately pine trees are on both sides of the trail, you'll be in the open for a while. On dreary winter days, this hike can brighten your mood as the evergreens cast a touch of color, and after the leaves have fallen from the trees, the reservoir—on your right—is much in evidence.

A series of short ups and downs follow and at 0.5 mile feel free to sit for a while on one of the many sawed logs that have been set up facing the reservoir. At 0.6 mile, with pines all around, there's a great view of the reservoir.

Ice sailing in winter at Round Valley

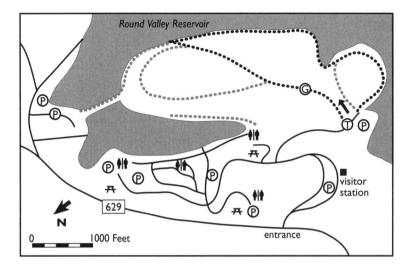

Round Valley Reservoir

visitor
station

629

N

0   1000 Feet

entrance

Ahead on the left are benches for visitors who attend classes here. (Ask for a schedule of events at the visitor station before leaving.) White birch appear deeper in the woods on the left. At 0.8 mile a trail appears on the left; but continue straight and a few yards farther, look to the right for a well-worn footpath. Turn right onto it to continue downhill past attractive white birch and oak trees. This leads to the Shore Line Trail, but be careful because it's steep and can be slippery in places. Even on a hot day, this area can feel cool because the trees form a natural canopy overhead. At the bottom of the hill, you'll reach the water's edge at 1.1 miles. Turn right, and follow the narrow path with the water on the left and magnificent views of hills in the distance. More pine trees grow along the water's edge, and just a short distance away, after climbing a tiny hill, is an interesting place to stop, have a snack or drink, and admire the vastness of the reservoir. A well-placed bench provides a good place to stop and gaze out onto the splendid scenery.

Small ups and downs follow. At 1.7 miles you'll be at a cove—a lovely spot with pines and another grand view of the reservoir and rolling hills in the distance. In a few yards, cattails appear at the water's edge, but from here some places along the trail may be muddy if you've come after a heavy rain. The dam comes into view at 1.8 miles. Another bench just ahead is a good vantage point to relax, breathe in the fresh air, and actually see for yourself the millions of gallons of water within this mighty hole in the ground and how beautiful and peaceful it is.

After leaving the bench, continue along the shoreline. Just before the parking lot comes into view, you'll find a lot of scorched pines at 2.2 miles. Continue 0.2 mile to your car.

52 LORD STIRLING PARK

Location ▪ Lord Stirling Park
County ▪ Somerset
Type ▪ Day hike
Difficulty ▪ Easy
Distance ▪ 3.9 miles
Elevation gain ▪ Negligible
Hours ▪ Trails, dawn to dusk; visitor center, 9 A.M.–4:30 P.M., closed holidays
Information ▪ Lord Stirling Park, 190 Lord Stirling Road, Basking Ridge 07920; (908) 766-2489
Website ▪ www.park.co.somerset.nj.us
Admission ▪ Free

Driving directions: From Basking Ridge, go south on South Maple Avenue, turn left on Lord Stirling Road, and proceed to the park entrance.

Children are often reluctant to walk one step farther when they get to the start of this trail. They'd much rather admire the antics of the Canada geese in man-made Branta Pond. Who can blame them? The beauty and constant honking of these creatures is exhilarating. However, there are many more treasures to be found on these easy, level trails within the 400 acres of Lord Stirling Park. Deer, meadow voles, and rabbits are frequent visitors. This trail is a pleasant warm-up for the more interesting things to come. A magnifying glass is helpful for examining insect-eating plants in the boggy area, one of five major plant communities in the park. If you love birds, bring binoculars; you'll probably also spot deer, pheasants, raccoons, skunks, opossum, and sometimes fox.

Nearly 8000 feet of boardwalk extend over the high-water areas. One section leads to an observation tower in a remote, marshy bend of the Passaic River where kayakers can sometimes be seen paddling by. Plan on having lunch here; you'll never forget the experience of looking out to the east at the quiet, mysterious depths of the Great Swamp National Wildlife Refuge. During spring, chain pickerel flip out of the water, briefly suspended in midair, as they journey upstream into the swamps and marshes where they spawn. There are also spring beauties such as trillium and lady's slipper, nine species of nonpoisonous snakes, and painted and snapping turtles (don't handle any; they may bite). The trails can be buggy during the summer, so be sure to wear long sleeves and pants and carry bug repellant. Before you begin, pick up a trail map at the Environmental Education Center. When you complete the hike, spend some time examining the seasonal displays in the 18,000-square-foot center.

The parkland was originally owned by William Alexander. Born in New

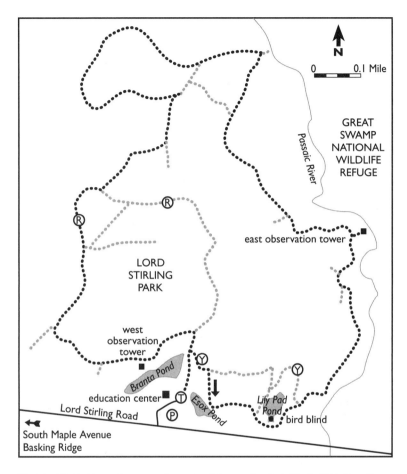

York in 1726, Alexander wanted to gain rights as the sixth Earl of Stirling (Scotland) after his father died in 1756. Both the British House of Lords and the British courts refused to acknowledge him, but he falsely used the title of Lord Stirling nevertheless. Despite this one vanity, Alexander was a man of great accomplishment; he not only served as surveyor general and one of Columbia University's founders, but he also gave his last dollar to outfit the New Jersey militia. A variety of owners occupied the land after Lord Stirling's death in 1783. In the 1970s, with the possibility of a jet port being constructed on these grounds, the Somerset County Park Commission purchased the property and built the Environmental Education Center "to educate the people about open space values and public land use management."

The entrance to the trail is to the right of the center, via a straight gravel path dividing Branta Pond from Esox Pond. During fall the field ahead is

Wonderful trails await hikers at Lord Stirling Park.

aglow with an enormous variety of wildflowers, including daisies, chicory, and Queen Anne's lace. Children are usually amazed to learn how important these wildflowers are to field dwellers. Moths, butterflies, and bees prize the nectar, while birds dine on the seeds and strip the leaves to line their nests.

At 0.2 mile, just before entering the woods, look to the right for a post with yellow reflectors, which indicates a right turn onto the yellow trail. (There will be a series of trail junctions; bear right at each one until you hit the red trail.) Don't be surprised if a huge bird, the great blue heron, flies overhead as you approach. It's probably looking for a tasty morsel in Esox Pond, just ahead.

From this area, there's an excellent view of the education center. The wide, grassy trail leads to the edge of Lily Pad Pond, another good viewing area with access to a bird blind. If the feeders are filled, you'll spot some beauties here. The next right turn takes you off the yellow trail and into deep woods at 0.5 mile. The topography changes from woods to open field and back again. After another right turn at 0.9 mile, grasses appear; these can be hypnotizing when they sway in the slightest breeze. In the spring, have children study a blade of grass under a magnifying glass. They'll see that grasses actually bloom! After a long stretch on the boardwalk, you'll reach the east observation tower at 1 mile. The climb up the staircase is steep, but the view is magnificent.

Walk back to the trail and turn right. At 1.2 miles, the woods become so dense that it almost feels like evening. The trail enters a wetter region, and at 1.5 miles a boardwalk meanders through wooded areas and open fields. Turn right to go past a field of cattails when the boardwalk divides. Kids usually like to hear about how their parents smoked these "punks" when they were children and how Native Americans prepared cereal by chopping the pretty stalk. At 1.7 miles take a right for another closeup view of the Passaic River. When you've finished examining the mushrooms and lichens that thrive in this peaceful area, turn around and continue, keeping to the right when the trail forks. The trail goes through woods and over more wet sections. At 2 miles a boardwalk goes over a stagnant body of water with a thick crust of algae, bright yellow waterlilies, and hundreds of cattails. This is one section of boardwalk that truly delights children; they love hopping over the sections that are partially submerged, and they even like getting their feet wet!

In another 0.25 mile you'll arrive at a junction with three boardwalks. Turn right and continue for an additional 0.25 mile to a junction with the red trail. From this point, follow the red blazes back to the Environmental Education Center. The swampy section encountered at 3 miles is eerie; hundreds of cattails appear, along with standing dead wood. The trail passes the west observation tower before skirting open field. At the T turn right, cross over the bridge, and head toward the center and the parking lot.

HEMLOCK FALLS

Location ▪ South Mountain Reservation
County ▪ Essex
Type ▪ Day hike
Difficulty ▪ Moderate
Distance ▪ 5.25 miles
Elevation gain ▪ 440 feet
Hours ▪ Dawn to dusk
Information ▪ Essex County Department of Parks, 115 Clifton Avenue, Newark 07104; (973) 268-3500
Website ▪ Not available
Admission ▪ Free

Driving directions: The hike begins in Millburn at a parking area northeast of the intersection of Glen Avenue and Lackawanna Place, about a block northeast of the railroad station.

Thanks to the Sierra Club and the Essex County Department of Parks, Recreation, and Cultural Affairs, the yellow-blazed Lenape Trail will eventually cover 30 miles and link dozens of county, municipal, and historical areas. This hike, open only to foot traffic and cross-country skiing, begins on the first completed segment of the trail at the western corner of the South Mountain Reservation. The trail rambles over the same land George Washington surveyed during the Revolution, when he realized the mountain range we know today as the Watchungs would offer his troops perfect cover from the British. You'll be crossing many scenic streams, where you'll see water tumbling over boulders. Hemlock Falls creates an impressive cascade, especially after a heavy rain or snowmelt. There are also scenic overlooks and dense woods chock-full of plants and wildlife.

Several trails merge near the start. Take the second from the left, an old carriage road. As you gradually ascend this rocky trail that follows the ridge, you'll see an old quarry below. At 0.3 mile, turn right at the T, then go left to follow the yellow-blazed Lenape Trail. A deep, lush ravine appears in another 0.3 mile, where you'll hear the melodious sound of Maple Falls long

Getting ready for the trail ahead

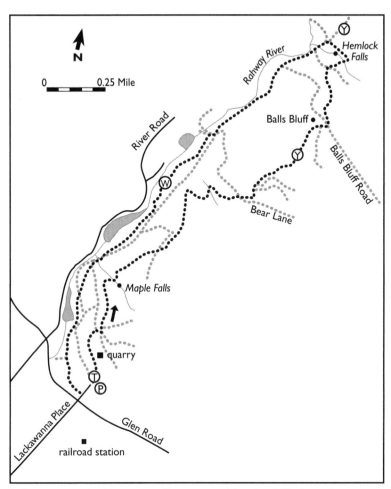

before you see it. Cross a small stream and head uphill along the narrow, rocky trail. Stands of green-leafed mountain laurel stand out on even the bleakest winter's day.

After crossing another old carriage road—now known as Pingry Trail and closed to traffic—and before climbing again, you'll pass more inviting streams. Where the trail descends and widens, there is new growth, and after the trees have shed their leaves, the view of the surrounding country is outstanding. The sound of gently flowing water is heard once more at 1.6 miles, especially after a heavy rain or when the snow is melting. The small waterfall provides a peaceful spot to rest or listen to the birds. It's also a good place to turn around if you don't feel like going on to Hemlock Falls.

To continue, proceed uphill and cross a dirt road, Bear Lane, at 1.9 miles.

Pause for a few minutes when you reach Balls Bluff and the remains of a shelter erected by the Civilian Conservation Corps in 1934. Only the stone support columns have survived. The trail descends steeply from this point, crosses a carriage road, Balls Bluff Road, and leads to an area with downed trees, mountain laurel, and a stream. Keeping your balance on the natural rock bridge across the stream at 2.9 miles is a lot of fun; the bridge leads to a short uphill section that bears left on a narrow trail leading to a beautiful stand of rhododendron. Cross another old road and then a bridge near Hemlock Falls. The trail turns left and follows a carriage road for a short distance. Leave the trail when the carriage road turns right. After crossing a bridge, continue straight along the wide path, River Road, to a magnificent spot where you can admire the Rahway River.

The trail is now level and wide, with dense woods providing a lovely backdrop. The sound of the flowing water can be heard even when the river temporarily disappears from view, and beautiful hemlocks tower overhead. Turn right on the wide path, an old carriage road, at 3.8 miles, and then make a quick left onto the white-blazed Rahway Trail. The path passes by small ponds, good places for youngsters to try their skill at skipping rocks. Lush rhododendrons surround the trail in another 0.2 mile. Delightful woods and water continue to work their magic; but gradually, you'll hear hints of civilization's return as you follow the path back to the starting point.

54 WATCHUNG RESERVATION

Location ■ Watchung Reservation

County ■ Union

Type ■ Day hike

Difficulty ■ Moderate

Distance ■ 2.4 miles

Elevation gain ■ 150 feet

Hours ■ Trails, dawn to dusk; science center, 1–5 P.M.; closed weekdays from the fourth week in November through March

Information ■ Trailside Nature and Science Center, 452 New Providence Road, Mountainside 07092; (908) 789-3670

Website ■ www.unioncountynj.org

Admission ■ Free

Driving directions: From Watchung, go north on Valley Road and continue straight on Sky Top Drive, which becomes Coles Avenue. Proceed straight into the parking lot for the Trailside Nature and Science Center.

The Lenni-Lenape Indians referred to the area that lies between two ridges as the *Wach Unks*, meaning "high hills." We know them today as the Watchung Mountains. On the trails, you'll be able to spot deer, birds, and wildflowers while walking beside a beautiful babbling brook. An added bonus is passing through the remains of Feltville, a nineteenth-century village ruled by David Felt. Until an archaeological dig in 2004, Felt was believed to have lived in a mansion away from the village. Now, thanks to evidence found in the dig, Matthew Tomaso, the center's associate director, says he is "100 percent certain" that Felt lived in the village in a modest house "among his workers," in this paper-manufacturing village.

After the hike, plan on exploring the Trailside Nature and Science Center, adjacent to the parking area. Enjoy a nature film, lecture, or planetarium show; browse various exhibits including live reptiles, pond life, geology, and local plants; and watch birds in the observation area. Outside are compact herb, wildflower, and butterfly gardens.

Walk away from the center on the blacktop road leading downhill, to the Nature Trail sign on the left side of the road. Follow the white-blazed Sierra Trail down the hill and over the bridge. Go slightly uphill, and this narrow trail, also marked with green blazes, soon levels. Blue Brook can be heard at approximately 0.1 mile. Oaks and tulip trees tower overhead, and the area is always alive with birds. An orange-blazed trail joins in, just after a left turn. Examine the growth on the forest floor for evidence that life does goes on after death as mushrooms grow profusely on fallen and decaying trees.

The trail turns to the right at 0.3 mile, but this is easy to miss because it

Climbing over rocks is always a challenge.

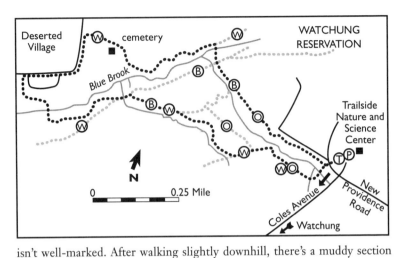

isn't well-marked. After walking slightly downhill, there's a muddy section that soon levels out; a gully will be on the left. The blue trail joins in at 0.6 mile. Exercise **caution** and hold on to little ones at this point; there's a steep drop-off into the gully on the left. Still following the Sierra Trail, cross over the stream at 0.7 mile; on the other side, leave the marked trail and take the right fork onto an unmarked path. To the right is a fantastic view of Blue Brook. The trail is slippery as it leads downhill, and it soon follows the brook, a perfect place to stop to play or look for wildlife. As the trail climbs up the hillside, it becomes slippery again; **use caution.** Bear right at the top of the hill at 0.9 mile. You'll be following along the brook again, where, during late winter, skunk cabbage pokes up from the ground. This remote area is very peaceful but also where you can easily get lost. You may have to bushwhack, bearing in mind that the stream should be on your right. Cross the bridge over the brook at 1 mile. As soon as you reach the other side, look for a trail going up the ridge to see the remains of Feltville, now referred to as the Deserted Village.

Turn right onto the paved road at 1.1 mile, where the Sierra Trail joins in again, and follow it to a combination residence, church, and post office—all that remains of Felt's reign, which at one time included thirteen double houses, two dormitories for single men and women, a manor house, a school, a barn, and a blacksmith shop. The paper-manufacturing venture thrived until 1860, when Felt tired of running the operation and people started moving away.

Proceed uphill through the village. A few yards after the last house at 1.4 miles, follow the Sierra Trail, which bears right into the woods where the road continues straight. Turn right in a few feet and follow the double blaze to a cemetery where members of the Wilcox family are buried. Peter Wilcox, a Dutch settler, erected a gristmill and lumber mill here in the 1700s; during the American Revolution and the War of 1812, the mill was converted into a gunpowder plant.

Walk downhill away from the cemetery and take the right fork onto an old road at 1.9 miles. Cross the brook, and at another junction take the middle path leading to the blue-blazed trail. The orange-blazed trail joins in at 2.1 miles, where it climbs gradually to reach the paved road. Turn right to return to the parking area.

55 SIX MILE RUN

Location ■	Six Mile Run Reservoir Site
County ■	Somerset
Type ■	Day hike
Difficulty ■	Easy to moderate
Distance ■	3 miles
Elevation gain ■	Negligible
Hours ■	Trail, sunrise to sunset; office, 8:30 A.M.–4:30 P.M
Information ■	Six Mile Run Reservoir Site, D&R Canal State Park, 625 Canal Road, Somerset 08873; (732) 873-3050
Website ■	*www.dandrcanal.com*
Admission ■	Free

Driving directions: From Somerville, take US 206 to Hillsborough, and then take CR 514 East (Amwell Road). Turn right onto CR 533 South (Millstone River Road), continue 2.1 miles, and turn left across the bridge onto Blackwells Mills Road. Cross the Canal Bridge and turn right onto Canal Road. The office is the second structure on the left. Parking is adjacent to the office.

A New Jersey Division of Parks and Forestry brochure refers to the Six Mile Run Reservoir Site as "a hidden treasure in Somerset County." Indeed it is a treasure and virtually unknown. Although the 3000-plus-acres were first acquired as a future reservoir site by the State of New Jersey in 1970, the property—administered by the New Jersey Division of Parks and Forestry—now serves as a marvelous recreation area used by equestrians, bicyclists, and hikers. Stop at the office to pick up a free trail map. If it's closed, maps are sometimes available in an outside box.

Begin the hike by walking around the building to face the Delaware and Raritan Canal, turn left, and continue straight ahead; an open field will be on your left. At 0.1 mile, cross a bridge over Six Mile Run, which appears as a narrow stream. On the left look for a sign for the red trail. Reserved for hikers only, this lovely trail is narrow with a lot of protruding tree roots. Six

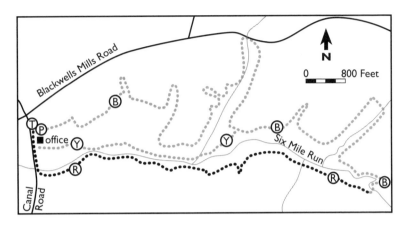

Mile Run will now be on your left. Beech trees hug the bank, while an open field is on the right. During summer months the beech and oak trees ahead form a natural canopy providing welcome shade on the warmest day. The nearby hearty sugar maples can be identified by the 3- to 8-inch, five-lobed leaf that turns a brilliant yellow-orange in the fall. Treasured for producing hardwoods, the sugar maple can reach heights of 100 feet or more and produce delicious sap that turns into sweet maple syrup when boiled.

After a slight climb, you'll reach an area where cedars and sugar maples blend together, and you'll find a large, flat rock that's perfect for sitting and listening to the water's melody. In the early 1700s, Dutch settlers farmed this area, and a few of the eighteenth-century farmhouses and Dutch-framed granaries and barns can still be seen. The soil is so fertile here that more than half the land in the Six Mile Run Reservoir Site is leased for agricultural purposes, while the remaining woodland and open fields provide habitat for a variety of plants and wildlife.

Watch your footing as you walk along the next section of trail, because it's very narrow and angled toward the water. Some gradual ups and downs follow. When you reach 0.4 mile, lush shrubs hide the field on the right, and the water can now be seen in the distance. Ahead you'll see how poison ivy grows as a hairy vine on tree trunks. When the field comes into view again, watch for deer who favor this area. A steep but short climb follows, taking you high over the river again. You're now approaching one of the state's bow-and-arrow hunting areas, and before choosing the day to hike here, it's best to either check the Division of Fish and Wildlife's website (*www.njfish andwildlife.com*) for the dates hunting is allowed.

Autumn is a great time to hike here, for at 0.7 mile you'll find pin oaks adorned with scarlet-colored leaves. **Use caution** ahead: soil erosion caused by rain has created a deep trench. After descending you'll have a couple of ups and downs. The yellow trail can be seen to the left, and when you reach another steep hill, it's best to hold on to the tree trunks for support and balance.

Once in the open, the dirt path changes to grass and proceeds through a wet area surrounded by shrubs on both sides. At the edge of the woods, you'll see the trees, but you'll no longer be under their canopy. At 1 mile turn left at the sign for the red trail, following a narrow, dirt path without rocks and only a few tree roots. Poison ivy abounds in this section, so remember, "Leaves of three, let it be." Six Mile Run appears again on the left, and before ascending slightly at 1.1 miles, you'll have fun crossing over rocks. You'll encounter the remains of an old fence with its support poles still standing, but be careful of barbed wire. High over the water once again, the sight of maples and oaks are most welcome as are the junipers hugging the trail.

At 1.4 miles sumac sports bright red twigs and leaves in the fall. The sign post at 1.5 miles marks the end of the red trail. Return the way you came.

Note: For a longer hike, cross the canal to the blue trail—used by hikers, mountain bikers, and equestrians. The trail is 3.8 miles one way and follows the forest edge, occasionally turning into the woods. There are two stream crossings without bridges on this trail. The yellow trail—reserved for hiking and bicycling—is 0.9 mile one way and passes through the lowland floodplain and a wooded area. The yellow trail, which is muddy during a wet season, connects with the blue trail in two places to form a loop trail.

56 DELAWARE AND RARITAN CANAL

Location ▪ Delaware and Raritan Canal State Park
County ▪ Somerset
Type ▪ Day hike
Difficulty ▪ Easy
Distance ▪ Up to 4.5 miles
Elevation gain ▪ None
Hours ▪ Dawn to dusk
Information ▪ Superintendent, D&R Canal State Park, 625 Canal Road, Somerset 08873; (732) 873-3050
Website ▪ *www.dandrcanal.com*
Admission ▪ Free

Driving directions: From Rocky Hill, take CR 518 east for a short distance, and just after crossing the Delaware and Raritan Canal, turn left on Canal Road. At Griggstown, turn left after the canal and park. To spot a second car, continue north on Canal Road, turn left at the T on Suydam Road, and right on Canal Road to Blackwells Mills Road. Cross the canal and park next to the towpath.

For more than 150 years the Delaware and Raritan Canal has been a tribute to the hundreds of laborers who created it. Armed with only picks and shovels, the crews spent countless grueling hours digging the long, deep trench. Many died on the job from exertion, poor hygiene, and cholera. Opened in 1834, this waterway—with more than sixty pivot bridges, fourteen locks with centrally pivoted shutter sluices, an extra lift lock at Lambertville for the narrow feeder canal, guard locks, and aqueducts—was built to allow coal barges to move between Philadelphia and New York City. The canal was closed in 1933 when trains made shipping faster and more economical. Today the canal is a major source of drinking water for residences and businesses in twenty-two towns, and since becoming a state park in 1974, it has been used by hikers, canoeists, fishermen, and bicyclists. Trees have sprouted up along the towpath, but in the days long gone, when barges plied the water, vegetation was controlled to prevent mule reins from getting tangled.

The hike, through a pretty, secluded area, begins at Griggstown. It can be done either as a 4-mile out-and-back or a 4.5-mile through-hike by leaving a second car at Blackwells Mills. As you walk near the water's edge, you'll find thick beds of pickerelweed, identified by their elongated, heart-shaped leaves and, from May to October, by their showy, blue-flowered spikes. Largemouth bass, pickerel, rainbow trout, and catfish can be hooked in this murky water. A fishing license is required.

Although you won't see many houses along this stretch today, stories abound about the old houses with their tall picket fences that prevented children from falling into the water. One owner placed empty whiskey bottles on the pickets as a decoration and much to his surprise found that passing coal barge crews would take aim at the bottles with pieces of coal. It didn't take him too long to collect a free supply of coal for the winter!

When ready, walk to the towpath and head north. The buildings on the opposite side of the canal soon disappear, giving way to woods. Surrounded

Along the towpath of the canal, you can see a variety of trees, birds, canoeists, and more.

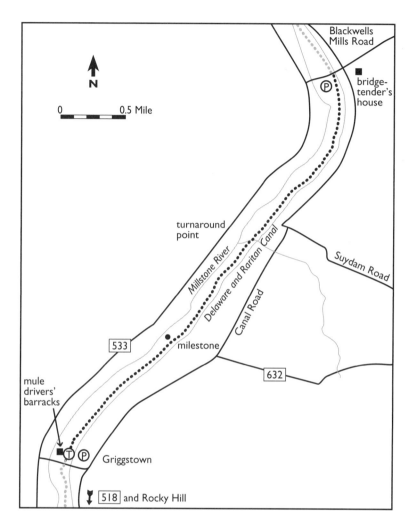

by trees, with the silence broken only by the chirping of birds, the calm water evokes the ambience of a quiet day perhaps a century ago. As you proceed
on the wide, packed-dirt trail beneath a canopy of yellow birch, red maple,
and tulip trees, be careful not to brush against poison ivy; it not only grows
along the entire length of the canal's bank but occasionally wraps itself around
tree trunks.

Stand quietly for a few seconds and you'll probably spot a frog just before it plunges into the water. On sunny days turtles bask on the bank or on
a log. No matter which season you come, you'll hear beautiful melodies;
more than 150 species of birds frequent the area. At 1.3 miles you'll reach a

concrete milestone placed for the mule team leader to figure the distance to New Brunswick or Trenton, depending on where the barge was going. The first sign of civilization—a farm—appears on the other side of the canal at a little over 2 miles. In the same area a pretty brook flows under the canal. This is a convenient spot to turn around, although it is possible to continue for as many miles as desired. If you continue 2.5 miles to Blackwells Mills, you'll have an opportunity to see the bridge-tender's house, which still stands.

57 SOURLAND MOUNTAIN

Location ▪ Sourland Mountain Preserve
County ▪ Somerset
Type ▪ Day hike
Difficulty ▪ Moderate
Distance ▪ 4.5 miles
Elevation gain ▪ 200 feet
Hours ▪ Dawn to dusk
Information ▪ Somerset County Park Commission, 355 Milltown Road, Bridgewater 08807; (908) 722-1200
Website ▪ *www.park.co.somerset.nj.us*
Admission ▪ Free

Driving directions: Drive 2.8 miles south on US 206 from its junction with CR 514, and turn right onto East Mountain Road. Continue 1 mile to the park entrance and parking lot.

Sourland Mountain Preserve—owned and administered by the Somerset County Park Commission—sits atop a ridge that extends from Hopewell to Hillsborough. Thanks to the efforts of volunteers, the preserve opened in 1995 and offers hikers a choice of three trails ranging in difficulty from easy to moderate. Along these trails you'll find massive boulders, dense forest, numerous ups and downs (some steep), a lot of boardwalks, flowing streams, and silence—except for the sweet melody of the birds. You may also spot a deer, bear, or other critters.

No one knows for certain where the name *Sourland* came from. One theory is that the word was derived from "sorrel-land," which describes the sorrel-colored (reddish brown) soils encountered by the pioneering German farmers who once occupied this area. Or perhaps because the land isn't too fertile, it was considered "sour." Whatever the origin, one thing is certain— hiking in these lush woods is a sweet experience!

From the parking lot, walk to a small booth where trail maps are some-

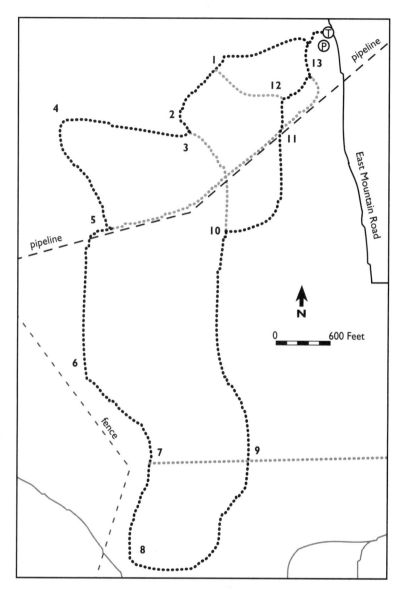

times available, and look for a nearby trailhead signpost. A level path leads to the right of the pond and as you head immediately into the woods, you'll pass an impressive tall tulip tree with Virginia creeper, identified by five leaves in a circle, climbing up its trunk. The understory along the trail is loaded with poison ivy, so stay on the path and remember: "Leaves of three, let it be." The trail climbs gradually, and on a hot summer's day when the temperature is soaring, it's unbelievably cool beneath the shade of towering trees. The surroundings are gorgeous, complete with fallen trees and huge boulders. At 0.2 mile you'll cross over a short wooden bridge, pass by a small stream on the left, and walk beneath beech and tulips trees looming high. At this point you have a choice—the 0.5-mile circle-blazed Pondside Nature Trail, which is level to gently sloping, the 1.1-mile triangle-blazed Maple Flats Trail, which is mostly level, or the rectangular-blazed Ridge Trail, which is moderate with numerous ups and downs.

Bear left for the Ridge Trail and at signpost 1 turn right, making your way uphill over natural steps—tree roots. At 0.5 mile and signpost 2 the trail curves to the left and immediately begins meandering to the right. When you reach signpost 3, you can shorten the hike to 1.5 miles by turning left and following signposts 10, 11, 12, and 13. Otherwise, go right. Rocks make walking a bit difficult, so a little concentration is necessary to avoid stubbing toes. While looking down you may find pretty flowers resembling tulips at your feet signaling that tulip trees are overhead. If you spot trees with "toes" spread out beside the trunks, you've found the black birch. There are less rocks and roots in this section, and it's usually so quiet in the woods that you can hear the rustle of leaves in the slightest breeze. Just ahead stands a magnificent old oak with a truck so broad that even three people can't get their arms around it.

Oops. Just when you thought you passed all the rocks, they're back along the trail. Although the trail is still level at signpost 4, you'll be walking over thick tree roots and some boulders, followed by a gradual downhill section. Kids love this next section of trail where they'll have to walk over several boulders in order to keep their feet dry, and then they'll shout with glee when they see the huge fallen maple that became a bridge over the stream. When filled with enough water, the stream sounds like a Japanese garden—so take a break to listen and enjoy. At 1.4 miles the trail is a bit rough, and at signpost 5 the Texas Eastern Gas Transmission Corporation's right-of-way pipeline appears in a large, open field. Walk to the middle of the clearing and turn right. In the wet area phragmites wave in the breeze. Rocks have been carefully placed on the trail so you won't have to get your feet wet while crossing the water. Take a left and continue with the phragmites on either side and then head into the shady woods again. It's very exciting hopping across the flat boulders that lead to a boardwalk at 1.6 miles, and it's a great place to examine the skunk cabbage that is profuse in this area during spring. Another boardwalk follows and where it ends, hikers have laid out single planks to make crossing during wet weather easier. More boardwalks, long and short, follow, and squirrels and chipmunks can often be seen scurrying across them. If you don't see a boardwalk or recognize a path, look around carefully since it's easy to lose your way.

After going steeply downhill over rocks that may be slippery after a rain, the trail levels out at 2 miles, but it descends steeply again at signpost 6. Fortunately, the railing that was built in 1997 by Todd Waters, a member of Scout Troop 89, as part of his Eagle Scout service makes all the difference in managing this difficult spot. The trail continues to descend gradually at this point, but do exercise **caution** because there are many small rocks to negoti- ate. Turn right at signpost 7, where the trail widens and climbs gradually for a few yards without too many rocks. Just when you thought you stepped upon the last one, the rocks are back as the trail levels at signpost 8. When you reach a log across the path and a small cairn (a pile of rocks that indicate trail direction), turn left, cross another boardwalk at 3.1 miles, and head uphill past a majestic maple on the left. The rocks suddenly disappear as the trail gradually climbs.

A series of short boardwalks follow. At 3.8 miles turn right at signpost 10. The trail levels and continues gradually downhill, crosses several boardwalks, and at signpost 11 you'll be back in the open area and the pipeline. Before reentering the woods at 4.2 miles, look for a pretty lilac tree that bursts into bloom in late spring. After a few ups and downs, you'll reach the last board-walk, a wide opening, the pond, and the parking lot.

58 HERRONTOWN WOODS

Location ▪	Herrontown Woods
County ▪	Mercer
Type ▪	Day hike
Difficulty ▪	Moderate
Distance ▪	1.8 miles
Elevation gain ▪	180 feet
Hours ▪	Dawn to dusk
Information ▪	Mercer County Park Commission, 640 South Broad Street, Trenton 08650; (609) 989-6559
Website ▪	www.princetontwp.org/herron.html
Admission ▪	Free

Driving directions: From Nassau and Witherspoon Streets in the center of Princeton, go north on Nassau Street (NJ-27) for 1.1 miles. Turn left at the light onto Snowden Lane, continue 1.5 miles, and look for a sign for the woods and parking on the left. If you come to Herrontown Road, you've gone too far.

Mention Princeton and most people automatically think of the univer-sity. But in the heart of this thriving college community, there's a hidden

Herrontown Woods offers a delightful challenge: how to cross a narrow stream.

oasis, Herrontown Woods, offering easy hiking year-round. Owned by Mercer County and run by the County Park Commission, it's a place of peace and quiet, where the birds are always flying about and where you're guaranteed a bountiful display of bright mountain laurel as well as a variety of colorful wildflowers in the spring. Jack-in-the-pulpit, violets, and marsh buttercups are only a few of them. Summer is the ideal season to take advantage of the shade provided by oaks, maples, and beeches, while fall is when Mother Nature paints the leaves bold colors. If you want to brave the cold plan a visit in the winter, when the ice crackles beneath your feet as you walk along the meandering trails, and you have a better opportunity to spot deer.

This densely wooded property was owned by Oswald Veblen, an internationally known mathematician who taught at Princeton University. He and his wife lived here, and they deeded their land to the Mercer County Park System in 1957 to be maintained as a wildlife and plant sanctuary with nature trails so that hikers could enjoy it as they did. In the 1970s the county purchased additional acreage, which brought the woods to 142 acres. The red trail follows the original property line and most likely was blazed by Dr. Veblen; the blue trail winds through the Levine Tract that the county purchased.

Sneakers will do, but sturdy shoes are recommended to prevent stubbing toes on the tree roots and rocks.

Begin from the right side of the map board located at the eastern end of the parking area, and walk slightly uphill on the narrow, red-blazed trail. A wire fence is on the right. Huge sweet gums, which turn a dazzling crimson in autumn, soon appear. When you reach a clearing with a cottage on the right and a barn on the left, pass between them and take the blue-blazed trail. The numerous odd-shaped boulders on and alongside the trail date back to the Triassic period, while the softer red shale underlies the southeastern corner of the woods.

At the wide swath of open land at 0.3 mile, the trail crosses the underground Transco Gas Pipeline right-of-way, marked by yellow posts, and heads back into the woods. The trail, which has been leading gradually uphill, soon levels. In this area are beautiful beech trees; a few of their golden leaves stubbornly cling to branches adding a touch of color through winter. Sassafras and ironwood trees follow, and at 0.5 mile is a stand of tall, shagbark hickory, identified by ragged gray bark curling away from the trunk. This hickory is valued commercially for smoking meats and for making ax handles.

Turn right onto the red trail at 0.8 mile. As the red trail makes several sharp turns, watch for the blazes; they are sometimes difficult to see against the dark tree trunks. Also watch for wildlife—the gray fox, opossum, cottontail rabbit, and white-tailed deer—that occasionally has been spotted here.

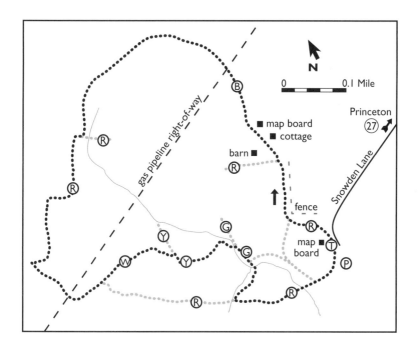

Cross the pipeline right-of-way once again at 1.1 miles. The white trail appears shortly. Stay left to follow the white blazes as the trail descends steeply. Rocks and tree roots in this area are sometimes covered by leaves, so watch your step. Turn right at the junction with the yellow trail, and after crossing the stepping-stone bridge at 1.4 miles turn right at the T onto the green trail. This short trail ends at a poorly marked junction with the red trail; it can best be recognized as the spot where the green markings disappear. Turn left; a red blaze will eventually come into view and you'll be heading southeast along a boundary fence. Cross a narrow stream in a few yards; you'll soon see a grove of white pine and the parking lot where deer can frequently be seen.

59 WASHINGTON CROSSING

Location ▪ Washington Crossing State Park
County ▪ Mercer
Type ▪ Day hike
Difficulty ▪ Easy
Distance ▪ 1.3 miles
Elevation gain ▪ Negligible
Hours ▪ Trails, dawn to dusk; interpretive center, Wednesday–Saturday, 9 A.M.–4 P.M., Sunday, noon–4:30 P.M.
Information ▪ Washington Crossing State Park, 355 Washington Crossing-Pennington Road, Titusville 08560; (609) 737-0623. Interpretive Center; (609) 737-0609
Website ▪ www.njparksandforests.org
Admission ▪ Free; fee for parking, Memorial Day to Labor Day

 Driving directions: From I-95 South take exit 3, bearing right onto Scotch Road. Continue to the light and turn left onto CR 546 West. Go through the light at the intersection with CR 579 to the park entrance on the right side of the road, and follow signs to the interpretive center.

Washington Crossing State Park offers ideal trails for first-time and expert hikers, who frequently spot white-tailed deer, raccoons, and squirrels. Migrating birds as well as the screech owl, great-horned owl, red-shouldered hawk, and Eastern bluebird can often be seen or heard along the stream and ravine. You'll see the forest in different stages of development, in addition to a variety of shrubs and wildflowers. Plan on stopping at the 1700-square-foot, barrier-free interpretive center for exciting and educational hands-on exhibits as well as a classroom and learning lab, computer station, live-observation beehive, and live and preserved wildlife specimens. A naturalist is available to answer any questions.

A young hiker stands under a huge, impressive tree near the interpretive center.

Look for the counterclockwise Red Trail access sign, across a wide, grassy lawn opposite the interpretive center. Natural succession hasn't taken place in this area because regular mowing has prevented the usual growth stages. The beginning of the Red Trail, identified by red blazes either on tree trunks or on brown plastic poles, is fairly level and wide enough for two people. As the trail ascends and descends, tall maples and oaks provide a welcome canopy sure to please on the hottest summer's day.

Turn right onto the White Loop Trail, crossing a short wooden bridge a few yards ahead. This area is a favorite among catbirds, those slate gray, black-capped noisemakers that sound like cats meowing. Take the side trail leading to the wildlife blind, and once inside stand quietly at one of the multi-level windows and be patient. You're bound to be rewarded by several species. When ready, return to the trail junction and continue on the white-blazed trail.

If you're here during autumn, the leaves of the birch trees will be a dazzling bright yellow. Stand still for a few minutes and you may spot chipmunks going through the brush or simply listen to and enjoy the sound of the birds. A bit farther the Green Trail Loop joins in with some easy ups and downs; take this trail to the Blue Trail Loop. Soon you'll cross a stream with lush growth on both sides. Spicebush, which flowers in March or April, grows profusely here. Its dried and crushed fruit was used as a liniment. At the

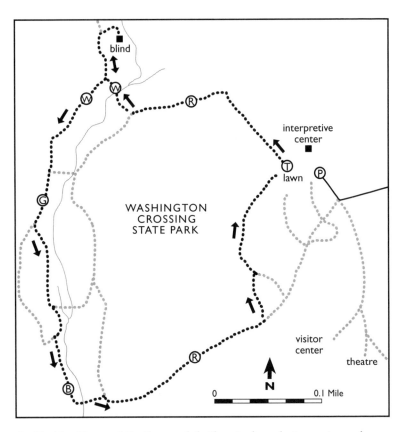

double-blue blaze at 0.8 mile, turn left; if you're here during spring and summer, you'll smell the sweet aroma of honeysuckle.

In a short distance, cross the stream again and pause to take in the beauty of the surroundings. When you reach the Red Trail at 1 mile, turn left. A well-placed bench is a good spot to take a quick break or sit back and listen to the sound of the wind as it blows through overhead branches. What a pleasure it is to hear nothing but the sound of leaves fluttering in the breeze and the birds calling to one another. Along the way, you'll reach stations 8 and 9, part of the self-guiding trail loop off the Red Trail. At station 8 notice how the woods have changed; you've left the mixed-oak forest for a late-succession field taken over by red cedar, flowering dogwood, wild rose, bayberry, black haw, and others. If left undisturbed, in a hundred years it will become the same as the northern mixed-oak forest you passed through before.

A sign for the Clockwise Trail Access is just ahead, continue to the parking lot.

60 CHEESEQUAKE CEDAR SWAMP

Location ▪	Cheesequake State Park
County ▪	Middlesex
Type ▪	Day hike or overnight camping
Difficulty ▪	Easy
Distance ▪	2.7 miles
Elevation gain ▪	200 feet
Hours ▪	Dawn to dusk
Information ▪	Cheesequake State Park, 300 Gordon Road, Matawan 07747; (732) 566-2161
Website ▪	*www.cheesequakestatepark.com/*
Admission ▪	Free; fee for parking, Memorial Day to Labor Day; fee for camping

Driving directions: Take the Garden State Parkway to exit 120 and follow signs to the park. Continue straight, past the entrance booth less than 0.1 mile ahead, to the trail parking area on the left.

Opened in 1940, Cheesequake State Park is Middlesex County's only state park. It lies between New Jersey's northern and southern vegetation zones, making it a transitional area with unique plant and animal life over diverse terrain. While hiking the green-blazed Cedar Swamp Trail, the longest in the park, you'll have closeup views of pine barrens similar to those in the southern part of the state; a freshwater swamp with outstanding specimens of Atlantic white cedar, sweetbay magnolia, and red maple; and a mature hardwood forest, where American beech, black birch, and white and red oak predominate. More than 180 species of birds have been sighted in these woods, as well as many mammals, including red foxes, white-tailed deer, and chipmunks.

There's still a lot of speculation about how the park was named. Some believe its origin is from the Lenni-Lenape Indian word *chichequaas*, meaning "upland village." But because Cheesequake lies on a fault where tectonic movement has been recorded as recently as 1979, others think it was named because the earth trembles like cheese! When you explore the quaking bogs in the marshes, you may agree with this explanation.

Start from the trail map in the parking area, head gradually downhill over a long boardwalk, and turn left at 0.1 mile, following red and green blazes. After crossing a brook and a slight rise, you'll reach the interpretive center, an excellent place to learn about the flora and fauna of the area before continuing on the sandy, level trail. If the interpretive center's Jim Faczak is available, you're in for a special treat. He is so knowledgeable and will introduce you to many

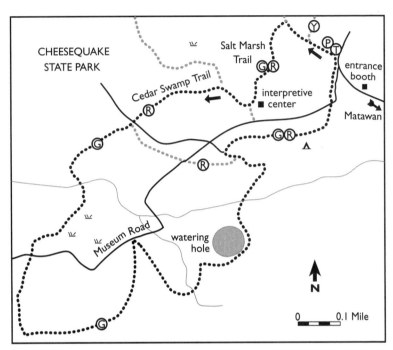

live species of wildlife including painted turtles, a pine snake, and an African clawed frog, just to name a few. Mountain laurel, abundant in this area, provides a lush green backdrop against the fallen snow in winter, while its pink blooms burst with a dazzling display each spring.

Cross a boardwalk over a wet area where skunk cabbage abounds. Although this plant is known for its rank odor, its spathe (a large, enveloping, green, stalklike leaf) is quite attractive. A rich, bright green carpet of sphagnum moss also thrives in this swampy section. Fern and sassafras appear a short distance ahead.

After a series of easy ups and downs, bear right where the trail divides to follow the green blazes. Take the steep stairs at 0.8 mile and hold on to little ones; sand between the steps makes them slippery. You'll immediately be on a level boardwalk, which keeps your feet dry in this wet area. You're now entering the dark, mysterious Atlantic white cedar swamp, where sweetbay magnolia, swamp azalea, and highland blueberry thrive. Some naturalists believe that the fallen cedar logs are still intact after many years because the tree is impregnated with resinous oil, protecting it from insects and fungi and slowing its decay. Woodpeckers hunting for insects in the dead trees are frequent visitors, and if you come late in the day, you may be lucky enough to spot a great horned owl.

A hiker takes some time out to admire the marsh.

The tall, century-old white pines nearby are a treat for the eyes and the nose. During the 1600s the British Crown took the straightest, tallest trees and used them as masts for the Royal Navy's ships, but their supply was cut off when the American Revolution began. Take a deep breath and begin the steepest climb of this hike at 1.3 miles. Fortunately, it's short and levels after a few yards. Deer sometimes hang out at the watering hole on the left at 2 miles; early morning or evening are the best times to spot them.

You'll be out in the open at 2.4 miles, at the group campsite. The trail, indicated by red and green blazes, leads back into the woods in a few more yards. Pass the interpretive center on your return to the parking area about 0.1 mile farther.

61 HOLMDEL PARK

Location ▪ Holmdel Park
County ▪ Monmouth
Type ▪ Day hike
Difficulty ▪ Moderate
Distance ▪ 1.2 miles
Elevation gain ▪ 120 feet
Hours ▪ Dawn to dusk
Information ▪ Holmdel Park, Longstreet Road, Holmdel 07733; (732) 946-2669 or (732) 842-4000
Website ▪ *www.monmouthcounty.com/parks/holmdel.htm*
Admission ▪ Free

Driving directions: From the Garden State Parkway, take exit 114. Coming from the south, take a left; coming from the north, take a right. Continue on Redhill Road until you reach Everett Road, turn right. Follow Everett Road to Roberts Road and turn left. Turn right onto Longstreet Road to the park entrance on the left.

To capture the flavor of what the Garden State was like during the nineteenth century, stop at Longstreet Farm before or after this pleasant, short

Spring is a glorious time to visit Holmdel Park.

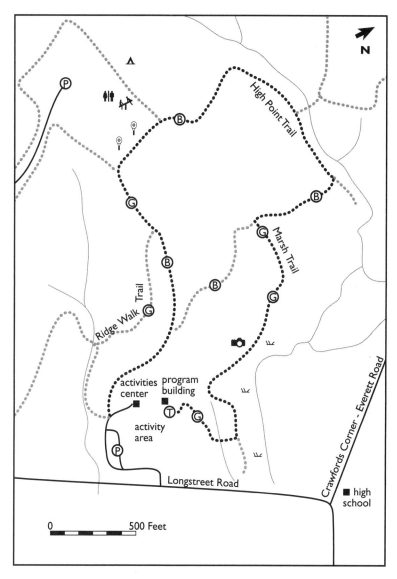

N

High Point Trail

Marsh Trail

Ridge Walk Trail

activities center

program building

activity area

Longstreet Road

Crawfords Corner - Everett Road

high school

0   500 Feet

hike. This nine-acre living history farm with nature and fitness trails, play-grounds, picnic areas, a shelter with snack bar, fishing and skating ponds, a sledding hill, and an impressive arboretum make up Holmdel Park—a 347-acre site nestled in the rolling hills of suburban Monmouth County. In 1965 the Monmouth County Park System purchased the farm and adjoining land from Mary Longstreet Holmes Duncan—the sixth generation of the

Longstreet family. Preserving a page from the state's agricultural past, the inside of an eighteenth-century farmhouse is on display, while outside horses, mules, hogs, sheep, Jersey milk cows, and other farm animals roam around. As if this wasn't enough to excite visitors, costumed interpreters work the farm as it was done a century ago.

Beautiful trails meander over much of the land the Longstreet family hiked a century ago. Highlights include magnificent stands of trees, including beech, which are easily recognized by their smooth bark and down-sweeping branches.

From the parking lot, walk to the activities center and pick up a trail map. Leaving the center, bear left across the vast lawn toward a brown-roofed building. Logs on the ground point the way to the green-blazed Marsh Trail. Starting from a high ridge the trail steeply descends a series of steps that gradually wind in and out past oak and tulip trees. Take your time; there's a sharp drop-off on the left, so hold children by the hand in this area. Where the trail bends continue straight, going up over a couple of steps next to a huge tree. In the wet area to the left, there's a sea of skunk cabbage that pops its green spathe through the snow as early as February and grows profusely in the marshy areas. Listed in *The United States Pharmacopoeia* in the 1800s, it was used to treat a host of illnesses, including epilepsy and asthma. It might also have been one of the first contraceptives, because those indulging in a daily dose believed it caused sterility.

After crossing a short bridge, you'll find an abundance of skunk cabbage that you can examine close-up and a boardwalk to keep your feet high and dry. At the T, turn left. If you're here during spring, you'll find violets and other wildflowers as well as skunk cabbage everywhere you walk in the wet areas. Watch your step when the boardwalk ends, for tree roots abound. Viewing platforms are to the right and left of the trail just ahead. Where a dirt trail appears on the left, continue straight over a boardwalk.

Leave the marsh behind when you reach a T and signpost for the blue-blazed High Point Trail. Turn right, go up the dirt trail, and when you reach the top of the hill with a narrow fence on the left and a huge birch on the right, gradually head downhill. At the next fence, at 0.5 mile, turn left. The trail starts out fairly level and then climbs gradually. A brook flows in the ravine to the right, and you can walk across a long wooden bridge for a better look at the brook. When ready, return to the trail to continue straight. The trail now ascends steeply, and at 0.8 mile the brook is left behind as you make your way beneath a canopy of red maple and beech trees. In a few yards the trail dips slightly followed by a gradual uphill climb as it winds in and out of the woods.

When you come to the tennis courts, bear left, hugging the perimeter of the woods, and pause for a few moments at the top of the hill to catch your breath and enjoy this spot where there's usually a welcome breeze. Should you have extra energy, try the fitness station on the left.

At the end of the tennis courts, turn left into the woods onto the wide and sandy green-blazed Ridge Walk Trail. At the next signpost, continue straight to follow the blue blaze. At 1 mile the trail gradually descends and when you reach the V, take the right fork (marked HPAC) and continue steeply downhill. When you spot the activities building and a picnic table in a lovely area on the right, turn right toward the table and follow the trail as it bears left toward the building. When you reach the concrete walkway, follow it to the parking lot on the right.

62 PORICY

Location ■ Poricy Park
County ■ Monmouth
Type ■ Day hike
Difficulty ■ Easy
Distance ■ 1.7 miles
Elevation gain ■ Negligible
Hours ■ Trails, dawn to dusk; nature center, Sunday, 12:30–3:30 P.M., Monday–Friday, 9 A.M.–4 P.M., closed Saturday
Information ■ Poricy Park, Oak Hill Road, P.O. Box 36, Middletown 07748; (732) 842-5966
Website ■ www.monmouth.com/~poricypark
Admission ■ Free

Driving directions: From the Garden State Parkway, take exit 114 and go west on Red Hill Road toward Middletown. Turn right on Bamm Hollow Road, which becomes Oak Hill Road. Park at the Poricy Park Nature Center to the right off Oak Hill Road.

This is a perfect outing for introducing children to hiking. You'll meander through Poricy Park's marsh and deep woods, pass a pond teeming with wildlife, and tramp through a field that's bursting with wildflowers during spring and summer. Children will also enjoy seeing soaring hawks, plump woodchucks, a farmhouse and barn dating back to colonial times, and the visitor center, which features fossils found in the area, an active beehive, and several hands-on exhibits. At the nature center you can rent a Nature Discovery Pack—consisting of binoculars, field guides, quick identification sheets, and magnifiers. Ask for a free plant, bird, or butterfly list and a self-guided trail booklet. Trail guides are usually available in the kiosk.

At the end of the hike, stop by the nature center to rent fossil screens for a dollar (with a $25 refundable security deposit), and then surprise your children by driving a few minutes to Poricy Brook, where they can search for

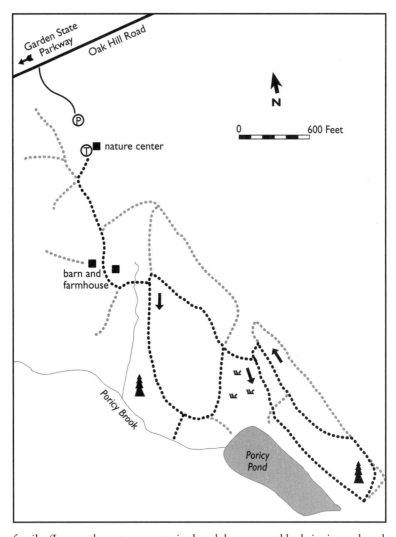

fossils. (In case the nature center is closed, be prepared by bringing a shovel, strainer, and towel and feel free to dig, but call first to check on the regulations.) Occasionally, the remains of duckbilled dinosaurs have been found preserved in the green sand and clay, but more common finds are the bivalved-animals with hinged double shells. Shark's teeth, snails, sea urchins, and sponges have also been found. Park officials say that the best way to find fossils is to sift the sand and gravel in the streambed. Please refrain from digging in the banks because this causes erosion. You're welcome to take home any specimens you find.

Rabbits are a common sight on and off the trail.

It's believed that this area was a shallow ocean during the Cretaceous period, approximately 65 million to 135 million years ago. Poricy Brook is part of the sea layer that finally receded. As the water receded, ocean animals died and sank to the bottom, where their bones, teeth, and shells were buried. The cutting action of the brook helps expose those fossils you'll discover.

From the center, walk past the barn along the Habitat Trail. Joseph Murray, a Scotch-Irish immigrant who enlisted in the Monmouth Militia during the Revolutionary War, built the barn and nearby farmhouse. He was murdered here in 1780, but his family owned the land until 1861. In 1969 the Poricy Park Citizens Committee was formed in an effort to save 250 acres of open space threatened by development. The group independently raised funds and then donated the land to the township so that everyone could enjoy the outdoors. The Murray Farm is now registered as a New Jersey historic site.

Shortly after crossing a small brook, turn right at 0.3 mile onto a wide, grassy path. To your right is a ravine where skunk cabbage thrives in spring. Stay to the right. At 0.5 mile a beautiful view of Poricy Brook appears. In spring the surrounding apple trees are adorned with pink blossoms and the tall tulip trees provide a natural umbrella to ward off the sun. The wooden staircase a short distance ahead leads down to the water's edge, an excellent spot to enjoy the flowing stream.

Climb back up the steps to return to the trail and bear right onto the open lawn area. The ravine will again be on the right. Look for a huge tree at 0.8

mile and take another wooden staircase down to the brook. A boardwalk crosses the swampy area and is flanked on both sides by skunk cabbage. Climb up more steps before turning right to follow the edge of the pond. At the end of the trail at about 1 mile, turn left, and at the fork bear left again, continuing along the railroad tracks. Make another left at the sign to Poricy Park and follow a level path. Look for the staircase leading to the marsh area at 1.3 miles. If you're here on a sunny day, you may see a turtle sunning on a rock or a garter snake darting out of the marsh grass. Concentrate on the water for a while; you can often spot frogs, tadpoles, or insects. Bear slightly right after you've climbed up the staircase on the opposite side, walking slightly uphill and straight for about 0.25 mile. Bear right when you see the nature center and proceed to the parking lot.

63 HUBER WOODS

Location ▪ Huber Woods Park

County ▪ Monmouth

Type ▪ Day hike

Difficulty ▪ Easy to moderate

Distance ▪ 2 miles

Elevation gain ▪ Negligible

Hours ▪ Trails, 8 A.M. to dusk; environmental center, Monday–Friday, 9 A.M.–4 P.M., except holidays

Information ▪ Huber Woods Park, c/o Monmouth County Park System, 805 Newman Springs Road, Lincroft 07738; (732) 872-2670

Website ▪ *www.monmouthcountyparks.com*

Admission ▪ Free

Driving directions: Drive east from Keyport on NJ-36, exit at the sign for Navesink, and take Grand Avenue, which turns into Navesink Avenue. Pass the Navesink United Methodist Church, make a right turn at the stop sign, and take the first left onto Brown's Dock Road. Turn left at the sign for Huber Woods, following Browns Dock Road as it changes from pavement to dirt. Turn left at the sign for the environmental center and park in the lot.

If you have only a couple of hours to spare and want an easy to moderate hike in pleasant surroundings, head to Huber Woods Park. Situated on a hill in the Locust section of Middletown overlooking the Navesink River, the trails aren't too taxing while offering a great opportunity to teach children tree identification in a hardwood forest of oak, tulip, beech, and poplar. The original 118 acres donated by the Hans Huber family in 1974 have grown to 258 acres

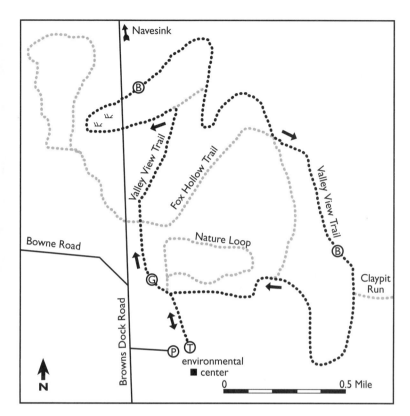

that have been permanently preserved as open space for nature education. In addition to the picturesque farm complex, the German-Swiss-style manor house, built in 1927, is currently used for environmental education, nature programs, and cross-country ski clinics as well as hands-on displays of plants and animals and details about the history of the park. Interior rooms feature a weather station, bird-viewing area, and restrooms. The Reptile House, with a variety of reptiles native to Monmouth County, is adjacent to the center.

The park's 6 miles of multiuse trails—designed for walking, hiking, mountain biking, and horseback riding—include a short, easy Nature Loop highlighting the diversity of the woods. Spring is an outstanding time to visit when the mountain laurel and pink azalea are in bloom. The Discovery Path, south of the environmental center, is a great place for younger children. Pick up a brochure (available between the parking lot and the environmental center) and stop at numbered posts to learn the history of the park, bird identification according to song, how forests grow on dry, sandy soils, and many more educational facts.

To begin this hike, walk north away from the environmental center and across the meadow toward a white sign at the trailhead. The huge meadow is

Hikers love checking out the huge meadow designed to attract wildlife.

designed to attract wildlife, and according to staff members, no matter which season you visit, this pretty meadow provides "an outdoor classroom for learning about wildlife habitat, plant adaptations, and seed dispersal." It takes years for a meadow to evolve. Annuals thrive during the first year, followed by perennials, and other seeds blow or are carried by birds into the meadow. Changes, depending on the season, are obvious. For example, during autumn, late-bloomers open their flowers, as the early-bloomers develop their seedpods and change color. Today wildflowers such as black-eyed Susan, butterfly-weed, and white yarrow thrive in the meadow, while birds, including the bobwhite, Eastern goldfinch, and mourning dove, feed here along with butterflies, honeybees, the white-footed mouse, cottontail rabbit, box turtle, and garter snake.

If you arrive on a hot summer's day, you'll feel the temperature drop as soon as you enter this lush forest on the green-circle-blazed, narrow, hard-packed sand trail. At 0.1 mile bear left onto the Fox Hollow Trail, descending gradually in a few yards. An outstanding pair of towering holly trees, at least 25 feet tall, are on the right. Capable of growing more than 50 feet in height, the holly's spiny-tipped leaves are 2 to 3 inches long. In winter the plant's pretty red berries add a glow to the forest and provide food for songbirds. At 0.3 mile continue straight, switching onto the blue-square-blazed Valley View Trail, which is rated moderate for hikers. Beautiful stands of mountain laurel surround the trail. Follow the Valley View Trail as it turns left and the climb becomes steeper. As you near a road, watch for bicyclists and cars, although it's rare to see either. Continue straight onto the flat, narrow, dirt trail and turn right as the trail loops around. The trail widens at this point with a lot of birch, oak, and mountain laurel as well as cedars scattered here and there in a field on the right.

Cross the road again, walk slightly to the left, and look for a signpost indicating the Valley View Trail. Heading downhill gradually at 0.8 mile, a valley appears far below on the left. A sign points to the view several yards ahead, but bear to the left and descend steeply. At 1 mile the trail levels after a steep single-file rocky path. This is a good place to sit, rest, have a snack, wait for a deer to appear, and note the many downed trees in this particular area. After the white fence on the left at 1.1 miles, the trail is sandy and easy hiking once again. At 1.2 miles the Fox Hollow Trail bears right but proceed left along the Valley View Trail. Proceeding gradually uphill this section is lovely during winter with the greenery of the mountain laurel adding a touch of warmth. Leveling off at 1.4 miles, the trail almost immediately descends again with a steep stretch at 1.5 miles followed by a level path for a few yards before another gradual climb.

The blue blaze and the Claypit Trail sign is reached at 1.6 miles, bear right. Spruce reach up to the sky at 1.7 miles, followed by a gorgeous wooded area and a gradual series of ups and downs. Turn left at the sign for the parking lot and trailhead, and watch out for tree roots in this section, particularly in fall and winter when it's difficult to see them beneath the fallen leaves. Return to the meadow at 1.9 miles; the parking lot is immediately ahead.

64 BUTTERMILK VALLEY

Location ▪ Hartshorne Woods Park
County ▪ Monmouth
Type ▪ Day hike
Difficulty ▪ Moderate
Distance ▪ 1.9 miles
Elevation gain ▪ 100 feet
Hours ▪ Dawn to dusk
Information ▪ Monmouth County Park System, Newman Springs Road, Lincroft 07738; (732) 842-4000
Website ▪ www.monmouthcountyparks.com
Admission ▪ Free

Driving directions: Drive east from Keyport on NJ-36 to a sign for Rumson, and turn right onto Navesink Avenue. The parking lot is on the left side of the road.

Families hiking the trail system within Hartshorne Woods Park for the first time are usually surprised by the steep overlooks, sloping valleys, and dense, dry, upland forest in the heart of New Jersey's coastal plain. In 1973 this 736-acre wilderness tract was purchased by the Monmouth County Park System for use as an undeveloped area. It was named for Richard Hartshorne, who purchased it from the Lenni-Lenape Indians. Wildlife abounds; if you hear a series of loud, sharp noises, it's probably an osprey. Also called a fish hawk, it plunges feet first into the water for its meal. Osprey have an impressive 4- to 6-foot wingspan, a brown body, and a broad black cheek patch across its white face. Because children usually concentrate on things at ground level, there's a good chance they'll spot one of the resident raccoons, opossum, or white-tailed deer. A variety of trees, including oak, maple, tulip, and immature chestnuts, fill the woods.

A large map board, and usually a good supply of brochures, is located next to the parking area at the start of the trails. It's best to come on a weekday to avoid the mountain bikers. Starting at the Buttermilk Valley Trailhead, walk to the right onto the red-blazed Laurel Ridge Trail. Follow the wide gravel path as it turns left and goes uphill gradually. Don't forget

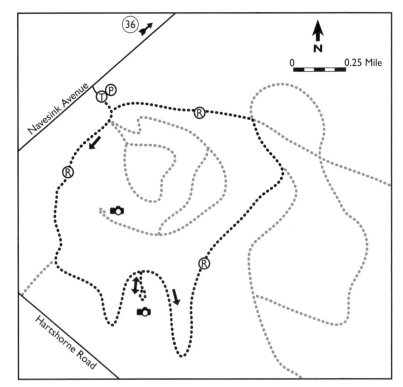

to look down every so often for raccoon or deer tracks. A gradual climb follows at 0.4 mile as the trail soon bears left over a lot of rocks and, at the turn, stands a tall holly recognizable by its characteristic sharp-pointed leaves.

Masses of mountain laurel and sassafras are ahead, and again you'll be climbing uphill to the left, as the land seems to fall away on the right. A blue blaze and an arrow at 0.7 mile points you to a side trail and to an overlook a short distance ahead. If you've come during the winter when the trees are bare, you'll have a fabulous view of the Navesink River.

When ready, return to the main trail and turn right. At 1 mile, stop and listen for a while and look down into the ravine. Trees tower about 50 feet above you. From here the descent is quite steep with a drop-off on the right. Watch out for the tree roots. Gorgeous tulip trees await at 1.4 miles just before the trail bears left at a junction. At the next junction, turn left to stay on the Laurel Ridge Trail. You'll pass a picnic table just before arriving at the parking lot.

65 THE HOOK

Location ▪ Gateway National Recreation Area
County ▪ Monmouth
Type ▪ Day hike
Difficulty ▪ Easy
Distance ▪ 3.6 miles
Elevation gain ▪ Negligible
Hours ▪ Trail, dawn to dusk; Sandy Hook Visitor Center, 10 A.M.–5 P.M
Information ▪ Gateway National Recreation Area, Sandy Hook Visitor Center, P.O. Box 530, Highlands 07732; (732) 872-5970
Website ▪ www.nps.gov/gate
Admission ▪ Free; fee for parking, Memorial Day to Labor Day, 7 A.M.–4 P.M. for beach parking at lots B, C, D, E, Gunnison, and the three lots for North Beach

Driving directions: From Atlantic Highlands, take NJ-36 east and follow signs to Sandy Hook. Summer weekends can be busy.

Sandy Hook, part of Gateway National Recreation Area, is a mixture of natural and historic wonders. While breathing in fresh ocean air at "the hook," you'll see dozens of fishing boats and freighters and hear buoys echoing mournful sounds in the distance. Take along a bag to collect treasures that have washed ashore. After a storm, you may find an old bucket, a twisted tree limb, a fishing net, or an unusual bottle. There are always shells, but

Treasures lie at your feet on the way to "the hook."

remind children to make certain they're collecting uninhabited ones. Common shells include those of the quahog clam, which was used by the Lenni-Lenape Indians for making wampum; the large "house" of the whelk snail; and the molted shell of the horseshoe crab, which resembles a perfect horseshoe when turned over. Shells with holes in the lower part are known as jingle shells, and when strung together, they make a dandy wind chime.

Ghosts of the past arise on this hike as well. Although calm today, the hook wasn't always peaceful. Between 1839 and 1848 shipwrecks were so common that Congress appropriated funds to build lifesaving stations, including the one built here in 1894 which now serves as the visitor center. The oldest continuously operating lighthouse in the United States can be seen on the hike, which ends past a section of Fort Hancock. The crumbling concrete bunkers and gun emplacements of the fort, built in the 1890s and early 1900s to protect New York Harbor, stand today as a reminder of days long gone. While miles of beach are available for exploration, this hike goes to the "hook" of Sandy Hook, east of Battery Gunnison, which is frequented by nudists during summer months.

Stop in first at the Sandy Hook Visitor Center for a nine-minute program about the U.S. Lifesaving Service. If you want to limber up, try the 1-mile circular Old Dune Trail just outside the building; it passes by one of the largest stands of American hollies on the Eastern Seaboard. The main park road leads past the visitor center to Fort Hancock. Turn right on Atlantic Drive and park in lot K, and start walking along the paved road from the north end, following

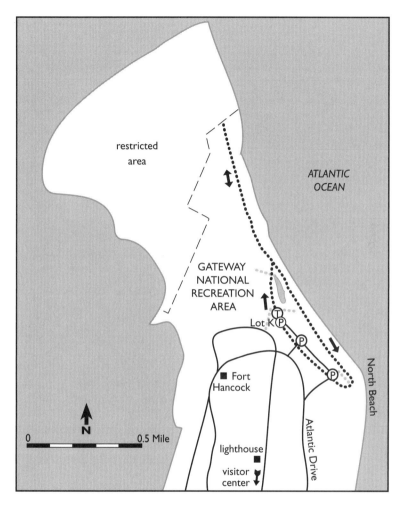

restricted
area

ATLANTIC
OCEAN

GATEWAY
NATIONAL
RECREATION
AREA

Lot K

Fort
Hancock

North Beach

Atlantic Drive

N

0   0.5 Mile

lighthouse

visitor
center

the fence and the old gun battery marked "Battery Peck." Passing the battery, take the wood chip path on the right leading to an observation platform with a panoramic view of New York Harbor and New York City.

Where the trail divides, go straight and climb briefly over to the dunes, where you'll have a good view of the long, narrow pond below and the ocean in front of you. Walk down to the pond, turn left, and as you trudge along the flat sandy trail, you'll see muskrat lodges built along the edge of the pond and phragmites. Native Americans used the oozing sap contained in stalks for chewing gum. In 0.25 mile the pond is obscured by the thick reeds and more dunes appear at 0.4 mile. Look for the chain-link fence and continue to the beach. At the water bear left (north) toward the tip of the hook. You'll be very close to the hook, which is restricted to the public because it is Coast Guard property.

Retrace your steps and bear left, continuing along the beach past the opening in the fence through which you entered the beach. To the right, at 2 miles, you'll see the 103-foot-tall lighthouse in the distance. This National Historic Landmark, completed in 1764 to guide ships sailing into New York Harbor, has a 45,000-candlepower lighted Fresnel lens that is visible for about 19 miles. On certain days visitors are welcome to climb to the top (call ahead for times).

When you reach North Beach, go around the fence and head west toward the parking lot exit. From here, with the lighthouse ahead to the left, you'll see a few of the houses in Officers' Row, the quarters for married officers who commanded the troops manning the fort in the late 1800s. Turn right to return to the beach parking lot and your car.

Note: Swimming is recommended only at beaches supervised by lifeguards, who are on duty 10 A.M.–6 P.M., daily from Memorial Day to Labor Day. While here, pay a visit to the Sandy Hook Bird Observatory, staffed by the New Jersey Audubon Society. Call (732) 872-2500 for details.

66 DORBROOK

Location ▪	Dorbrook Recreation Area
County ▪	Monmouth
Type ▪	Day hike
Difficulty ▪	Easy
Distance ▪	1.6 miles
Elevation gain ▪	Negligible
Hours ▪	Dawn to dusk
Information ▪	Dorbrook Recreation Area, (732) 542-1642, or Monmouth County Park System, (732) 842-4000, ext. 257 or 237
Website ▪	www.monmouthcountyparks
Admission ▪	Free

Driving directions: From the Garden State Parkway, take exit 109 southbound, turn right onto CR 520 (Newman Springs Road); for northbound traffic, turn left onto CR 520. Follow CR 520 1.5 miles to Swimming River Road and turn left. Follow Swimming River Road to CR 537 West. Turn right and continue to Dorbrook Recreation Area in the town of Colts Neck.

If you're looking for an easy hike over level terrain, this is the perfect place, especially during spring and fall. Dorbrook, consisting of 534 acres of open and cultivated fields, hedgerows, and woodland bordering the Swimming River

Reservoir, offers other outdoor opportunities as well. Thanks to the homes of the former owners, there's a lot of space for indoor activities ranging from Tai Chi, arts and crafts, plus science and sports programs during the summer months for children and adults. An activities directory newsletter published six times a year is available by calling (732) 842-4000, ext. 239.

After parking, follow a chain-link fence to the visitor center. This is a good

Pause and watch the action when you reach this unique bird house.

place to obtain a trail map, fill your canteen, and use the restrooms. Walk toward the tennis courts and playground to start the hike. When you reach the blacktop trail in front of the baseball field (a white house will be on the left), turn right continuing with the tennis court on the right. Veer to the left at 0.1 mile, cross the road, and check out the beautiful Eastern white pine trees that are easily recognized by the 3- to 5-inch-long needles in bunches of fives and its drooping cones ranging from 4 to 10 inches in length. Nearby borders of Queen Anne's lace are spectacular, with specimens ranging from tiny to huge. To the left are stands of cattails and chicory. Chicory, commonly found along highways and empty lots, was brought here by the early colonists who considered it a useful plant. Capable of reaching 3 feet in height, it produces pretty blue flowers about 1 1/2 inches in diameter that bloom between July and October. When its root is dried and ground, chicory is used commercially as a filler or flavoring agent in coffee.

Soon you'll probably notice dozens of purple martens flitting back and forth. Park personnel have erected a house for them situated atop a tall pole. Stand here for a while and watch the action.

At 0.5 mile turn onto the unmarked side trail (next to a road) that leads to the Swimming River Reservoir. Managed by the North Jersey American Water Company, the reservoir provides drinking water for residents of Monmouth County. Completely shaded by a canopy of tall tulip and oak trees, this is the perfect spot to rest and admire the scenery. Stay left with the short arm of the reservoir on your left. The dirt trail leads to another good spot, and just a bit farther the reservoir comes into view again. When you've soaked in enough of this beautiful scene, return to the main trail and go right.

During spring the vast field on the right is aglow with wildflowers. At the

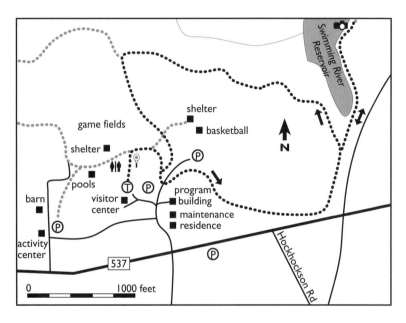

T at 1.4 miles, turn left. A short distance ahead, on the left, the hockey field can be seen, and you'll recognize where you were before. Continue walking through the recreation area to the parking lot.

67 TURKEY SWAMP

Location ■	Turkey Swamp Park
County ■	Monmouth
Type ■	Day hike or overnight camping
Difficulty ■	Easy
Distance ■	2.7 miles
Elevation gain ■	Negligible
Hours ■	8 A.M. to dusk
Information ■	Park Ranger, Turkey Swamp Park, Georgia Road, Freehold Township 07728; (732) 462-7286
Website ■	www.monmouthcountyparks.com
Admission ■	Free; fee for camping

Directions: From US 9, continue to CR 524 west to Georgia Road, turn left, and follow 1.7 miles to the park. From the New Jersey Turnpike, take exit 7A to I-195 East to exit 22. Turn left onto Jackson Mills Road North, follow it to

Georgia Road, and turn left. Go 1.7 miles to the main park entrance.

Heavy rains came down the first day we camped at Turkey Swamp Park. History repeated itself the second day, but we decided to hike in the rain because a great portion of the trails are usually wet anyway! Although the soil is sandy here on the northern fringe of the Pine Barrens, the water table lies just beneath the earth's surface, which often makes for swampy conditions; hence the name Turkey Swamp. Most hikers are disappointed when they don't encounter any turkeys, but the 1180-acre park was named for the town of Turkey, now known as Adelphia. Flat, sandy trails

A post at Turkey Swamp Park notes the way to the Old Lenape Trail.

and a variety of vegetation—pitch pine, scrub oak, young white oaks, sweet gum, and a thick understory of pepper bush, huckleberries, and blueberries—makes up for it. The second part of this walk follows the edge of a man-made lake, where you can rent canoes and paddleboats during the summer. The multiuse trails are open to hikers, bicyclists, and equestrians. Pick up a trail map at the office next to the parking area.

Walk across the parking lot to the road you entered the park on. At the sign pointing left to the campground and right toward the exit, go right and look for a circular green blaze indicating the start of the Old Lenape Trail, which was named for the early inhabitants of this area and for the pinelands forest that was their home. A dense carpet of pine needles covers the narrow path. Tall, handsome sweet gums make their presence known on the ground with an abundance of round seed capsules that appear as dry brown husks with deep pits where the seeds have escaped their cells. The sweet gum's foliage is unforgettable, especially during autumn when its star-shaped leaves turn crimson and orange. Named for a sticky substance that oozes from cuts made in the trunk or branches, its seed clusters are favored by goldfinches, pine siskins, bobwhites, and other birds, and its wood is prized for making furniture.

After crossing a short bridge over a wet area, turn right at the fence. The campground is far to your left at 0.3 mile and, after crossing another bridge, the trail ascends and descends gradually, followed by a short climb. Check for

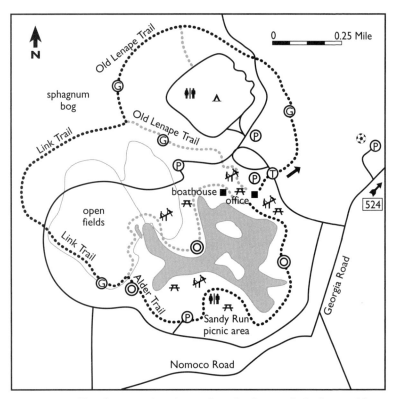

oncoming traffic when crossing the sand road a few yards farther, and keep checking for green blazes with white arrows; they're placed high up on the trunks of trees.

As the trail turns, you'll be deeper into the pine forest. Turn right at the trail post; the campground will be in view straight ahead. Throughout this hike, you'll hear nothing but the songbirds and the swishing of pine needles beneath your feet! The trail zigzags in and out of the trees, and when you reach the signposted junction, turn right onto the Link Trail. At 1 mile a huge grassy field appears on the left; just ahead is station 15, one of the twenty exercise stations found along the Link Trail. Red blazes—remnants of old trail markers—now appear, just before station 14. At 1.2 miles, station 13 and the green-blazed Link Trail are to the left of another trail post. As the trail widens, station 12 follows. Cross a road and go straight toward the open field. Turn right and walk along the edge watching for more stations. A small section of the lake can be seen on the left at 1.4 miles. When you reach station 10, use the railing to take a brief rest and listen to the geese honking and foraging in the field. When you reach a tree with a green blaze at 1.6 miles, turn left keeping the woods on the right. Station 8 is ahead as well as a signpost for the Alder

Trail and the Link Trail. Turn right onto the orange-blazed Alder Trail, which leads through many bogs and swampy areas. Boardwalks will keep you high and dry. As you continue hiking, watch for an abundance of grayish green sphagnum moss on the swamp floor. Native Americans used sphagnum moss as a natural diaper; it's still prized today by plant nurseries as packing material because it can hold ten times its weight in water. With a magnifying glass, you can find two carnivorous plants, the sundew and pitcher plants, in the moss.

A picnic area is on the left.

At a trail post 1.8 miles turn left toward the Sandy Run Picnic Area parking lot. A playground and the lake will be on the left; restrooms on the right. Take the path alongside the lake. Pass a narrow footpath going down to the water's edge, and continue straight, crossing another boardwalk at 2.1 miles. Two more boardwalks are ahead, with the trail following close to the edge of the lake with pine and birch trees overhead. Another boardwalk follows; this one is a good place to pause at a flooded area to spot ducks and geese and decaying tree trunks in the water. At the fence, turn right following the trail, which leads to a small beach area where anglers usually try to reel in dinner. The parking lot is within sight. At the end of this hike kids get a special treat—another play area.

Note: Camping for tents and trailers is available by reservation or on a first-come, first-served basis from March 1 to November 30. The wilderness campground area is a favorite of organized youth groups.

68 MANASQUAN RESERVOIR PERIMETER TRAIL

Location ■ Manasquan Reservoir
County ■ Monmouth
Type ■ Day hike
Difficulty ■ Easy to moderate
Distance ■ 5 miles
Elevation gain ■ None
Hours ■ Trail and visitor center hours change depending on the season. It's best to call before going.
Information ■ Manasquan Reservoir, c/o Monmouth County Park System, 805 Newman Springs Road, Lincroft 07738; (732) 919-0996 or (732) 842-4000
Website ■ www.monmouthcountyparks.com
Admission ■ Free

Driving directions: From the Garden State Parkway, take exit 98, I-95 West, to exit 28B, US9 North-Freehold. At the first traffic light, turn right

While hiking, you'll spot many birds putting the trees along the shoreline to good use, such as this osprey who has built a nest.

onto Georgia Tavern Road, turn right onto Windeler Road, and continue 1.5 miles to the reservoir, on the left.

Fishermen can strike it rich here with bass, trout, and panfish. Sailors with electric motorboats, sailboats, kayaks, and canoes can glide through the water. Bikers can pedal with ease. But hikers are the luckiest of all—for they can combine various exercises with a close look at a variety of habitats while hiking along the Manasquan Reservoir Perimeter Trail. They can also try their luck spotting a few of the more than two hundred species of birds that have been identified here as well as one or more of the nocturnal animals or a muskrat building its nest. The land around the New Jersey Water Supply Authority's 770-acre reservoir consists of wetland, grassy plains, and a hemlock grove. From the visitor center's second-level observation deck, you can also enjoy a spectacular view of the reservoir, and then rest your feet near the fireplace in the comfortable lounge. Or if you still have energy left over, rent a kayak or rowboat (available from April through October).

Starting from the right side of the parking lot as you face the reservoir, the trail goes between two wooden posts. With the water to your left, bear

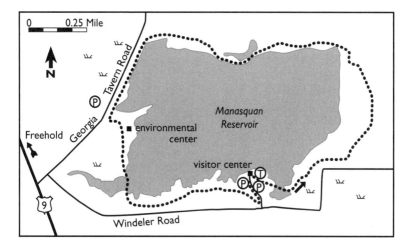

right onto the wide, grassy trail. Cross over the dike through an area frequented by ducks. At the T in 0.25 mile, turn left onto the gravel road heading toward the water. The trail soon becomes a wide dirt path that passes junipers, known for their wonderful aroma and their use in cedar closets and chests. These trees can reach a height of 50 feet at maturity. Scattered stands of mountain laurel at 0.6 mile make a colorful appearance each spring, and at 0.8 mile hollies flank both sides of the trail. Even on the dreariest winter's day their red berries add a bright touch of color to the surroundings. If you've come during spring, frogs will be sounding their mating call; if you get too close, they'll leap into the water.

Although the trail sometimes meanders near the roadway, it won't detract from the woodsy atmosphere, especially at the 1-mile mark after you've crossed a bridge into the swampy area. At this point, you'll see a large dam across the water, and a bit farther ahead, you will come to a lovely hemlock grove. The trail turns left and away from the road again 0.25 mile later and faces the main dam. Every so often a seagull, letting out a mournful cry if it hasn't yet found dinner, can be seen flying low over the reservoir. You might even spot a majestic osprey as well. The trail swings to the water's edge at 1.9 miles and is almost directly opposite the parking area. Ahead, the contrast is amazing. On the left side is open water; on the right, a stagnant, wet area with ghostly trees that were here before the dam was built. Eventually they'll die, but for now they make an eerie sight.

Turn left before the road. The sound of traffic nearby may be intrusive at this point, but the beauty of the trees standing in water is some consolation. Continue past the parking lot at 3 miles and cut back left into the woods onto a gravel trail. The reservoir is blocked by trees but reappears at a spot where Canada geese often hang out. Crossing on a narrow dike that separates the marsh from the reservoir, you'll feel as though you're walking on water. The trail goes through some wet spots before entering deep woods. Continue until it intersects the main entrance road. Turn left to return to the parking lot.

Note: Plan on visiting the Manasquan Reservoir Environmental Center located on the western shore of the Manasquan Reservoir. To reach the center after your hike, go west on Windeler Road to the stop sign, turn right on Georgia Tavern Road, and drive to the entrance on the right. (Open daily, 10 A.M.–5 P.M. and on Fridays until 8:30 P.M.; closed on Thanksgiving Day.) Call (732) 751-9453 for details.

69 ALLAIRE

Location ▪ Allaire State Park

County ▪ Monmouth

Type ▪ Day hike or overnight camping

Difficulty ▪ Easy

Distance ▪ 3.25 miles

Elevation gain ▪ Negligible

Hours ▪ Memorial Day to Labor Day, 8 A.M.–8 P.M., spring and fall, 8 A.M.–6 P.M., winter, 8 A.M.–4:30 P.M.

Information ▪ Allaire State Park, P.O. Box 220, Farmingdale 07727; (732) 938-2371

Website ▪ www.njparksandforests.org

Admission ▪ Free; fee for camping and fee for parking, Memorial Day to Labor Day

Driving directions: From the Garden State Parkway, take exit 98 near Belmar and follow I-195 west to exit 31B (CR 524, Allaire Road). Follow signs to Allaire Village.

Although you'll be arriving and parking at Allaire Village, explore this historic site after the hike is completed. While hiking, you'll be passing through lush woods beside tiny streams where ninety-four varieties of wildflowers can be seen. For bird lovers, there's always the possibility of spotting a blue-winged warbler, a ruby-throated hummingbird, or dozens of other species.

The village and land James P. Allaire purchased in 1822—along with the Monmouth Furnace, which he renamed Howell Furnace—is within Allaire State Park and is managed by the State of New Jersey. Allaire was a man of great vision and talent. At the age of nineteen, he was credited with having built the brass air chamber in Robert Fulton's steamship, the *Clermont*. He turned the Howell Furnace operation into one of the finest bog ironworks in the country. Layers of bog ore, charcoal, and seashells were added to the furnace, and the intense heat of the fire turned these ingredients into a molten mass. The chemical reaction caused the iron to separate and fall to the bottom, and the molten iron poured out through another opening and became solid. In time Allaire rebuilt the original village, adding row houses for the three hundred to four hundred workers and their families, as well as shops and a church. Unfortunately, when anthracite was discovered in Pennsylvania in 1846, bog iron was no longer in demand and the workers eventually left. Allaire's son stayed on, but after he died in 1901 Arthur Brisbane, a top editor under William Randolph Hearst, bought the land. Upon Brisbane's death and per his wishes, his widow donated the land to the state in 1941. The Episcopal church Allaire built for his community, visible from the parking lot, is unusual in that the steeple was built over the pulpit because the front of the building couldn't support it!

As a bonus after the hike you might want to board the Pine Creek Railroad,

The trail passes through lush woods, tiny streams, and a pond where ducks and birds hang out.

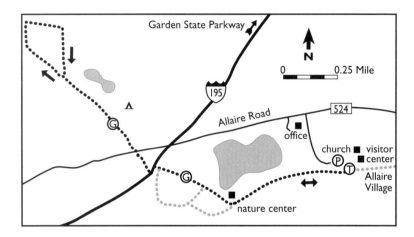

the first operating steam train exhibit in New Jersey and one of the earliest in the United States. Or you might want to camp to enjoy another day here. The fifty-five tent and trailer sites and the two yurts in this state park are spacious and shaded—perfect for overnight or a weekend.

Walk toward the row houses and the visitor center, where you'll see a trail sign pointing to the nature center. Follow the green blaze onto a wide, sandy trail. To your right you'll find the remnants of a canal—obvious after a rain, but at other times it's completely dried out. After passing a picnic grove at approximately 0.25 mile, turn right over the wooden bridge if you want to explore the nature center. Otherwise, continue straight. Here and there are stands of mountain laurel, and at 0.5 mile is what has become a burial ground for trees. The area has been flooded repeatedly, and the trunks stand like soldiers in the water. I-195 appears overhead briefly at 0.8 mile, but the scenery more than makes up for this intrusion.

In another 0.1 mile turn left on Allaire Road walking toward traffic, but exercise **caution,** as cars come by at high speeds. In a few yards at a break in the wooden fence on the opposite side of the road cross over and follow the green blaze. Almost immediately on the right you'll see an impressive sycamore, its peeling white bark standing out against a clear blue sky on a winter's day. At 1 mile a campground appears, and a short distance ahead is another tree graveyard at the edge of a wide expanse of water. At 1.6 miles check out both sides of the trail for impressive holly trees; during winter their red berries add a brilliant splash of color against the snow. The water disappears from view in a few yards, and this area containing pine and oak is usually good for birding. A lovely pine grove is just ahead.

At the crossroad in another 0.2 mile, turn left and follow the green-blazed trail continuing back the way you came.

70 SHARK RIVER

Location ▪ Shark River Park
County ▪ Monmouth
Type ▪ Day hike
Difficulty ▪ Easy to moderate
Distance ▪ 2.4 miles
Elevation gain ▪ Negligible
Hours ▪ 8 A.M. to dusk
Information ▪ Shark River Park, Monmouth County Park System, Newman
Springs Road, Lincroft 07738; (732) 842-4000
Website ▪ *www.monmouthcountyparks.com/parks/shark*
Admission ▪ Free

Driving directions: From the Garden State Parkway, take exit 100 onto NJ-33 East and turn right on Schoolhouse Road. Turn right at the Shark River Park entrance and proceed to the parking area.

This beautiful 588-acre family-oriented park opened in 1961 and has a lot to offer anglers as well as those who love to cross-county ski or ice skate during winter months. Best of all, it's a great place for hiking. There are three loop trails, and this pleasant hike samples each one. The first part of

Kids enjoy the playground at Shark River Park before or after the hike.

the trip along the Rivers Edge Trail is demanding, but the rest of it is fairly easy. If you're feeling energetic you can do the various exercises at the fitness stations. The trail passes through several habitats, including a coastal river and floodplain, gravel-capped sandy hills, a cedar swamp, and several sphagnum bogs. Wildflowers are abundant here in spring, but the hike is great any season. Waterproof shoes are recommended because the trail is often wet; bring binoculars because this is a great birding area year-round.

From the parking area cross the road to the trailhead. Turn left, walking parallel to Schoolhouse Road. Pitch pine, sporting three needles to a bundle and cones armed with sharp prickles, is dense in this area. Even after shedding their seeds, the empty cones cling stubbornly to the branches for years. The tree is named for that sticky, black pitch oozing out of the buds and branches. As you head downhill, you'll see oaks and mountain laurel and a thick understory of bracken fern, pepperbush, blueberry, sheep laurel, and catbrier.

After crossing a wooden bridge over a small brook, walk uphill and stay left passing a couple of trail junctions. Your goal is the Rivers Edge Trail, marked by black diamonds. The trail quickly reaches a long wooden staircase leading down to a narrow, meandering, sandy path along the bank of the Shark River. Climb the steep stairs at 0.5 mile, and after climbing another staircase return to the riverbank. Duck under overhanging vines and cross a short boardwalk and stairs. Check the trail carefully just after this point: It makes an immediate right turn away from the river but then returns again in a short distance. At 0.75 mile follow the staircase uphill and continue winding left; the trail levels before veering away from the bank, descends gradually, and levels again in another 0.25 mile when the river reappears. Bear right; the water will be in sight on the left. A group of buildings mars the view to the left, but you'll quickly reach the river's bank and then head away from the water for the last time. Civilization is left completely behind once you reach the steps and head southwest along a wide, level trail through the forest. Turn left at the signpost onto the Hidden Creek Trail, a narrow dirt path marked by blue squares.

A series of steps leads down to a bog, an excellent area to pause and search for insect-eating sundew and pitcher plants as well as frogs and turtles. Continue through an impressive 12-foot-high stand of mountain laurel. After crossing a brook, continue uphill to a long boardwalk and a staircase that leads to a large, grassy field. Turn right immediately, and in a short distance, turn right again into the woods. Steps gradually descend to a T; turn right once more, heading west. This widening trail cuts through a cedar swamp. You'll be crossing a boardwalk over a lovely stream at 1.7 miles; just after a bench at the T turn left onto the wide sandy path in the direction of the trailhead.

If you're feeling energetic, practice a few exercises at one of the fitness stops or walk straight ahead to the abandoned quarry at 1.9 miles. At the T, turn right into the woods. After reaching the very wide sand path, turn left and then turn left again to follow the arrows pointing toward the trailhead. The play area near the parking lot is open from 8 A.M. to 5 P.M. and is perfect for a cool-down period—while you sit on a bench, your children can enjoy the swings, climbing wall, and other activities.

71   **CLAYTON WOODS**

Location ▪ Clayton Park
County ▪ Monmouth
Type ▪ Day hike
Difficulty ▪ Easy
Distance ▪ 1.8 miles
Elevation gain ▪ Negligible
Hours ▪ Dawn to dusk
Information ▪ Monmouth County Park System, Newman Springs Road, Lincroft 07738; (732) 842-4000
Website ▪ *www.monmouthcountyparks.com*
Admission ▪ Free

Driving directions: Take I-195 to exit 11 (Imlaystown/Cox's Corner) toward Imlaystown and follow to the T. Turn left onto CR 526 and make an

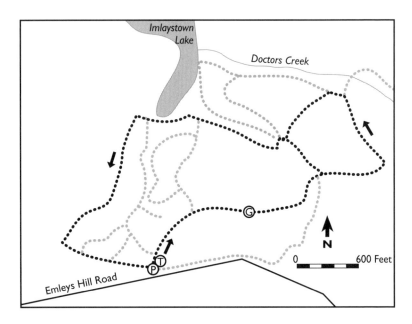

immediate right onto Imlaystown–Davis Station Road. Continue to Emleys Hill Road, and turn left. Follow it to the park entrance on the left side of the road.

This 417-acre park is a hidden gem. Although a couple of the trails are designated as multiuse and are used by mountain bikers and equestrians mostly on weekends, it's a good bet that you'll be alone on weekdays. With more than 7 miles of trails to explore—a very easy 0.7-mile trail skirting through a bit of the forest; an easy 1.8-mile trail over a mostly sandy gentle graded trail; a moderate 2.2-mile multiuse trail with steeper grades and more primitive trail conditions; and a 3-mile primitive and challenging trail—there's a wide choice as well as a lot to see and admire.

Eager for a short hike, I chose the Bridges Trail, which begins to the right of the map board in the parking lot opposite the entrance road. Don't worry if it's a hot, humid day, the towering beech and tulip trees form a welcome canopy during summer months.

At 0.3 mile cross a short bridge where stately tulip trees stand tall. The tulip tree bears flowers with six petals crossed by a bright orange band with yellow borders during May and June, has an odd-shaped leaf, and conical clusters of winged seeds in late fall. Known as the yellow poplar in the lumber industry, its light wood is made into crates, cabinets, and boxes. Continue right at the T, with gradual ups and downs ahead. Occasionally you may hear a plane, but for the most part there is silence except for the

A walking stick sometimes comes in handy, as does a tripod!

sound of leaves rustling in the breeze and birds singing. Continue straight at the post with green blazes. A deep gully appears on the right at 0.9 mile, and ahead are two bridges. The first is very short, but the second is longer and will keep you high and dry as you cross over a swampy area. A gradual uphill climb follows, with excellent specimens of Virginia creeper growing up a few trees on the left. With five joined leaflets, it forms the shape of a fan.

At 1.2 miles you'll reach a huge cornfield, a pretty body of water, and a bunch of posts adorned with bluebird houses. In this open area, sumac abounds, and if you're here on a hot, sunny, summer's day, listen for the buzzing of honeybees, who love the greenish white flowers. The plant's fruit clusters make a great home for insects. Hundreds of grasshoppers usually gather in this area as well and will hop out of your way with each step you take. It's fun to walk slowly and see how far they can leap.

The level trail ascends slightly now. A long hill follows; be careful not to leave the trail because poison ivy flourishes here—as do more tulip trees that have grown so tall it's difficult to see their tops. Another gully as well as lovely beech trees appears on the right at 1.4 miles. When you reach the top of the hill, rest for a while, and take in the beauty of the fields you just came from.

At 1.6 miles, with the main traffic road ahead, turn left to return to the parking lot.

72 FOREST RESOURCE EDUCATION CENTER

Location ▪ Forest Resource Education Center
County ▪ Ocean
Type ▪ Day hike
Difficulty ▪ Easy
Distance ▪ 3.4 miles
Elevation gain ▪ Negligible
Hours ▪ Dawn to dusk
Information ▪ Forest Resource Education Center, 370 East Veterans Highway (Route 527), Jackson 08527; (732) 928-0029
Website ▪ www.njparksandforests.org
Admission ▪ Free

Driving directions: Take I-195 to exit 21 for Jackson/Siloam, and follow CR 527 south for 5 miles. The New Jersey Forest Tree Nursery is on the right side of the road, just past Meadowbrook Village. Look for the Smokey Bear sign. For the interpretive center, continue south and follow signs to the entrance on Don Connor Boulevard.

The day I decided to hike through the Forest Resource Education Center's property turned out to be my lucky day because the Fall Forestry Festival was in progress. Celebrated annually on the first Saturday of October, it proved to be great fun as well as educational for all ages. Although I've always appreciated the beauty of trees, on this day, I learned many new facts. According to the New Jersey Forest Service, "Trees help supply oxygen we need to breathe;

Learn how to tap the red maple trees in the maple grove at the Center.

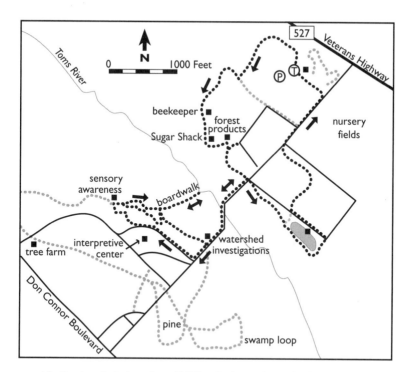

provide food and shelter for wildlife; shade us from the hot sun; act as a barrier against cold winds; provide the material for many products, including paper, food cartons, film, and furniture; help absorb pollution and purify water; tree roots help stabilize soil and prevent erosion; and trees beautify our communities and help conserve energy." In addition, trees provide beautiful scenery when fishing, camping, biking, picnicking, and, of course, hiking!

Having gained a greater appreciation for trees, I was eager to hike a portion of the more than 5 miles of trails that meander through these 650 acres, located in the Pinelands National Reserve Woods. Starting on the level 0.25-mile, white-blazed Project Learning Tree Trail, I followed numbered markers corresponding to shrubs and trees described in a free booklet that can be obtained at the office (when it's open). Highlights include the tall shadbush, also known as juneberry or serviceberry, located at marker 1. Sporting showy white flowers in early spring, its fruit is ideal for making jams and jellies and is devoured by birds as well as fox, bear, turkey, chipmunk, and deer.

Lightning damage can be seen at marker 5; the crown of the tree that was struck is now rotting on the ground, but it provides a good home to mosses, lichens, ants, termites, salamanders, moles, and more. Another outstanding find in this area from May until early June is the pink lady's slipper, a member of the orchid family.

Study the poison ivy at marker 14. The entire plant—leaves, berries, roots, and vines—can cause watery blisters and a severe itching rash if touched. Learn to recognize and avoid this plant by remembering: "Leaves of three, let it be," or if it looks like a rope climbing up a tree trunk, the saying, "Looks like a rope? Don't be a dope!" can save you days of agony.

 The pitch pine, a hearty, fire-adaptive tree found in the sandy Pine Barrens and all forest communities of the outer coastal plain, stands at marker 24. Prized for making tarpaper, turpentine, flooring, and charcoal, its seeds are sought after by quail, grouse, wild turkey, squirrel, rabbit, nuthatch, and other wildlife.

Bear right at 0.2 mile to follow the white blazes to the New Jersey Beekeepers Association's beehive boxes and the Sugar Shack, with its prominent smoke stack. During certain times of the year when the nights are below freezing and the days are warm, visitors can learn how to tap red maple trees in the grove and then turn the sap into delicious syrup. Conditions must be perfect in order for pressure to increase in the sap, which in turn forces it to flow.

At the road at 0.3 mile turn right into the open area adorned with mountain laurel and the Toms River on the right. Turn right again, the trail leads to a boardwalk crossing the Toms River. This is a perfect spot to gaze out upon the lush scenery. When ready, continue straight and turn right at the hill toward the new interpretive center. A map board describes the water resources and excellent trout fishing opportunities, thanks to the Division of Fish and Wildlife, which stocks the river annually with brook, rainbow, and brown trout. This is known as a riparian buffer area, where plants act as a buffer between the waterway and the surrounding upland area.

 Pass the interpretive center on your left or stop in to see the exhibits. When ready, follow the wide, sandy Bluebird Trail. Every so often you'll see one of the twenty-eight bluebird nesting and roosting boxes.

At 0.5 mile you'll arrive at the unique Sensory Awareness Trail. Symbols have been carved for each of the five senses to assist those with physical or visual limitations and for hikers who want to understand the problems people with disabilities encounter in their everyday lives. When kids sit next to the Talking Tree and press the button, they'll be delighted to hear the sounds of the forest, including birds chirping, squirrels chattering, and trees creaking. The perfect place to check out simulated animal tracks is the sandbox located at one end of this area. You can feel the pattern of deer tracks on the trail marker and then duplicate them in the sandbox! A kiosk describing each

of the five senses offers a few ideas on how to enjoy the trails even more.

Follow the white blazes heading northeast and turn left onto a boardwalk that brings you to the edge of the river. This is a small portion of the Toms River watershed, which includes the river itself and the encompassing land area. Return to the trail and turn left. Turn left again at the T at 1 mile onto the wide, sandy road. **Use caution:** Although traffic is extremely light, be aware of vehicles coming toward you. After recrossing the bridge over the Toms River, continue straight. When you reach an opening, turn right and cut into the woods. Go through a cedar swamp, followed by a hardwood area containing shrubs and trees, including the red maple, sour gum, sweet pepperbush, dangleberry, and highbush blueberry. A different habitat appears shortly as well as a boardwalk in the corner of the agricultural fields. A 57-acre spring-fed pond serves as the irrigation source for the seedling production operation, and a pumping station is located at the west end. You may be here when the water is high or low; it depends on the season and when water has been diverted to the seedlings. As you walk around the pond, you may see ducks, great blue herons, or deer. In a few yards, another bridge and picnic tables await as well as a gorgeous place to sit and wait for wildlife or just watch birds flitting about.

The trail joins a sand road leading to stands of sweet pepper and blueberry bushes. The blueberry, New Jersey's official state fruit, was originally cultivated from the wild at nearby Whitesbog and today is a major agricultural crop in the Pinelands. If you've arrived during winter, the last tree with bright red berries is the shade-tolerant American holly, an evergreen that provides food for wildlife and a gorgeous sight for visitors on the dreariest day. At the end of the boardwalk is a large bench area and a pleasant place to sit and study the hardwood swamp and the red maple trees that produce maple syrup. Ferns sprout in the moist soil of the forest floor, and in spring the cinnamon fern starts sprouting fuzzy fiddleheads that grow into dark green fronds up to three feet tall by summer.

Continue following the sand road, and when you come to an irrigation house on the left, take the white-blazed trail heading to the right. Turn right on a wide road where a grassy field appears in front of you. From here it's an easy hike back to the parking area along the sandy road. A house painted green will be in front of you; the parking lot is on the left.

Note: The Forest Resource Education Center is dedicated to enhancing awareness, knowledge, and understanding of forest resources toward the development of a conservation ethic. Besides hiking, a variety of recreational and educational opportunities are open to the public year-round, including fishing, hunting, kayaking, cross-country skiing, horseback riding, and mountain biking. Call (732) 833-9816 for a schedule.

73 CATTUS ISLAND

Location ▪ Cattus Island Park
County ▪ Ocean
Type ▪ Day hike
Difficulty ▪ Easy
Distance ▪ 2.9 miles
Elevation gain ▪ Negligible
Hours ▪ Trail, dawn to dusk; office, 8:30 A.M.–4:30 P.M.
Information ▪ Cattus Island Cooper Environmental Center, 1170 Cattus Island
Boulevard, Toms River 08753; (732) 270-6960
Website ▪ *www.co.ocean.nj.us/parks/cattus.html*
Admission ▪ Free

Driving directions: From Toms River, take Fischer Boulevard north from NJ-37, turn right on Cattus Island Boulevard, then left into the park.

Cattus Island Park is on a peninsula dividing Silver Bay from Barnegat Bay. If you could see it from above after the tide has flooded the marsh, you'd see why it's called an island. The last private landowner was New York importer John V. A. Cattus who used the property as a private retreat for hunting and fishing. The area was first opened to the public as a county park in 1981.

Salt marshes make up 70 percent of the 500-acre tract, with cordgrass and marsh elder the primary salt-tolerant plants. Among the other three hundred species are false heather, lady's slipper, turkey beard, sweet pepperbush, and blueberry. Prickly pear cactus makes a brilliant appearance in June, while holly and pine add a touch of color during winter.

Stop in at the Cooper Environmental Center upon arrival. The 5000-square-foot solar energy building houses excellent educational exhibits and affords a closeup look at some of the critters you're likely to meet on the trail. These include the eastern king snake, the most common in the area, and the black rat snake, which can grow up to 9 feet and is one of New Jersey's largest. Hands-on displays and a mural of life beneath

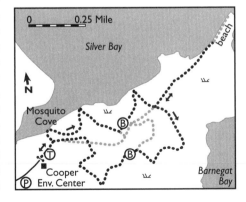

Barnegat Bay add to the enjoyment. A naturalist is always on hand to answer questions.

From the front of the environmental center turn right onto a dirt road, pass through the gate or go around it, and continue across the salt marsh. Binoculars come in handy for viewing the birds that usually congregate in this section, which has several small circular trails. Note that transfers from one trail to another generally involve left turns.

Turn left onto the wide, sandy blue trail at 0.2 mile; Mosquito Cove will be on the left as you walk through pine and oak woods. A tiny beach appears at 0.4 mile. In another 0.2 mile Silver Bay is on the left, and tall hollies form a living canopy. After rounding the bend, you'll find cedars along the water's edge. The narrow, meandering trail reaches a wide path and at 1 mile turn left. Look for deer and birds in the salt marsh on the right. In 0.25 mile a long strip of beach is a perfect place for lunch or a rest. When you've had your fill of the pleasant sound of water slapping against the shore, return through the salt marsh and turn left at the blue blaze leading back into the woods at 1.6 miles. The water and holly trees disappear from view as oaks take over on this narrow, winding trail. There are a lot of cedars and a pretty view of the marsh at 2 miles, and then you'll be back in pine, oak, and holly woods. At the main trail, at 2.7 miles, turn left, heading back to the parking area.

74 DEEP HOLLOW

Location ■ Brendan T. Byrne State Forest

County ■ Burlington

Type ■ Day hike or overnight camping

Difficulty ■ Moderate

Distance ■ 6.3 miles

Elevation gain ■ Negligible

Hours ■ Dawn to dusk

Information ■ Brendan T. Byrne State Forest (formerly Lebanon State Forest), P.O. Box 215, New Lisbon 08064; (609) 726-1191

Website ■ *www.njparksandforests.org*

Admission ■ Free

Driving directions: From the junction of NJ-72 and NJ-70 at Four Mile Circle (about 10 miles southeast of Mount Holly), take Buddtown Road north 1.7 miles to Ongs Hat and turn right on a small road marked by pink blazes to a parking lot.

Don't drive too fast or you may miss the trailhead, located in the tiny town of Ongs Hat. A mere pinhead on the map, Ongs Hat consists of a few houses

Taking a rest break in the heart of the Pine Barrens

and a family restaurant. In the 1840s, however, it was widely known for its cranberry cultivation. The town was supposedly named for Jacob Ong, a robust Pennsylvania Quaker who loved to drink and dance. Ong ran a tavern in the 1700s and one night, when he might have had one drink too many, he tossed his hat high up onto the limb of an oak tree. Too high to retrieve, the hat became a conversation piece. Customers would yell to newcomers, "There's Ong's hat." By 1828 this cry was officially adopted as the town's name.

Ongs Hat is the northern terminus of the Batona Trail, a 50-mile-long, pink-blazed path through the pinelands of southern New Jersey that was

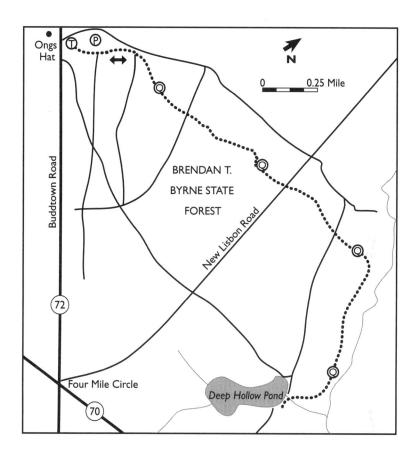

charted and built by the Batona Hiking Club of Philadelphia in 1961. The trail was designed to offer a true wilderness experience, despite the fact that it cuts across several roads and is accessible by car at a number of points. It passes through some of the most scenic areas of the Pine Barrens, a section of the state noted for its unusual plants, including several insect-eating species.

The pink blazes of the Batona Trail lead back to the main road and then indicate left turns into the woods. At the beginning you'll be walking under tall, thin pitch pines. Although the trunks have been charred by repeated fires, this hearty tree always springs back to life again. Scattered about are luscious blueberries and huckleberries, but you'll have a lot of competition if you want to grab a handful because the woods are teeming with wildlife.

Use caution when crossing the sand roads, although they're usually not busy. The first of these is encountered at 0.25 mile. Follow the pink blazes at the next sand road and then immediately reenter the woods continuing along the well-makred trail. Pine is the dominant tree here, with an occasional oak, until 0.6 mile when the oak becomes more profuse. Stands of mountain laurel burst into a spectacular display during spring. As the trail narrows, pines take over again. Another sand road crosses the trail at 1 mile.

 From this point, the trail meanders in and out of a mixed pine and oak forest, and the only sound is the cry of a bird or an occasional plane. **Use caution** when crossing paved New Lisbon Road at 1.4 miles and a wide sand road 0.4 mile later. The trail descends gradually at 2 miles and is flanked on both sides by mountain laurel. If you've come in July or August, you'll also find wintergreen sporting brilliant red berries. From here you'll be walking along a ridge with slight ups and downs for about a mile. A gully will be to the left and a hill to the right.

As you approach Deep Hollow Pond at 3 miles, watch for cars along the blacktop road. If there aren't too many insects, the beach makes a nice spot to take a break. Bullfrogs usually monopolize the pond in spring, when their bellowing mating call can be heard. Return to the parking area the way you came.

75 PAKIM POND

Location ≡ Brendan T. Byrne State Forest
County ≡ Burlington
Type ≡ Day hike or overnight camping
Difficulty ≡ Easy
Distance ≡ 6.5 miles
Elevation gain ≡ Negligible
Hours ≡ Dawn to dusk
Information ≡ Brendan T. Byrne State Forest (formerly Lebanon State Forest),
P.O. Box 215, New Lisbon 08064; (609) 726-1191
Website ≡ *www.njparksandforests.org*
Admission ≡ Free; fee for camping

 Driving directions: From the traffic circle (near Pemberton) linking NJ-70 and NJ-72, take NJ-72 south for about 1 mile, turning left at the sign for Brendan T. Byrne State Forest. Drive to park headquarters and park in the large lot.

Each winter we hike a small section of the 50-mile-long, pink-blazed Batona Trail that leads to Pakim Pond—a crown jewel within the 34,725-acre Brendan T. Byrne State Forest. The water, stained by iron deposits in the soil, may be the color of dark tea, but it's clean. It's best to come during fall and winter when the insects are gone and the rich green color of the pines add warmth on the bleakest day. If you do visit during the buggy summer months,

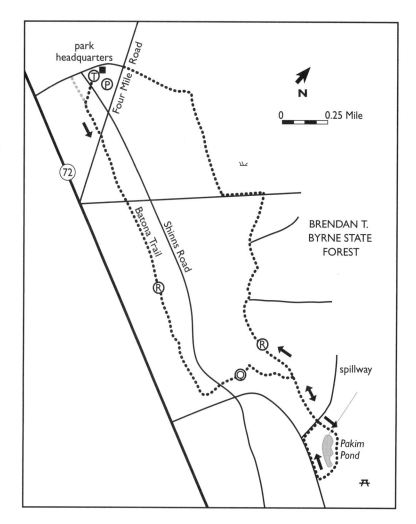

be sure to bring insect repellant and check yourself for ticks.

Beneath this ground lies a huge aquifer believed to contain 17 trillion gallons of clean water. Aboveground this wilderness area is unique with its vast array of rare plants, pine stands, cedar swamps, and more than 350 species of birds, reptiles, amphibians, and mammals.

After picking up a map from park headquarters, turn right and look for a sign showing the way to the Batona Trail. Follow this short connecting trail and then turn left onto the pink-blazed Batona Trail toward Pakim Pond. **Caution:** Several sand roads cross the trail; be certain to check for traffic before crossing.

Hikers always pause to take in the beauty of Pakim Pond.

Walking on a carpet of pine needles over fine, white sand, you'll pass many red oaks mixed in with the pines. In 1 mile you'll come to two small hills. Following the well-marked trail, turn left at 1.9 miles to cross Shinns Road, and then turn right at 2.2 miles. Cross over a boardwalk and turn right at 2.5 miles where the trail widens. The next right, at 2.8 miles, leads to the pond, a picnic area, and a grove of pine trees. Pakim Pond, bearing the Lenni-Lenape Indian word for "cranberry," was previously used as a reservoir to store water for flooding a nearby cranberry bog. When it was abandoned, pitch pine, red maple, and Atlantic white cedar overtook this wetland. However, when a family of beaver took up residence in the 1980s, the dam they built downstream flooded the area, killing most of the trees and creating a marsh. In the late 1930s, the Civilian Conservation Corps developed the pond as a swimming and picnic area, but as of this writing swimming is no longer allowed. The picnic grove is a good place to stop for lunch. In late fall or winter, take your pick of where to sit and observe the reflections of the evergreens in the brownish water.

After sharing lunch with friends on a chilly winter day, or cooling off beneath a canopy of pine and oak in warm weather, it's always a pleasure to hike around the pond. Start in a clockwise direction beginning on a narrow trail marked with pink blazes. The pines emit a wonderful aroma, while the understory is ablaze with colorful mountain laurel during spring. When you reach a wooden bridge, look carefully for patches of grayish green sphagnum moss. Native Americans used this as a natural source of diapers, and it's still prized today by plant nurseries as packing material because it can hold ten times its weight in water!

Where red cedars hug the water's edge, you can scout for more clumps of sphagnum moss, along with insect-catching plants—the sundew and pitcher plant. The sundew traps insects with the sticky hairs on the upper surface of its leaves, while the pitcher plant traps its prey by luring it with its color and odor. Once the insect lands in the pitcher plant's water-filled, pitcher-shaped leaves, it drowns. The sundew and the pitcher plant digest the insect to supply the nitrogen and other nutrients not available from the soil.

Farther ahead you may see painted turtles basking in the sun or another insect-loving plant, the purple bladderwort. Identified by tiny yellow flowers growing out of the water, the tiny bladderwort has miniscule sacs on its underwater leaves to trap insects. As insects and tiny organisms float by, the wavelike motion they create breaks the vacuum seal on the plant's bladder. The victim then floats in and once the bladder cells pump out the remaining water the trap is set and the prey is doomed.

The long boardwalk ahead is a great place to sit and listen to the sound of an entering stream, listen to the frogs, and simply relax and absorb the beauty of the pond on one side and the swamp on the other. Continue to the road junction and turn right to walk against traffic. On the right are three cabins on the shore of Pakim Pond that are furnished with bunks, a kitchen with running water, toilet and basin, and a living room with a fireplace. They're available from April 1 though October 31.

When you pass the picnic area, bear right on a sand road, and turn left at the pink blaze onto the Batona Trail. Leave the Batona Trail where it turns left and continue straight on the red-blazed trail.

The red trail follows old sand roads and paths through thick woods and is wide enough for several people to walk abreast. At 5 miles, the trail turns left and passes through a cedar swamp for about 0.25 mile before thick stands of pine emerge again. Watch for blazes; the soft white-sand trail makes several turns. At 6.4 miles the red trail ends at a blacktop road. Park headquarters is visible just to the left.

Note: Camping is by reservation only and requires a permit. There are designated campsites along the Batona Trail and in Wharton State Forest as well as individual campsites, group campsites, cabins, and yurts (circular tents built on a wood frame featuring a Plexiglas skylight, lockable wood door, window screens and flaps and two double-deck bunks) within Brendan T. Byrne State Forest.

76 ISLAND BEACH STATE PARK

Location ▪ Island Beach State Park
County ▪ Ocean
Type ▪ Day hike
Difficulty ▪ Easy
Distance ▪ 3 miles
Elevation gain ▪ Negligible
Hours ▪ Trails, dawn to dusk; nature center, 8 A.M.–4 P.M.
Information ▪ Island Beach State Park, P.O. Box 37, Seaside Park 08752; (732) 793-0506
Website ▪ *www.njparksandforests.org*
Admission ▪ Fee

 Driving directions: From Toms River, take NJ-37 South to the park entrance (or take exit 82 from the Garden State Parkway) and turn right onto NJ-35 South following signs to Island Beach State Park.

The best time to explore this barrier island is between Labor Day and Memorial Day, when the crowds are gone and parking is plentiful. During spring and winter months, dress warmly because the breezes off the ocean can make the temperature seem quite chilly. Binoculars will come in handy for zooming in on a few of the 240 species of birds that frequent the area; among them are three on the endangered species list—the black skimmer, least tern, and piping plover. You'll feel the salt spray from the waves breaking onshore, and the hike will lead you to a fine view of the Barnegat Lighthouse, built in 1858.

To learn more about the fauna and flora of Island Beach, make the nature center your first stop. Here, view slide shows, browse through numerous hands-on exhibits, and limber up on the excellent 0.2-mile-long nature trail, where you'll find prickly pear, aglow in June with brilliant yellow flowers and in autumn with bright red fruit; a dwarf red cedar forest; bayberry shrubs, a favorite source of food for migrating myrtle warblers as well as the source of wax for fragrant bayberry candles; and the shadbush, always a gathering site

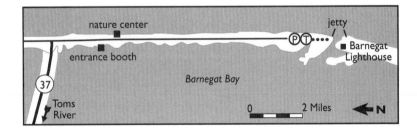

Shell collecting on Island Beach

for catbirds and brown thrashers when the berries ripen over the summer. You'll also see magnificent holly trees and pass a large clump of poison ivy (look but don't touch) among the beautiful white sand dunes.

After stopping at the nature center follow the main park road till it ends.

As you walk past the Barnegat Beach Buggy Access sign toward the beach, the going will be slow for a while because of the soft sand, but once you reach hard-packed sand along the water's edge, hiking is a snap. Anglers, who are allowed in this section with four-wheel-drive vehicles (after obtaining a permit at the main office; fee), stake out their favorite spots and sometimes land striped bass or bluefish. Watch for the sandpipers; they dart to and fro searching for a meal of sand fleas as the waves retreat.

If you can pull your eyes away from the ocean, you'll no doubt find many treasures at your feet, such as the cast left by a horseshoe crab from one of its fifteen or so molts. This scary-looking crab—thought to be one of the oldest living fossils—sports a long, sharp tail, swims upside down, and has five pairs of legs. Once caught for use as fertilizer and chicken feed, today their blue blood is important for cancer and spinal meningitis research studies. You may also find jingle shells, oysters, or the quahog, used by Native Americans for beads and wampum.

On the primary dune, created by the never-ending winds carrying sand, you'll find outstanding plants. Examine them carefully and from a distance (walking on the dunes is not permitted), and you'll find old dune grass, which can survive the driest season because its leaves have the ability to roll up tightly when water is scarce. This grass not only bears pretty yellow flowers in the spring, but it helps to stabilize the dunes by spreading horizontal roots beneath the sand. You'll also find the edible sea rocket and the Japanese sedge. Along the secondary dunes are black cherry, prickly pear cactus, magnolia, trumpet vine, and beach plum.

In the 1750s, Island Beach was known as Cranberry Inlet and was part of an island created when the sea opened a sliver between the ocean and Barnegat Bay (near the northern end of the park). In the 1780s shipping was a big industry here, and Barnegat Bay was used by the New Jersey Privateers, a group sanctioned by the government to raid British ships. To lure vessels ashore, these pirates would tie a lantern onto an animal's back and lead it along the dunes parallel to the coast. An unsuspecting captain, thinking it was another vessel, would turn toward the light. As soon as the vessel ran aground, the pirates would grab its valuables. A series of storms closed the inlet in 1812, but life went on peacefully for the two farmers who raised livestock on the land and grew cranberries in the boggy areas. After the lifesaving service was established to aid distressed ships, speculators attempted to promote the land as a dream resort. In 1910 squatters erected shacks in an effort to cash in on a new seaweed industry. Each would collect eel grass by boat from the shallow waters of Barnegat Bay, hang it and pick it clean of clinging crabs and shrimp, and then dry it in the open to get rid of any odor. Because it was a fire retardant, it was commercially used as mattress stuffing and as insulation in the walls of theaters. Eelgrass was even used inside the upholstery in the Model T Ford! Disease finally wiped out the supply, but today the grass is alive and well once again.

Thanks to Francis Freeman, the beach is here for everyone to enjoy. Freeman took over management of the Phipps estate in 1929 and preserved its natural beauty, according to park officials, by allowing only certain people to enter—those who followed his rules of "no berry picking, dune destruction, littering, and reckless plundering of natural resources." He also allowed a few squatters to lease sections, provided they paid an annual fee to the Phipps estate. However, when the War Department took over in the 1940s, they forced everyone to leave while they worked on antiaircraft rocketry. These efforts led to the launching of a supersonic ramjet rocket in 1945 that traveled more than 9 miles at one and a half times the speed of sound. The property was purchased in 1953 by the state and various fishermen's groups so that the natural beauty of Island Beach would be preserved.

At 1.5 miles, you'll reach the jetty. **Use caution** if you walk onto the jetty to watch the fishermen; it's slippery from the spray and moss. Directly across Barnegat Inlet is a landmark in these parts, the Barnegat Lighthouse, affectionately called "Old Barney." When you're finished enjoying the action— the scuba divers, birds, and sandcastle builders—turn back the way you came to return to the parking area.

 ## RANCOCAS WOODS

Location ■ Rancocas State Park
County ■ Burlington
Type ■ Day hike
Difficulty ■ Easy
Distance ■ 1.4 miles
Elevation gain ■ Negligible
Hours ■ Trails and visitor center, Tuesday–Saturday, 9 A.M.–5 P.M., Sunday, noon–5 P.M., closed Mondays and major holidays
Information ■ Rancocas Nature Center, 794 Rancocas Road, Westhampton 08060; (609) 261-2495
Website ■ www.njaudubon.org or www.njparksandforests.org
Admission ■ Free; donation accepted

Driving directions: From I-295, take exit 45A and head east on Rancocas Road. The center is 1.8 miles from I-295 on the right-hand side.

A father and his children pause to admire the dense woods.

When the temperature plummets, the Rancocas Nature Center is the perfect place to begin a short, brisk hike that's guaranteed to warm the body as well as the spirit. Located in a century-old house and operated by the New Jersey Audubon Society, the center has an extensive reference library in addition to numerous please-touch exhibits of the flora and fauna of the area. It also contains a gift shop and not-to-be-missed bathrooms where you can view gorgeous outdoor murals that were painted by a fourteen-year-old boy. If you don't want to brave cold weather, come during spring or fall since summer tends to be buggy. More than 200 plants, approximately 150 species of birds, a vast array of trees, abundant deer, and other critters have been spotted in the various habitats found along the trail—in addition to a closeup view of Rancocas Creek.

Ask for a trail guide before leaving the nature center. If you prefer picnicking before or after the hike, picnic tables are located beneath several American holly trees located just outside the building.

The trail starts from the front of the nature center and follows the diamond-shaped blazes to the right (east) leading through an impressive grove of fifty-year old Douglas firs. You'll soon enter an open field with dominant shrubs and sun-loving trees including the thorny multiflora rose, persimmon, and sweet gum. About two decades ago this was a cultivated field, but as these trees shade out the shrubs, hickories and oaks will move in, changing the plant community in a process known as succession.

Continue along the narrow, hard-packed, dirt trail. During spring, just past the wooden bridge on the left at 0.1 mile, masses of bright yellow daffodils can be seen nodding their heads. Bear right at the intersection and, when you reach the dense thicket of young trees, shrubs, and vines on the right, pause and stand quietly a few minutes. This area, where several habitats come together, is referred to as an ecotone. It is a favorite hangout for meadow voles, cottontail rabbits, woodchucks, ring-neck pheasants, and bobwhites because there's food and cover. The birdhouse perched on a tall pole to the left was especially designed for the American kestrel, a bird of prey that feeds on insects and small rodents. Pass by the side trail on the left and continue through another thicket. When the wide road appears at 0.2 mile, continue straight with young forest on either side. The sweet gum, identified by its distinctive star-shaped leaves and its spiny ball-shaped fruit scattered on the trail, is common along the trail and was named for the sweet, sticky substance that exudes from injuries to its bark.

Soon you'll enter an older section of forest where the trees are larger and include oaks and hickories with an understory of spicebush. The leaves, berries, and inner bark of the spicebush have a distinctive spicy smell when crushed. Native Americans used the dried berries as a seasoning, and the colonists made an herbal tea from its leaves. Beautiful holly trees abound at 0.4 mile. An unmarked section of trail leading to the west crosses a bridge over a small, pretty stream. The water is so clear that the brown sandy bottom can be observed as well as insects that resemble tiny boats as they swim in every direction.

When ready, return to the main trail and continue, gradually climbing until you enter the floodplain of Rancocas Creek at 0.6 mile. Its main channel is about a quarter of a mile to the south, and several times a year when the high tides coincide with high stream flow the water rises almost to the edge of the trail—as it did when I was there. Cinnamon fern, sensitive fern, bog fern, and netted chain fern can be found growing in this area. As you continue downhill, with holly trees on both sides, the water will be on the right. A huge log at 0.7 mile is the perfect place to sit, gaze out upon the open water, and watch and listen to the honking of the Canada geese. You may also hear but not see bull frogs. On a hot summer's day, this is a great place to relax because the trees form a natural canopy.

When rested, continue along the trail. During winter skunk cabbage is the first plant to poke out of the ground in the wet areas, and by summer its leaves are huge. In almost any area you'll find fallen trees. Although they're dead and rotting, they are vital to the forest, providing shelter to many animals and food for wood-eating insects and insect-eating birds. Within a few

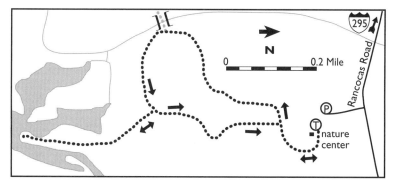

steps you'll soon have a grand view of Rancocas Creek. Depending on rainfall you may be able to walk farther than I did. This is a good spot to sit on the wooden walkway over the swampy area and watch turtles sun themselves on the logs. The thickets surrounding the water's edge are loaded with fragrant spicebush, sweet pepperbush, and arrowwood.

When you can't go any farther, head back the way you came, passing the log you may have rested on. The water will now be on your left. At the top of the hill at 0.9 mile, go right at the trail junction. During spring mayapples, resembling tiny umbrellas, dot the forest floor, and you'll no doubt smell the rich aroma of the conifer plantation. Here you'll find white pine, identified by long needles growing in bundles of five; the Austrian pine, with long needles in bundles of two; the Norway spruce, with short, sharp-pointed needles that grow singly; and the European larch, with short needles that grow in bunches on short spur branches. When you reach the trail junction at 1.1 miles, turn right, and at the V bear left following the blazes on the trees back to the starting point.

78 THE PLAINS

Location ▪ Penn State Forest
County ▪ Burlington
Type ▪ Day hike
Difficulty ▪ Moderate
Distance ▪ 4.9 miles
Elevation gain ▪ Negligible
Hours ▪ Dawn to dusk
Information ▪ Penn State Forest, c/o Bass River State Forest, 762 Stage Road, P.O. Box 118, New Gretna 08224; (609) 296-1114
Website ▪ state.njparksandforests.org
Admission ▪ Free

Driving directions: From Chatsworth, drive 7 miles south on CR 563. Turn left onto Lake Oswego Road in Jenkins Neck at the Penn State Forest sign and follow it for 3 miles. Park in the lot at the top of the hill.

When the colonists first came upon the dwarf trees of the Pine Barrens, they assumed—because none were taller than 5 feet—that they had entered a forest of immature trees. However, after all these years the trees still haven't grown much taller. As you hike into the Plains section of the Pine Barrens, also known as the Pygmy Pine Forest, you'll probably be standing taller than even the tallest tree! No one knows exactly why they haven't grown, but possibly the poor, sandy soil conditions, wind, and frequent forest fires are responsible

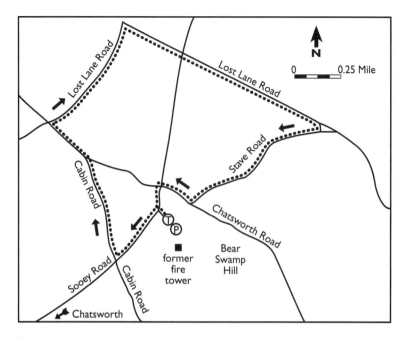

for stunting their growth. A true survivor, the pitch pine, with its thick bark, is resistant to fire. Soon after a fire, it sprouts needles from its trunk, and since the cones open only in extreme heat, fire allows the trees to reseed themselves. Some theories as to why these pitch pines remain stunted include poor and acidic soil, toxic ground minerals, and constant wind. A recent theory suggests that since the soil surface is always dry and pines are instant fuel—even when badly charred from the frequent fires in this area—the trees continue growing but are stunted, or dwarfed have kept the trees dwarfed. Fortunately, these pines have a thick bark and the ability to sprout new needles from dormant buds on the trunk and branches. In addition to the stunted trees, you'll have an opportunity to spot white-tailed deer in unusual terrain that boasts 800 plant species, 91 butterfly species, and 23 types of orchid. This hike through the Pine Barrens follows sand roads, and although the map shows names for all, not a single one along the route is marked. Use your compass to check directions with those on the map. All roads are open to traffic, and an occasional vehicle may pass by. It's wise to stay to the side of the road and listen for the rumble of an engine. Access to the trailhead is via a sand road, generally passable by car. Check driving conditions before entering this road.

   Start the hike by walking a few yards to the top of Bear Swamp Hill. Standing next to concrete pillars—evidence of a fire station that was destroyed when a plane crashed through its tower—you'll have a bird's-eye view of the pitch pine and oak forest 150 feet below. Hike along the entrance road to the fork at

A hiker stands taller than full-grown pines in the heart of the Plains.

0.1 mile and turn left onto the wide, level sand road. Occasionally an oak pops up amid the tall, thin pines, or you might see a pine snake, which makes its presence known with a loud hiss and by vibrating its tail. Although it acts bravely by flattening its head and puffing its body, this nonpoisonous snake is all show; look it straight in the eye and it instantly goes limp.

Turn right onto Cabin Road at 0.5 mile and follow it to the **T**, turning left onto Chatsworth Road at 1 mile, then right onto Lost Lane Road at 1.3 miles going northeastward. The sand, accented by fallen pine needles, is very fine and white along this section. Hawks frequent the cedar swamp section 0.5 mile ahead. Follow the road as it turns to the right in another 0.3 mile.

The dwarf pines in the Plains appear at 2.6 miles, and there is something eerie about the wind whistling through the stunted trees. You'll find low-bush blueberries along the sides of the road. You may also see deer tracks. Turn right at the **Y** onto Stave Road at 3.6 miles and then turn right again on Chatsworth Road at the **T** a mile later. At the crossroad, turn left on Sooey Road and then left again onto Bear Swamp Hill and the starting point.

79 HOLGATE

Location ▪ Edwin B. Forsythe National Wildlife Refuge
County ▪ Atlantic
Type ▪ Day hike
Difficulty ▪ Easy
Distance ▪ 6 miles
Elevation gain ▪ None
Hikable ▪ Year-round, except during nesting season from April 1-August 31 (subject to change; call before going)
Hours ▪ Dawn to dusk
Information ▪ Refuge Manager, Edwin B. Forsythe National Wildlife Refuge, P.O. Box 72, Great Creek Road, Oceanville 08231; (609) 652-1665
Website ▪ http://forsythe.fws.gov
Admission ▪ Free

Driving directions: From exit 63 on the Garden State Parkway, take NJ-72 East and go straight onto Long Beach Island. Turn right on Long Beach Boulevard and follow it 9 miles to a parking lot at the end of the road.

You might not notice it unless you return year after year, but the beach at Holgate is constantly shifting and growing in length under the influence of changing tides and sporadic storms. This 3-mile strip, known as the Holgate

Besides the ocean, birds and Atlantic City skyline, Holgate hikers can see anglers trying for dinner.

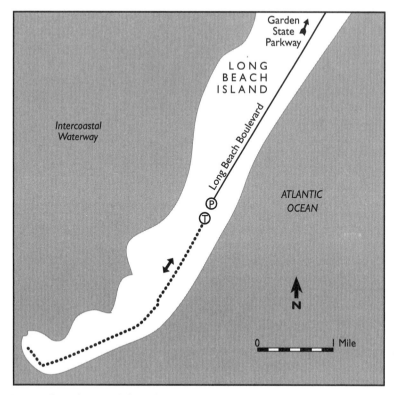

Peninsula and part of the Edwin B. Forsythe National Wildlife Refuge, is one of the few undeveloped beaches in New Jersey. Holgate was given to the U.S. Department of the Interior by the National Audubon Society in 1960.

Hiking with pounding surf on one side and large dunes on the other is tonic for the soul. Arrive a couple of hours before sunset to watch the sky suddenly come ablaze as the lights are switched on in Atlantic City's casinos across the water. Bring a pair of binoculars; this is prime nesting territory for three birds on New Jersey's endangered species list—the piping plover, the black skimmer, and the least tern. You won't be allowed to roam near the nests, but during nesting season (April 1–August 31; subject to change; call before going), you can watch the birds in flight, along with the peregrine falcon, glossy ibis, snowy egret, and other beauties. Remember to bring insect repellent; the mosquitoes and greenheads are plentiful during this time of year. If you're not a birdwatcher, hike here after a storm and you may find a Spanish coin that's washed ashore. Or simply enjoy the fresh air, the sand dunes, and the sight of a fisherman landing dinner.

At the water's edge, sandpipers chase the retreating waves. That harsh cry you'll probably hear is from a laughing gull hovering overhead. On the way to the point, keep an eye open for a pretty shell, such as the Atlantic moon snail or blood ark shells. If you see jets of water spurting out of the sand during low tide, dig down quickly and you may find a soft-shelled clam. Round the point and continue walking for a short distance. Other sections of the refuge stretch out before you across the bay. During winter this is where the great black-backed gull, the largest gull on the East Coast, hangs out. It sports a white head and breast, black wings and back, and a yellow bill.

When you're ready, return to the parking area the way you came.

80 BATSTO LAKE

Location ▪ Wharton State Forest
County ▪ Burlington
Type ▪ Day hike
Difficulty ▪ Easy
Distance ▪ 2.2 miles
Elevation gain ▪ Negligible
Hours ▪ Trails, dawn to dusk; visitor center, 9 A.M.–4:30 P.M., closed New Year's Day, Thanksgiving, and Christmas
Information ▪ Batsto Village, c/o Wharton State Forest, Batsto, 4110 Nesco Road, Hammonton 08037; (609) 561-0024 or (609) 561-3262
Website ▪ www.batstovillage.org
Admission ▪ Fee for parking, Memorial Day to Labor Day

Driving directions: From the Garden State Parkway, exit at New Gretna, and take CR 542 west and turn right at the sign for Batsto Village.

You won't get "bogged down" hiking along the perimeter of Batsto Lake, but you will find spongy sphagnum moss in the boggy areas. Look closely to find insect-trapping pitcher plants and sundews as well as British soldiers, the tiny scarlet lichens named for the "redcoats" of the Revolutionary War. White sand, oaks, cedars, and towering pitch pines make this a delightful hike. The trail is very narrow with greenbrier as well as ticks in some areas, so it's best to wear long sleeves and light-colored long pants with socks pulled over the cuffs. Summer is a busy time, so consider visiting during the off-season if you want to avoid the crowds.

When you're finished hiking, explore historic Batsto Village, site of a former bog-iron and glassmaking industrial center from 1766 to 1867. Batsto is believed to have been derived from the Swedish word *Batstu* for "bathing place." According to park officials, it is believed that the Lenni-Lenape Indians borrowed the term "because old deeds of the area mention an 'Indian Batstu.'" The village is listed on the New Jersey and National Registers of

Historic Places. Batsto, as well as Wharton State Forest, are part of the Pinelands National Reserve. The reserve, established by Congress in 1978 to protect the unique natural and cultural resources found in the Pinelands, was the first of its kind in the nation.

It's a good idea to pick up a brochure describing the village, mansion tours, and the latest trail information from the visitor center (adjacent to the parking lot) before beginning the hike. The trail begins behind the visitor center, where you bear right taking the wide gravel path past the ironmaster's mansion looming high on the left. If you're here during winter months, stop for a while at the holly tree on the right side of the path, when the tree is often covered with hundreds of robins busily devouring its lush red berries. When ready, continue straight along the path until you reach the lake. Turn right, keeping the lake on the left. In a few yards, turn left at the wooden-rail fence at 0.3 mile onto a narrow trail with white and blue blazes. Stands of pitch pine, a cone-bearing evergreen with long, thick needles in clusters of three, abound. Here, too, is the sassafras sporting mitten-shaped leaves. Oil from its roots is used in flavoring root beer and various medicines. During May check the wet areas for the delicate pink lady's slipper. Admire this member of the orchid family but resist the temptation to touch it as the hairs covering the stem of this rare plant may cause a skin reaction.

In a short distance, just after crossing a boardwalk, you'll reach a trail junc- tion. You can shorten the hike to 1 mile by turning right onto the red-blazed trail; this route winds back to the village over a wide, finely crushed cinder path taking you over a long boardwalk, where you'll be surrounded by pines.

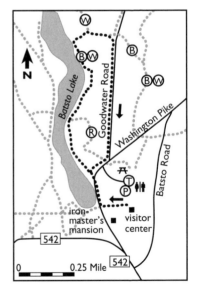

For the longer hike, continue along the blue-and-white-blazed lakeside trail. A good overall view of Batsto Lake, which was created in 1766 when the Batsto River was dammed, appears shortly. Water from this man-made lake was harnessed to provide power for the sawmill and the iron furnace when the village was in its prime. Shortly you'll come to a bog rich in sphagnum moss and carnivorous plants, such as the sundew and pitcher plants. Spend a few minutes at the wide clearing at the water's edge in another 0.5 mile and study the skeletons of southern white cedar destroyed by a fire in 1960. Today they're sprouting new growth from scattered wind-blown seed.

At the next trail junction, turn right to follow the blue blazes and then turn right again onto the sand road at 1.4 miles. As you walk through this lovely oak and pine forest, you'll get plenty of exercise because the sand is deep and soft. In 0.5 mile walk around the fence and continue straight. The lake comes into view again on the right at just under 2 miles. Next you'll come to the junction and the trail leading to the visitor center. Turn left and retrace your steps to the start or stop to explore the village.

Note: Camping is available at several sites within Wharton State Forest. Check at the visitor center for further details.

The ironmaster's mansion at the beginning of the trail

81 PARVIN STATE PARK

Location ▪ Parvin State Park

County ▪ Salem

Type ▪ Day hike or overnight camping

Difficulty ▪ Easy

Distance ▪ 3 miles

Elevation gain ▪ Negligible

Hours ▪ Dawn to dusk

Information ▪ Parvin State Park, 701 Almond Road, Pittsgrove 08318; (856) 358-8616

Website ▪ www.njparksandforests.org

Admission ▪ Free; fee for main beach parking; fee for camping; if camping, main beach parking is free

Driving directions: From Vineland take CR 540 west 6 miles. Park in the lot opposite the park office.

Parvin State Park is a product of the 1930s when the campground and trails

The rich aroma of the pine trees are intoxicating in these dense woods.

were built by young men in the Civilian Conservation Corps (CCC). The work was hard and the hours long, but the men were grateful to earn a few dollars to send to their families during the Depression. Few realized they'd soon be serving their country in yet another way during World War II—the barracks they built and lived in at Parvin were eventually used to house German prisoners of war.

If the CCC were to hike in this 1137-acre forest today, they'd no doubt be proud of their accomplishment. Much of the park has been dedicated as a natural area, with trails leading through a variety of habitats, including cedar swamps, pine forests, and holly groves with lush patches of mountain laurel. Parvin boasts 172 species of birds as well as an abundance of deer, salamanders, toads, and turtles. With more than two hundred herbaceous flowering plants, the opportunity to swim in Parvin Lake, and a profusion of club mosses and ferns, this hike is a winner.

Camping is available on Jaggers Point, along the south shore of Parvin Lake, and cabins may be rented on the west shore of Thundergust Lake. It's best to come during fall or winter so that the mosquitoes don't carry you away, and to wear long pants and sleeves year-round to protect against ticks.

To begin the hike, turn right in front of the park office onto the hard-packed sand trail so Parvin Lake is to your left and CR 540 is to your right. Tall hollies appear immediately. In winter their thick green, spiny-tipped leaves and brilliant red berries stand out against a backdrop of snow. These are followed by pitch pines, which provide a fine bed of needles, while mosses hold their heads high beneath the fragrant canopy. You'll come to a tree with a tuning fork–shaped trunk at 0.3 mile. Directly behind it is a chunky pitch pine, identifiable by its three-to-a-bundle curved needles. If you touch one of the buds or branches, a sticky substance, the pitch of its name, will ooze out. At an opening in the woods and an unmarked trail junction, bear right. The woods are filled with hollies and a few red maples and sweet gums. Turn left at the junction at 0.8 mile and follow the wide paved trail to Muddy Run, a pleasant stream that empties into Delaware Bay. Cross over the second landing bridge, a popular spot for birding, and continue on a very wide track for a few yards. Turn left past an impressive cedar stand onto a narrow, sandy trail beneath pines. Watch out for the greenbrier. In a few yards, walk over a few planks to cross the stream.

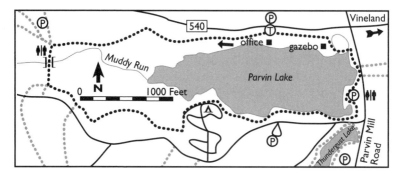

The campground appears at 1.5 miles. Continue following the green-blazed trail leading to Parvin Lake, which is soon visible on the left. This is another great place for bird observation. At an opening continue straight ahead, keeping the group campsite to the left and the restroom to the right. The sandy trail passes a log cabin before reaching a boat ramp and a good place to view the lake again. Turn left and cross the bridge. A few minutes' walk reveals a closeup view of the horseshoe-shaped dam from its retaining wall. Walk around the dam and cross the small bridge to head toward the picturesque gazebo and onto the wide, open lawn area. Ducks and geese are usually lazing about in this section. You'll reach a narrow trail heading into the woods again, with a picnic area on the left by the lake. Continue and you'll reach your car.

82 BELLEPLAIN CIRCULAR

Location ▪ Belleplain State Forest
Counties ▪ Cape May and Cumberland
Type ▪ Day hike or overnight camping
Difficulty ▪ Moderate
Distance ▪ 4.9 miles
Elevation gain ▪ Negligible
Hours ▪ Dawn to dusk
Information ▪ Belleplain State Forest, P.O. Box 450, Woodbine 08270; (609) 861-2404
Website ▪ www.njparksandforests.org
Admission ▪ Free; fee for parking, Memorial Day to Labor Day; fee for camping

Driving directions: From the town of Woodbine in northern Cape May County, take CR 550 west toward Belleplain. Turn left on Henkin-Sifkin

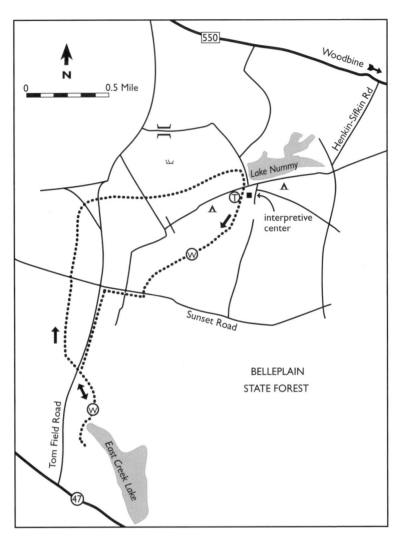

Road, and then turn right at the entrance to the Belleplain State Forest camping area. Park to the left of the interpretive center, opposite Lake Nummy.

Chief Nummy and his band of Lenni-Lenape Indians hiked through this area of the southern Pine Barrens many times, and some of it has been protected as Belleplain State Forest and the Pinelands Preserve. Today it includes 2320 acres of upland and wetland forest, bogs, lakes, and meadows. What mattered to the Native Americans was the excellent hunting and fishing in this area, and you can still find white-tailed deer, red foxes, and ruffed grouse here as well as a variety of fish in the lake. Lake Nummy, named for the last Lenni-Lenape Indian chief in Cape May County, is the starting point for this hike.

Hiking deep into the woods, you'll find trees typical of the coastal plain, including pitch pine, black and white oak, and American holly. In the low swamp areas, magnificent stands of Atlantic white cedar stretch toward the sky, and red-bellied turtles and a variety of frogs can be seen stretched out on logs. Bring a magnifying glass for a closeup look at sphagnum moss and cinnamon fern, or bring binoculars for spotting birds such as the bald eagle and warblers as they dart in and out of the underbrush. A swim in Lake Nummy is just the ticket after hiking on a hot day, but it's best to come during fall or winter to minimize exposure to mosquitoes, chiggers, and ticks. Wear long sleeves and pants year-round to safeguard against overgrown shrubs and overeager insects. Although this hike is on fairly level trails, be prepared to exert a great deal of energy in places where the sandy trail is soft.

Walk onto the paved road in front of the interpretive center toward the sign for the group camping sites, and turn left at the trash/recycling area. A white-blazed tree on the right guides you into the woods beneath a canopy of pine and oak. Stands of mountain laurel appear at 0.5 mile, and this section of the trail is easy walking. At 0.9 mile towering red-trunked cedars covered with bright green lichens appear. Immediately after crossing the short boardwalk ahead, watch for tree roots on the trail. Sunset Road, a paved auto road, is just ahead.

Turn right onto the pavement. Impressive stands of mountain laurel are on the left, and at 1.1 miles a pretty brook flows beneath the bridge. This is an excellent place to see birds, especially warblers. Turn left onto the wide, gravel Tom Field Road and continue for just over 0.5 mile until white blazes appear on trees on both sides of the road. The trail is also marked with brown trail markers topped with a white mark. Turn left into the woods, where a short walk leads to the edge of East Creek Lake, a serene, watery oasis surrounded by woods. When you've drunk in your fill of the beautiful scene, turn around and retrace your steps to cross the sand road into the woods. The trail, a narrow, meandering path, soon leads through a jungle of mountain laurel. After clearing this obstacle, oak, red maple, and a scattering of holly take over, followed by a pine grove at 3 miles. **Use caution** when crossing Sunset Road. After another 0.5 mile through woods, cross two sand roads before entering lovely holly and cedar stands.

A short boardwalk in the wet area at 3.7 miles helps keep feet dry, even though many of the boards may be under water. Sphagnum moss is very much in evidence beneath the cedars, while pitch pine dominates on slightly higher ground 0.1 mile later, with a hemlock popping up every so often. One-half mile after crossing a blacktop road, the trail reaches a cedar swamp. Pause for a few minutes because children—or the young at heart—will love examining this boggy area. Lake Nummy, a former cranberry bog that was dug out in the 1930s by the Civilian Conservation Corps, is just ahead. Today its western tip serves as a swimming area, while boaters and fishermen also take advantage of this small, pretty lake.

83 DIAMOND BEACH

Location ▪ Higbee Beach Wildlife Management Area
County ▪ Cape May
Type ▪ Day hike
Difficulty ▪ Moderate
Distance ▪ 2.5 miles
Elevation gain ▪ Negligible
Hours ▪ Dawn to dusk
Information ▪ Higbee Beach Wildlife Management Area, New Jersey Department of Environmental Protection, Division of Fish and Wildlife, P.O. Box 400, Trenton; (609) 292-2965 or (609) 628-2103
Website ▪ www.state.nj.us/dep/fgw/higbee.htm
Admission ▪ Free

Driving directions: From West Cape May, take CR 607 (Bay Shore Road) north. Turn left at the junction with CR 641, and continue to the parking lot at the end of the road.

Diamonds are forever—that is, unless they're Cape May diamonds. These ersatz gems, found along several Delaware Bay beaches, are actually quartz pebbles that have been broken up and deposited on the sands by thousands of years of waves. In earlier times there were so many of these "diamonds" on Higbee Beach that it was called "Diamond Beach." Other gems encountered

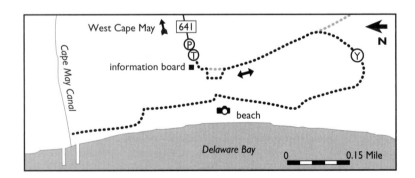

Horseshoe crab molt looks like the real living fossil.

on this hike include dense woods, meadows, and towering white sand dunes. While many serious birdwatchers flock to the tip of nearby Cape May, which is world famous for the fall bird migration, you'll be able to spot many of the same birds without the crowds. More than 250 species, including the bald eagle, are present at Higbee Beach Wildlife Management Area.

The hike is short, but trudging through the sand can sometimes be tiring. Allow extra time to linger and examine driftwood and pretty shells along the beach. While you can refresh yourself by dipping your feet into Delaware Bay during warm weather, don't swim; there are no lifeguards, and there's a strong undertow.

A number of unmarked trails originate at the parking area. Walk to the left of the information board and take the trail heading west into the woods. At the first fork bear left, and then make a second left a few feet later onto a narrow, level path beneath a canopy of oak, holly, and bayberry.

At the T, bear right onto a wide trail leading to a meadow dominated by common reed and flanked by dense woods. Occasional yellow blazes define the route. The trail narrows, briefly passes through woods, and just before it widens again at a yellow blaze, it continues through another small meadow.

Turn right into the woods at the yellow blaze at 0.5 mile. Follow the yellow markers as the trail makes several quick turns before reaching the dune area. It's difficult trudging through the soft sand, but you probably won't mind the exertion as you pass the beautiful beach plum, honeysuckle, and Virginia creeper found throughout the dune area. These plants help to keep the fragile dunes in place.

At 0.75 mile with the trail heading in a northerly direction, you'll hear the roar of the surf. Look to the left for a great view of Delaware Bay, which is so vast that many mistake it for the Atlantic Ocean. A detour down to the beach lies a few yards ahead. Higbee Beach is loaded with driftwood and shells, especially after a storm. Children are usually fascinated by the huge discarded shells the horseshoe crab leaves behind after each molt, and when they turn it over, they'll see how closely the rim resembles a horseshoe. Zoologists describe this creature as a living fossil with good reason: It dates back more than 300 million years to the Triassic period. Growing up to 20 inches in length, it swims upside down. It's also blue-blooded, which means its blood contains copper instead of iron and turns blue when exposed to oxygen.

Continue on the trail past shrub oak and seaside goldenrod. After a series of ups and downs along soft sand, you'll reach the end of the marked trail at about 1 mile. At this point walk to the left onto Higbee Beach, a good spot for beachcombing, and then turn right toward the jetty of the Cape May Canal. From the beach you can watch ferries ply the waters of Delaware Bay or be entertained by the aerial performances of the birds. You'll probably have a difficult time leaving this spot if children are busy searching the sand for interesting shells and the famous diamonds. Higbee Beach extends 1.5 miles south from this point toward Sunset Boulevard. During the summer, it's 30 yards deep, but in winter months the beach narrows due to tidal action that causes erosion.

Out in the bay you'll see what appears to be a blob of concrete in the distance. That's the 2500-ton SS *Atlantus*, which is, indeed, a huge piece of concrete. One of fourteen experimental vessels built by the government during World War I and used for a short time as a coal steamer, it was towed here after it began to sink during a storm in 1926. When ready, return to the parking area the way you came.

Note: Yellow-blazed trails head to the beach and the parking lots. A blue-blazed trail runs through the dunes parallel to the beach from New England Road south to Pond Creek. Observation platforms can be found on the way to the jetty parking lot and along the fields to the left of the main parking lot. A field of warm season grasses is found at the junction of the blue-blazed trail and Pond Creek, and a field of wildflowers is located near a trail at the first lot on New England Road.

84 BRIGANTINE ISLAND

Location ▪	Brigantine
County ▪	Atlantic
Type ▪	Day hike
Difficulty ▪	Easy
Distance ▪	5 miles
Elevation gain ▪	None
Hours ▪	Dawn to dusk
Information ▪	Superintendent, Bass River State Forest, P.O. Box 118, New Gretna 08224; (609) 296-1114
Website ▪	*www.njparksandforests.org*
Admission ▪	Free

Driving directions: From exit 40 on the Garden State Parkway, take NJ-30 east. Turn left on NJ-87 and follow it to a parking area at the end of the road.

If you haven't had any luck at the casinos, you may strike it rich hiking along the flat, well-packed sands at Brigantine Island, one of many barrier islands along the southern New Jersey coast. Maybe you won't find the leather-and-brass chest Captain Kidd purportedly buried here in 1698, but there are other treasures waiting to be discovered. These include the long, narrow Atlantic jackknife clam, strings of knobbed whelk egg capsules, and an assortment of shellfish found beneath rocks, planks, and driftwood.

Walk onto the beach and you'll immediately feel the invigorating effect of the fresh saltwater air and the roaring surf. Arrive early so you have time to search the beach for treasures. A plastic bag comes in handy for carrying

Sharing treasures found on the sands of Brigantine Island

shells, but please make certain they do not contain live specimens. Old pilings, lined up in an interesting pattern, are at 1.25 miles, and treacherous sandbars appear shortly before the point to the northeast.

 When you reach Brigantine Inlet at 2.5 miles, you'll see why fishing boats keep their distance; more than three hundred vessels have been wrecked on the shoals in this area since the late 1700s. In 1849, a Scottish ship carrying two hundred passengers hit a bar. Fortunately, it was equipped with a newly perfected breeches buoy—a device consisting of a pair of breeches within a floating ring. Using this, people could be rescued one by one via a line extending from ship to shore. Other ships, however, weren't as lucky; in 1854, the *Powhaten* broke in half, taking all aboard down with her.

Into the early 1800s, parts of the island were accessible only by sailboat and later by scheduled motorboat. Thanks to a new trolley line, visitors began coming to see the dunes in 1892, but the area didn't become popular until a 10-million-dollar bridge that connected the island to the city of Brigantine was completed in 1972. The northern end of the island

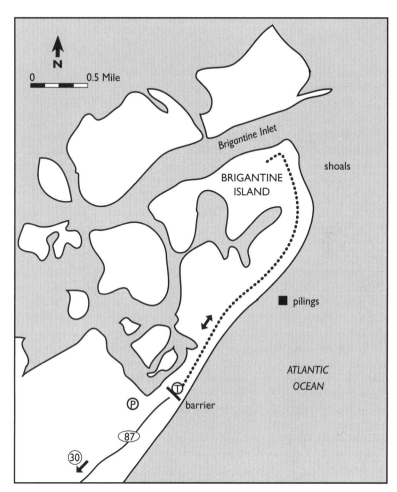

is uninhabited and contains part of the national wildlife refuge area.

James Baremore, the island's first official resident in 1802, liked the surroundings so much that he built a home on the beach. During the War of 1812 a British war party raided his garden, but his twelve-year-old son convinced the soldiers to pay for the vegetables. Because of erosion, the house vanished into the sea long ago.

Continue walking as far as you like before turning around and returning the way you came. Good timing will allow you to witness a glorious sunset as the sun slowly disappears and sets the sky aglow with vibrant colors. And if you linger, there's nothing quite as beautiful as watching a full moon rise over the ocean as the western sky glows a brilliant red. If you're here in the evening, you'll also see the lights of Atlantic City across the water.

85 WELLS MILLS

Location ▪ Wells Mills County Park
County ▪ Ocean
Type ▪ Day hike
Difficulty ▪ Easy to moderate
Distance ▪ 1.8 miles
Elevation gain ▪ Negligible
Hours ▪ Trails, dawn to dusk; nature center, 10 A.M.–4 P.M.
Information ▪ Wells Mills County Park, 905 Wells Mills Road, Waretown 08758; 609-971-3085
Website ▪ *www.co.ocean.nj.us/parks/wellsmills.html*
Admission ▪ Free

Driving directions: From the north, take the Garden State Parkway to exit 67. Turn right onto CR 554 (West Bay Avenue) and proceed to NJ-72. Go 0.25 mile to CR 532 and turn right; proceed 3 miles. The park is on the right.

From the south, take the Garden State Parkway to exit 69. Turn left onto CR 532 West and proceed about 2 miles to the park entrance on the left.

With more than 900 acres, Wells Mills County Park offers hikers 16 miles of trails with varying degrees of difficulty, including a Visually Impaired Persons (VIP) Trail and a Tree Identification Trail. Within the largest park in Ocean County's park system, you'll be traversing through extensive pine-oak forests interspersed with Atlantic white cedar swamps, freshwater bogs, and maple gum swamps in the heart of southern New Jersey's Pine Barrens. Dedicated by the Ocean County Board of Chosen Freeholders to "promote environmental conservation and education," the park's acreage has thankfully remained untouched by human development and is blessed with bountiful wildlife.

Since visitors are encouraged to make their first stop the Wells Mills Nature Center, follow signs to this unique three-story building, but be forewarned: On the way you'll probably have to shoo resident geese off the paved path! Inside you'll find a 1400-square-foot exhibit room, a lecture room, library, park offices, and, on the third floor, the impressive Elizabeth Meirs Morgan Observation Deck. Named for an active Ocean County naturalist and conservationist, the deck affords a fantastic view of the surrounding Pine Barrens and Wells Mills Lake. The park also offers a bike trail, canoe rentals, lake fishing, open playing fields, a picnic area, a playground, and restrooms.

As you peer at the lush surroundings, imagine the colonial era. Elishia Lawrence, a Tory, lost ownership of this land after having fought for the British during the Revolutionary War. In the late 1700s it's believed that the

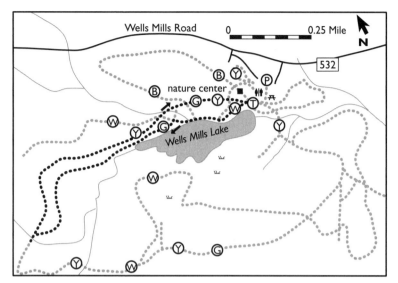

new owner, James Wells, dammed Oyster Creek—thereby creating today's Wells Mills Lake—and built the first sawmill in the area in order to harvest the huge stands of Atlantic white cedar, which were used for building ships, homes, and fences. By the late 1800s Wells Mills was purchased by the Estlow family. They're credited with building two sawmills side-by-side, thus the plural property name. Other activities performed at the mill and on the land included shingle making, firewood cutting, and sphagnum moss gathering. One of the last Estlows who lived here was also involved in clay mining. In 1936 the Conrad family purchased the land as a recreational retreat and built a rustic cabin overlooking Wells Mills Lake in 1937.

The Conrad family sold the land to the New Jersey Conservation Foundation in the late 1970s. In 1985 the Ocean County Board of Chosen Freeholders purchased about 200 acres from the foundation in 1985, as well as additional land from Ocean Township and other private landowners.

Before you leave the center, ask for a free trail map and an activities calendar. Walk toward the lake and look off to the right for a huge sassafras tree sporting various trail blazes. Follow the white-blazed Penns Hill Trail, keeping the lake to your left.

This part of the trail is so close to the lake that you'll hear the bullfrogs bellowing along the bank. Cross the narrow bridge in an area covered with lush ferns and lichen-covered trees. A nearby dock is a good place to sit, have a drink, and admire the passing ducks or kayakers enjoying 35-acre Wells Mills Lake. You'll know when you've reached the Atlantic white cedar swamp, for here, the tall, thin trees sport reddish bark, which combined with the surrounding mountain laurel, is a breathtaking scene during any season. A

Geese can usually be spotted from the trail adjacent to Wells Mills Lake.

bench has been thoughtfully placed a few yards away, and I guartantee you won't be able to resist sitting for a while to admire the lake or take a few photographs. You might even search for pitcher plants, a carnivorous plant that collects and holds rainwater and traps and consumes inquisitive insects. Occasionally musk turtles and snapping turtles can be spotted in the shallow water or on a fallen branch or log sunning themselves.

Bear right at the triple-white blaze at 0.2 mile. A series of narrow boardwalks follow but be careful; they can be slippery when wet or covered with ice during a cold spell. My favorite boardwalk is a very long one over a pretty brook. This is a great place to stand quietly for a few minutes to watch for deer or simply listen to the melodious sound of the water gliding over rocks. Another footbridge follows. With the lake still on the left, continue through the woods, ascending gradually at 0.3 mile and through a densely forested area consisting of pitch pine, blackjack oak, white oak, sassafras, and an understory of blueberry bushes.

At the trail junction, turn left onto the narrow, sandy, green-blazed Estlow Trail, which ascends and descends several times. You'll soon be on a yellow-and-green-blazed trail that's flanked by an understory of sweet pepperbush. This plant is easily recognized by its shiny leaves and long white flower spikes that mature from the bottom up with blossoms opening each day from July to September. When crushed, it smells like lilacs. Don't worry about the climb, the trail goes downhill almost immediately, depositing you beneath a canopy of oaks mixed in with the pines. Gazing to the left, the lake is still in view despite the dense woods. However, at 0.5 mile the gully is so deep and the tree foliage so dense, it's impossible to spot the lake. Gorgeous orange mushrooms dot the forest floor and, if you're fortunate, you may spot the endangered Pine Barrens tree frog or a timber rattler, toad, or deer. What you will definitely encounter is peace and the wonderful sound of birds.

Just when you think you've crossed all the boardwalks, you'll come to a short one ahead and then another long one at 0.9 mile beneath a canopy of tall tulip trees.

At the T, turn left for a short detour to Coon Bridge—a pretty spot with cedar trees sporting their unique "knees." When ready, return the way you came, but at the junction continue straight on the level, sandy yellow-blazed trail that leads back to the nature center and the parking lot.

APPENDIX: CAMPGROUNDS

STATE CAMPGROUNDS

Allaire State Park, P.O. Box 220, Farmingdale 07727; (732) 938-2371

Atsion (Wharton State Forest), 744 Route 206, Shamong 08088; (609) 268-0444

Bass River State Forest, 762 Stage Road, P.O. Box 118, New Gretna 08824; (609) 296-1114

Belleplain State Forest, County Route 550, Box 450, Woodbine 08270; (609) 861-2404

Brendan T. Byrne State Forest, P.O. Box 215, New Lisbon 08064; (609) 726-1191

Cheesequake State Park, 300 Gordon Road, Matawan 07747; (732) 566-2161

Delaware and Raritan Canal State Park (Bull's Island Section), 2185 Daniel Bray Highway (Route 29), Stockton 08559; (609) 397-2949

High Point State Park, 1480 State Route 23, Sussex 07461; (973) 875-4800

Jenny Jump State Forest, P.O. Box 150, Hope 07844; (908) 459-4366

Parvin State Park, 701 Almond Road, Pittsgrove 08318; (856) 358-8616

Round Valley Recreation Area, 1220 Lebanon-Stanton Road, Lebanon 08833; (908) 236-6355

Spruce Run Recreation Area, 1 Van Syckels Road, Clinton 08809; (908) 638-8572

Stephens State Park, 800 Willow Grove Street, Hackettstown 07840; (908) 852-3790

Stokes State Forest, 1 Coursen Road, Branchville 07826; (973) 948-3820

Swartswood State Park, P.O. Box 123, Swartswood 07877; (973) 383-5230

Voorhees State Park, 251 County Road 513, Glen Gardner 08826; (908) 638-6969

Washington Crossing State Park, 355 Washington Crossing Pennington Road, Titusville 08560; (609) 737-0623

Wawayanda State Park, 885 Warwick Turnpike, Hewitt 07421; (973) 853-4462

Wharton State Forest, 4110 Nesco Road, Hammonton 08037; (609) 561-0024

Worthington State Forest, HC62, Box 2, Columbia 07832; (908) 841-9575

MORE INFORMATION

For a listing of New Jersey's public and private campgrounds, contact the New Jersey Campground Owner's Association, 29 Cook's Beach Road, Cape May Court House, NJ 08210; (609) 465-8444, *www.NewJerseyCampgrounds.com*. Or request the latest copy of *Trailer Life RV Campground and Services Directory (www.tldirectory.com)* or the *KOA Kampgrounds Directory* (a free directory is available on their website, *www.koakampgrounds.com*).

INDEX

ABOUT THE AUTHOR

Writer/photographer **Arline Zatz** "knows New Jersey like no other," exclaimed a leading New Jersey newspaper. She is the author of a number of books, including *30 Bicycle Tours in New Jersey*, *New Jersey's Special Places*, *New Jersey's Great Gardens and Arboretums*, *Horsing Around in New Jersey: The Horse Lover's Guide to Everything Equine*, and *100 Years of Volunteer Wildlife Law Enforcement*.

Her books have won several first-place state and national awards by both the National Federation of Press Women and the North American Travel Journalist Association. Ms. Zatz was named Travel Writer of the Year by the Pennsylvania Travel Council, and her thousands of features and photographs have appeared in *The New York Times*, *Asbury Park Press*, *Star-Ledger*, *New York Daily News*, Amtrak's *Arrive Magazine*, *Sports Afield*, and *National Geographic's World Magazine*, among others. Contact her at *funtravels.com*

Joel Zatz, a member of the American Society of Media Photographers, specializes in travel and nature photography. He has been enjoying the natural areas of New Jersey for many years on foot and in a canoe or kayak. A sampling of his photographs can be found at *ecofocus.com*.